The Anglican Patrimony in Catholic Communion

The Anglican Patrimony in Catholic Communion: The Gift of the Ordinariates

Edited by Tracey Rowland

t&tclark

LONDON • NEW YORK • OXFORD • NEW DELHI • SYDNEY

T&T CLARK
Bloomsbury Publishing Plc
50 Bedford Square, London, WC1B 3DP, UK
1385 Broadway, New York, NY 10018, USA
29 Earlsfort Terrace, Dublin 2, Ireland

BLOOMSBURY, T&T CLARK and the T&T Clark logo are trademarks of
Bloomsbury Publishing Plc

First published in Great Britain 2021

Copyright © Tracey Rowland and Contributors, 2021

Tracey Rowland has asserted her right under the Copyright, Designs and Patents Act, 1988, to be identified as Editor of this work.

Cover design: Terry Woodley
Cover image: Gothic Arabesque textile by A.W.N. Pugin. England, mid-19th century. V&A Images / Alamy Stock Photo

All rights reserved. No part of this publication may be reproduced or transmitted in any form or by any means, electronic or mechanical, including photocopying, recording, or any information storage or retrieval system, without prior permission in writing from the publishers.

Bloomsbury Publishing Plc does not have any control over, or responsibility for, any third-party websites referred to or in this book. All internet addresses given in this book were correct at the time of going to press. The author and publisher regret any inconvenience caused if addresses have changed or sites have ceased to exist, but can accept no responsibility for any such changes.

A catalogue record for this book is available from the British Library.

A catalog record for this book is available from the Library of Congress.

ISBN: HB: 978-0-5677-0013-1
PB: 978-0-5677-0024-7
ePDF: 978-0-5677-0014-8
ePUB: 978-0-5677-0015-5

Typeset by Newgen KnowledgeWorks Pvt. Ltd., Chennai, India

To find out more about our authors and books visit www.bloomsbury.com and sign up for our newsletters.

For His Holiness Pope Emeritus Benedict XVI in gratitude for the Gift of the Apostolic Constitution Anglicanorum Coetibus.

CONTENTS

List of Contributors ix

Introduction 1
Tracey Rowland

1 Five hundred years after St John Fisher: Pope Benedict's initiatives regarding the Anglican Communion 9
William Cardinal Levada

2 The Anglican patrimony in *Anglicanorum coetibus* and the Complementary Norms 23
Rev. Richard Waddell

3 The worship of God in the beauty of holiness: A presentation of *Divine Worship* 45
Most Rev. Steven J. Lopes

4 The evangelizing mission of the Ordinariate 65
Very Rev. Timothy P. Perkins

5 The virtue of religion: The irreducible essence of the Anglican patrimony 75
Rev. James Bradley

6 Seedtime: St John Henry Newman, personal influence and the evangelizing mission of the Ordinariates 85
Clinton Brand

7 The spirit of *Anglicanorum coetibus*: Beauty in the development of Anglican patrimony 109
Robert M. Andrews

8 A rich heritage of sanctity: The cultural impact of pre-Reformation English and Welsh saints 131
Petroc Willey

9 Service in perfect freedom: The precious gift of the Caroline Divines 151
Jacob Phillips

10 The place of the Monarchy in Anglican culture 167
James Bogle

11 A personal reflection on Our Lady of Eton and the place of Marian devotion in English culture 185
Rev. Alexander Sherbrooke

Appendix: Benedict XVI – Apostolic Constitution
      Anglicanorum coetibus 207
Bibliography 213
Author Index 223
Subject Index 224

CONTRIBUTORS

Robert M. Andrews is a lecturer in Church History at the Catholic Institute of Sydney. He is the author of *Lay Activism and the High Church Movement of the Late Eighteenth Century: The Life and Thought of William Stevens, 1732–1807* (2015) and *Apologia Pro Beata Maria Virgine: John Henry Newman's Defence of the Virgin Mary in Catholic Doctrine and Piety* (2017). His research interests focus on Anglicanism and British Catholicism in the eighteenth and nineteenth centuries. He is a member of the Ordinariate of Our Lady of the Southern Cross.

James Bogle is a barrister of the Middle Temple, practising commercial and chancery law from chambers in London, and a former British cavalry officer and tank troop commander, later serving in Her Majesty's reserve forces, retiring with the rank of colonel. He is a fifth-generation Australian, his ancestor emigrating from Scotland during the Gold Rush of the 1850s. He is a convert from the Scottish Episcopalianism (Anglicanism) of his forebears who were lairds (minor nobility) in and around Glasgow since the Middle Ages, conforming to Protestantism but retaining their allegiance to the monarchy. He has co-written with his wife, Joanna, a biography of the last Habsburg Emperor of Austria and King of Hungary, Blessed Charles I. He is a former chairman of the Catholic Union of Great Britain, a knight of the Sovereign Military Order of St John of Jerusalem, Rhodes and Malta and a Constantinian Knight of St George.

The Reverend James Bradley, JCD, is Assistant Professor of Canon Law at the Catholic University of America, Washington, DC. He was a chorister at Winchester Cathedral and read music at the University of Bristol. After studies in Oxford he was ordained for ministry in the Church of England. He joined the Personal Ordinariate of

Our Lady of Walsingham in 2011 and was ordained a priest the following year. In 2017 he was awarded a doctorate in canon law from the Catholic University of America. He returned to England as a parish priest and university chaplain, before joining the faculty of the School of Canon Law in early 2020. He is presently undertaking a doctorate in liturgical studies at the University of Vienna.

Clinton Brand, PhD, KSG, is Associate Professor of English at the University of St Thomas in Houston, Texas, where he teaches medieval and Renaissance literature. In addition to his scholarly work on pre- and post-Reformation English religious culture, he served from 2010 to 2015 on the Holy See's interdicasterial commission Anglicanae Traditiones. He is the general editor of *St. Gregory's Prayer Book: A Primer of Catholic Devotions from the English Patrimony* (2019). For his contributions to the liturgical life of the Ordinariates, he was named in 2015 to the Pontifical Equestrian Order of St Gregory the Great.

William Cardinal Levada (1936–2019) was the Prefect for the Congregation of the Doctrine of the Faith (CDF) from 2005 to 2012 during the Pontificate of Benedict XVI. He had previously been the Archbishop of Portland Oregon (1986–95) and the Archbishop of San Francisco (1995–2005). The responsibility for the carriage of the Apostolic Constitution *Anglicanorum coetibus* fell within his jurisdiction at the CDF.

Most Rev. Steven J. Lopes is the first bishop of the Ordinariate of the Chair of St Peter and pastor of all its members in the United States and Canada. He holds a primary degree from the University of San Francisco with a major in theology and minors in philosophy and liturgy and a doctorate in sacred theology from the Pontifical Gregorian University. Bishop Lopes also studied philosophy and liturgy at the University of Innsbruck. In addition to his responsibilities for the Ordinariates, Bishop Lopes is a chaplain to the Sovereign Military Order of St John of Jerusalem, Rhodes and Malta.

The Very Reverend Timothy P. Perkins serves as vicar-general of the Personal Ordinariate of the Chair of St Peter. He holds a master of music degree from the University of Texas, San Antonio, and a master of divinity degree from Nashotah House Theological Seminary. Prior to his ordination to the Catholic priesthood in 2012, he served as an Anglican clergyman for over two decades and was the pastoral leader of the first group that was received into the Catholic Church for the Ordinariate in North America.

Jacob Phillips is a senior lecturer in Theology and Director of the Institute of Theology at St Mary's University, Twickenham, in the United Kingdom. His recent publications include *Mary, Star of Evangelisation: Tilling the Soil and Sowing the Seed* (2018) and 'Human Subjectivity in Christ' in *The Theology of Dietrich Bonhoeffer* (2019).

Tracey Rowland holds the St John Paul II Chair of Theology at the University of Notre Dame (Australia). From 2014 to 2019 she was a member of the Ninth International Theological Commission. Her publications include *Culture and the Thomist Tradition* (2003), *Ratzinger's Faith* (2008), *Benedict XVI: A Guide for the Perplexed* (2010), *Catholic Theology* (2017), *The Culture of the Incarnation* (2017) and *Portraits of Spiritual Nobility* (2019). She is a Dame of the Sovereign Military Order of St John of Jerusalem, Rhodes and Malta and of the Equestrian Order of the Holy Sepulchre.

The Reverend Alexander Sherbrooke is a priest of the Archdiocese of Westminster. Educated at Eton College, he then read for a master's degree at the University of Edinburgh. He commenced his studies for the priesthood at the English College in Rome receiving a licentiate in sacred theology from the Pontifical Gregorian University and MSt from the University of Oxford. He has been the parish priest of St Patrick's Church in Soho since 2002. St Patrick's has been an important contributor to the New Evangelization, particularly with works dedicated to the intellectual formation of young people and an extensive Eucharistic Adoration programme.

The Reverend Richard Waddell, JCL, was born and educated in Sydney. He studied theology at Trinity College, Melbourne, and was ordained to the ministry of the Anglican Church in 1983, subsequently serving in the dioceses of Newcastle, Wangaratta and Melbourne. Between 1991 and 2013 he worked as a barrister in Melbourne. In 2013, he was ordained a Catholic priest and completed a licentiate in canon law at the Pontifical Gregorian University. After his return to Australia in 2016, he led the Sydney Ordinariate Community which continues at St Joseph's Church, Newtown. In 2020, he was also appointed administrator of the parishes of Balmain and Rozelle by the Archbishop of Sydney and the promotor of justice in the Cause of the Servant of God Eileen O'Connor.

Petroc Willey has been the director of the Catechetical Institute and head of the Office of Catechetics at Franciscan University, Steubenville, USA, since 2014. He worshipped at his local Anglican Church in Chartham, Kent, for many years before being received into the Catholic Church in 1985. He received his bachelor's degree in divinity from King's College, London, and a doctorate in philosophy from Liverpool University. After teaching at Plater College in Oxford he moved in 1992 to the Maryvale Institute in Birmingham where he was Deputy Director for Academic Affairs and subsequently Dean of Graduate Research. While there, he completed the licentiate in sacred theology at Maynooth and a further doctorate in philosophy at the Pontifical Lateran University.

Introduction

Tracey Rowland

To celebrate the tenth anniversary of the promulgation of the Apostolic Constitution *Anglicanorum coetibus* by Pope Benedict XVI in 2009: this was the original idea for this collection of essays. The provision for Ordinariates for those attached to the Anglican Patrimony within the Catholic communion was one of the boldest initiatives of the Ratzinger pontificate – and one of the goals for which he had fought a tough battle within his own Curia. For there are always officials who like to 'keep things tidy', administratively speaking, rather than find creative solutions, coordinated with canon law, to meet the needs of exceptional faithful. Furthermore, the proposal of 'corporate reunion' which lies at the centre of the Constitution appears unfair to some who believe that it diminishes the sacrifices of individual Anglican converts who, as a direct consequence of their conversion, lost their professional and social standing – not to mention historically the many martyrs who lost their very lives. Yet others were concerned about the 'injustice' of allowing the Ordinariate to include priests who were married men before their conversion, while maintaining the tradition of priestly celibacy for cradle Latin Catholics. This is despite the fact that there has been the possibility of married former non-Catholic clergy to be ordained to the Catholic priesthood with special papal permission since the 1950s when Pius XII authorized the ordination of married ex-Lutheran pastors. Whatever Pope Benedict's thoughts on these and other objections, he judged that the provision of some form of corporate reunion for members of the Church of England was a high priority of his pontificate, and he accepted personal responsibility to achieve it.

At the heart of the idea of 'receptive ecumenism' is the notion that the Christian communities who found themselves out of communion with the See of Peter in the great ecclesial dramas of the sixteenth century sometimes preserved and developed valuable elements of the older Christian tradition to a high degree, and further, that these elements now form part of the patrimony, or inheritance, of these scattered communities. Since the patrimony is always of a cultural nature, it is not easily preserved and promoted when people convert on a one-by-one basis. With a corporate reunion – however, that is, with whole parish communities returning to communion with the See of Peter – it was possible to retain a good portion of that culture.

We have high testimony to the value of the Anglican patrimony from Yves Congar OP in the early half of the twentieth century. Speaking of England, Congar wrote:

> It is a country of ancient culture, a land of liberty where, apart from the factories and their smoke, things are individual and human. I love the Anglican Church for its admirable inheritance and its methods, which is at once both religious and humanist, reverent yet free. A stay at the theological college of Lincoln in 1937, where Dr Michael Ramsay, the present Archbishop of Canterbury, was my guide, was a revelation to me. In spite of the lapse of time, I am still under the spell of Evensong, which I have never forgotten. Later I came to know Mirfield, Ely (with its cathedral which has always attracted me) and more than one college at Cambridge where I was entertained during my exile. I have been told that the chapter on Anglicanism in *Chrétiens désunis* is the one which gives the greatest impression of having been written *con amore*. If that be true, it is due to the impressions of my first living contact with England.

Nonetheless, Congar went on to observe that Anglicanism has both strengths and limitations:

> However though I find the Anglican Church sympathetic and its ethos attractive, it seems to me relatively uninteresting from a dogmatic point of view. Anglican historical and exegetical works have taught me much, its theological treatises very little. Its

ecclesiological situation is weak. But what can be done to prevent the moral and religious riches of its heritage from perishing if it should eventually become united with Rome?[1]

That indeed is the question! Benedict XVI's gift of *Anglicanorum coetibus* has been the most pointed and substantial response to this question to date. It opened the door for Anglicans to return to full communion with the See of Rome in their parish groups and to bring the most cherished elements of their patrimony with them. They were no longer required to 'come home' one by one like stray sheep, only to join Catholic parish communities that were, culturally speaking, from another planet, especially in the language of their liturgy. Indeed the Anglican writer Digby Anderson went so far as to describe the typical liturgy of the Catholic suburban parish as 'oikish'.[2] In response to the question, 'What is it that Anglican Catholics could bring with them as a small gift on their trip to Rome?' Anderson suggested better translations of the Mass and the moral sensibility associated with the idea of the gentleman, including the cult of understatement and self-deprecation and traditional manners.[3] Ratzinger/Benedict is likely to have recognized such attributes in the character of St John Henry Newman, one of the intellectual heroes of his youth, who famously addressed the issue of the hallmarks of a gentleman in his *Idea of a University*.

While oikish may be a little harsh, the worryingly mundane character of many suburban parish Masses has been widely noted. At the time of the promulgation of the *Novus Ordo* Missal in 1969, Pope Paul VI justified the very non-hieratic quality of the translations by saying that 'modern man is fond of plain language'.[4] 'Folk liturgy', including folk music, became the fashion of the late 1960s and 1970s. It was not, however, universally popular, and since these times it has had been the subject of much critique, academic and otherwise. In particular, the English translation of the Missal of 1969 has been criticized for its use of asyndetic syntax.[5] This is the style of writing associated with government reports and other bureaucratic documents. It is conceptually clear, but it lacks the beauty of more poetic phrasing, cadence and rhythm. It is as unlike a hieratic language, understood as a priestly or sacred language, as could be. Instead of lifting the worshipper out of the realm of the mundane into the realm of the numinous, it keeps him chained to the everyday. Though some efforts were made to remedy the worst of this under the pontificate of Benedict XVI, with new translations of the English Missal restoring some of the hieratic language, dissatisfaction with mundane 'folk liturgy' remains one of the great pastoral issues of the anglophone world.

Into all this comes the gift of the Ordinariate. It meant that Anglicans who aspired to embrace the more 'dogmatically interesting' Catholic theology, to use Congar's expression, could do so without having to jettison their Anglican liturgical sensibilities and other cultural treasures. They did not have that anguished choice between beautiful liturgy and rich theology, but could enjoy both.

A second reason for this collection of essays is to showcase the Ordinariates as an example of 'receptive ecumenism' in operation. If receptive ecumenism is to be something more than a fashionable theological buzzword, it is necessary to give an example of it in operation. In this instance what is of interest is the Catholic Church's receptivity to elements of the Anglican patrimony. The creation of the Ordinariates is arguably the most ambitious attempt by the Catholic Church to receive and affirm graciously the 'gifts' or 'patrimony' of one of the Christian communities that fell out of communion with Rome in the sixteenth century. The early essays in this collection by Cardinal Levada and Bishop Lopes directly address this issue of the reception of the patrimony, and the paper by Clinton Brand considers the lessons that may be learned from St John Henry Newman on how to live out the patrimony within the ecology of Catholic communion. These themes of Newman as exemplar of the Anglican convert par excellence, and of reverent transcendent liturgy as the greatest gift of the patrimony, are tied together by the ecclesial historian Robert M. Andrews in his essay on the place of beauty in the Anglican patrimony.

As a general principle, Bishop Lopes explains that 'the Church is the ultimate arbiter of what is or is not to be considered patrimony … It is not what you or I, or this scholar or that community says it is, but involves discernment by the Church, which is then confirmed by the exercise of ecclesiastical authority.' The paper by Fr Richard Waddell follows upon this theme with an analysis of the patrimony concept as it appears in the Apostolic Constitution *Anglicanorum coetibus* and the Complementary Norms. The paper by Fr Timothy P. Perkins then drills down even further into the Constitution and Complementary Norms to provide an account of the Ordinariate's evangelizing mission while Fr James Bradley's paper marshals these various themes under the concept of the 'virtue of religion'.

No doubt there must be a kind of 'customs authority' within the Church with the power to declare that certain bits of baggage, that is, cultural practices, cannot be brought in, for particular theological reasons. This is a similar issue to that of whether certain practices of pre-Christian cultures can or cannot be 'baptized'. Catholicism is very incarnational. Matter matters! Some practices, like polygamy or child sacrifice or the worship of wooden idols, can have no entrance into the world of 'baptism into Christ'. It is quite clear from the contributions of the late Cardinal Levada and from Bishop Lopes that the elements of the Anglican patrimony which the ecclesial authorities were most keen to receive were the liturgical.

A third purpose of this collection is to consider some of the elements that may not be, formally speaking, part of the 'Patrimony' – understood in a capital P sense – and thus the subject of ecclesial regulation, but are nonetheless typical Anglican social sensibilities or cultural capital. The reason for this is that it is often difficult for cradle Catholics to understand why it is so hard for Anglicans to enter into communion with the Catholic Church as individuals. For many Anglicans it is not the Catholic theology that is a deterrent but, along with the language of the liturgy, more mundane matters like the modes of social interaction and thus the ethos of parish life and emotional connections to particular Anglican institutions.

One of the most insightful contemporary philosophers of culture is Alasdair MacIntyre, who ascribes his success in this academic field to the fact that he spent his childhood immersed in four different cultures: one Gaelic, one English, one Catholic and one Wee Frees Presbyterian. In many of his publications MacIntyre has emphasized the importance of living within a culture in order to understand its sensibilities from the inside. The final four papers in this collection seek to give some 'insider' insight into certain treasures of the English Christian centuries and their culture, though they are not, formally speaking, part of the patrimony. To this end Jacob Phillips has offered a paper on the Caroline Divines, and Petroc Willey contributes a reflection on the cultural impact of the pre-Reformation saints of England and Wales, while the last two papers deal with two great English Christian institutions – the Monarchy and Eton College. James Bogle's paper discusses the place of the Christian monarchy that began, in England, with Alfred the Great in 886 and, in Scotland, according to legend, with Fergus the Great (*Fergus Mòr Mac Earca*) in 498 or, by record, Kenneth I MacAlpin

(*Cináed mac Ailpín*) in 843. Canon Alexander Sherbrooke's paper moves across the road, so to speak, from Windsor Castle to the King's College of Our Lady of Eton, founded by King Henry VI in 1440, and explores the Marian foundations of this august institution and the place of Our Lady in English Christianity.

As a member of the British Army and currently a barrister of the Middle Temple Inn, Bogle has twice sworn oaths of allegiance to Her Majesty Queen Elizabeth II. He is not making the claim that support for the monarchy is part of the Anglican patrimony as *Anglicanorum coetibus* understands it, but he is making a claim that this typically Anglican social sensibility is part of the 'warp and weft' of English Christianity. Bogle's paper may help to explain to Catholics of a republican political persuasion, commonly found in Commonwealth countries like Australia and New Zealand, why so many members of the Ordinariate continue to feel a loyalty to the crown of the United Kingdom, precisely because of what the crown represents as a Christian institution. It may also be of general interest to the many Ordinariate members located in the United States who are perfectly happy with their country's constitutional arrangements but who nonetheless often regard the British traditions associated with Christian constitutional monarchy with affection. Similarly, the final paper by Canon Sherbrooke is also written from the perspective of an insider who has straddled both the culture of the Church of England and the culture of the Catholic Church. Sherbrooke attended Eton as the son of a Church of England father and a Catholic mother from a recusant family, that is, one of the families that refused to attend the Protestant services mandated during the reign of Queen Elizabeth I. Although the Scottish writer Gerald Warner of Craigenmaddie has suggested that British culture has been 'marinated' in anti-Catholicism since the sixteenth century, Sherbrooke's paper ends the collection on a hopeful note that the marinade has only buttered the surface. His experience of Eton College suggests that beneath the outer crust of the great English institutions, there lies buried Catholic treasure. It is there to be excavated by a generation adventurous enough to go digging. It is perhaps because he foresaw the possibility of the rise of such a generation that Benedict XVI pushed so hard to get *Anglicanorum coetibus* across the line. This collection of essays is dedicated to him.

Notes

1 Yves Congar, *Dialogue between Christians: Catholic Contributions to Ecumenism* (London: Geoffrey Chapman, 1966), p. 16.
2 Digby Anderson, 'English Gentlemen', *New Directions*, October 2008, p. 29.
3 Ibid.
4 Paul VI, general audience address, 26 November 1969.
5 See, for example, Catherine Pickstock, *After Writing: On The Liturgical Consummation of Philosophy* (London: Routledge, 1999).

1

Five hundred years after St John Fisher: Pope Benedict's initiatives regarding the Anglican Communion

William Cardinal Levada

Introduction

Of the fifty or so English cardinals, only one was a martyr: St John Fisher. I am honoured to be invited to give this St John Fisher Visitor Lecture to this assembly sponsored by Newman House at Queen's University in Kingston. I am reminded of the prayer with which our Holy Father imposed the cardinal's biretta or hat on my head some four years ago this month: 'Receive this red biretta as a sign of the dignity of the Cardinalate, by which you must be strong – even to the shedding of your blood – in working for the increase of the Christian faith, for the peace and tranquility of the People of God, and for the freedom and progress of the Holy Roman Church.'

As a way of celebrating these five hundred years since the time of St John Fisher's saintly and intrepid life, which brought him the martyr's crown, and of celebrating as well this year's promised beatification of the Venerable John Henry Cardinal Newman, whose search for the fullness of truth led him to Rome without requiring that he abandon the spiritual heritage that had nurtured him in the Anglican Communion, I entitled my presentation today 'Five hundred years after St John Fisher: Pope Benedict's initiatives regarding the Anglican Communion'.

Anglican–Roman Catholic International Commission and the *Catechism of the Catholic Church*

The recent Apostolic Constitution *Anglicanorum coetibus*, establishing personal Ordinariates for groups of Anglicans seeking full communion with the Catholic Church, was not created in a vacuum. For many Anglicans, the possibility opened by this initiative has seemed to be a logical development of the official dialogues between the Anglican Communion and the Roman Catholic Church during the forty-five-year period since the end of the Second Vatican Council. Any discussion of Pope Benedict's initiatives regarding Anglicans might therefore begin with a glance at this important history.

Just a few years after the close of the Second Vatican Council in 1965, the first Anglican–Roman Catholic International Commission (commonly referred to by a shorthand term 'ARCIC') was established in 1969, with a mandate to produce agreed statements on three issues: Eucharistic Doctrine, Ministry and Ordination and Authority in the Church. One notes immediately that these questions moved from areas of greater supposed agreement (Eucharist) to that of greater challenge, such as authority, which included discussions about papal primacy and infallibility.

The commission worked rapidly to produce its agreed statements: on Eucharist in 1971, on Ministry and Ordination in 1973 and on Authority in the Church in 1976. With the further clarifications on various points that were needed, ARCIC I prepared its responses, called 'Elucidations' (published in 1979 and 1981), and produced a second agreed statement, Authority in the Church II, in 1981.

The work of ARCIC I was thus completed, and received a largely favourable judgement both within the Anglican Communion and from the Catholic authorities. The Holy See would later approve the agreed statements on Eucharist and ministry, with their Elucidations.

The ARCIC statements on Authority in the Church stated that full agreement on certain issues (e.g. Papal primacy and infallibility) had not yet been achieved, and recommended that these issues be addressed by a new ARCIC.

The only outstanding question on Ministry and Ordination remained that of the ordination of women, an issue that was new: I note here that the ARCIC I statement on ministry was published in 1973, and only in 1976 did the first ordination of a woman priest occur in the Episcopal Church in the United States. In spite of the request of the Holy See for further elucidation on this question, the commission maintained that its mandate to examine the classical teaching on ministry and orders had been accomplished and asked that the question of the ordination of women be remanded for consideration by its successor commission. Until now, this question has not yet been examined by ARCIC.

As a result of the work of ARCIC I, hopes ran high in ecumenical circles. Many Anglicans and Catholics saw in the agreed statements a path leading to the recognition of a common expression of their own faith. Such has been the testimony of the Anglican members of the working group with whom the Congregation for the Doctrine of the Faith (CDF) consulted in the preparation of *Anglicanorum coetibus*, who see Pope Benedict's Apostolic Constitution as one of the fruits of the ARCIC agreed statements.

For many Anglicans, however, the question of women's ordination remains a source of tension and disagreement, particularly in the Church of England, where more than three hundred parishes have refused the ministry of bishops who ordain women, and for whom alternative episcopal oversight in the form of 'flying bishops' (suffragans to the Archbishop of Canterbury) have provided supplemental ministry. The decisions of the recent Synod of the Church of England to permit the ordination of women bishops, and the refusal to authorize continued alternative episcopal oversight, have made the problem for this minority of Anglicans even more acute.

For its part, the Catholic Church has clearly articulated its position on the ordination of women. In 1975 Pope Paul VI issued a formal appeal to the then Archbishop of Canterbury, Frederick Donald Coggan, to avoid taking a step which would have a serious negative impact on ecumenical relations. In October 1976, the CDF issued its declaration *Inter insigniores*, stating that the Church does not consider herself authorized to ordain women, not on account of sociocultural reasons but rather because of the 'unbroken tradition throughout the history of the Church, universal in the East and in the West', which must be 'considered to conform to God's plan for his Church'. This position was reiterated in 1992 in the *Catechism of the Catholic Church*,[1] and again in 1994 with the Apostolic Letter of Pope John Paul II, *Ordinatio sacerdotalis*. In October 1995, the CDF issued a *Response* affirming that the doctrine stating the Church has no power to confer sacred orders on women is *definitive tenenda* and thus is to be considered part of the infallible ordinary and universal Magisterium.

For Catholics, the issue of the reservation of priestly ordination to men is not merely a matter of praxis or discipline but is rather doctrinal in nature and touches the heart of the doctrine of the Eucharist itself and the sacramental nature or 'constitution' of the Church. It is, therefore, a question which cannot be relegated to the periphery of ecumenical conversations, but needs to be engaged directly in honesty and charity by dialogue partners who desire Christian unity which, by its very nature, is Eucharistic. Cardinal Walter Kasper, current president of the Pontifical Council for the Promotion of Christian Unity, addressed this very point in an intervention given in June 2006, to the House of Bishops of the Church of England during its discussions on the ordination of women to the episcopate. In his talk he affirmed:

> Because the episcopal office is a ministry of unity, the decision you face would immediately impact on the question of the unity of the Church and with it the goal of ecumenical dialogue. It would be a decision against the common goal we have until now pursued in our dialogue: full ecclesial communion, which cannot exist without full communion in the episcopal office.

Returning to the ARCIC process, in 1983 ARCIC II was established by the authorities of both communions, with a new group of representative theologians from each side. A list of the agreed statements produced by ARCIC II can provide an idea of the broadened scope of the Commission's mandate: *Salvation and the Church* (1987), *Church as Communion* (1991), *Life in Christ: Morals, Communion and the Church* (1994), *The Gift of Authority: Authority in the Church III* (1999) and *Mary: Grace and Hope in Christ* (2005). These documents, although rich in content, have not received the widespread attention of the statements of ARCIC I, nor, as far as I know, have they been submitted for evaluation by the 'authorities' of the two communions, as were the previous statements.

A more general analysis of the work of ARCIC II would go beyond the scope of this talk, not to mention the time available. But there is one statement – *Life in Christ: Morals, Communion and the Church* – that addresses the question of homosexuality, which has in the past decade become another Church-dividing issue within the Anglican Communion (and potentially between the two communions) and, thus, also touches our topic, since it motivated the need seen by some Anglicans to request the possibility of corporate union with the Catholic Church to which *Anglicanorum coetibus* is a response.

In *Life in Christ*, we read the following conclusions offered by the commission members as a statement of doctrinal agreement between Catholics and Anglicans on the question of homosexuality:

> (no. 87) Both our Communions affirm the importance and significance of human friendship and affection among men and women, whether married or single. Both affirm that all persons, including those of homosexual orientation, are made in the divine image and share the full dignity of human creatureliness. Both affirm that a faithful and lifelong marriage between a man and a woman provides the normative context for a fully sexual relationship. Both appeal to Scripture and the natural order as the sources of their teaching on this issue. Both reject, therefore, the claim, sometimes made, that homosexual relationships and married relationships are morally equivalent, and equally capable of expressing the right ordering and use of the sexual drive. Such ordering and use, we believe, are an essential aspect of life in Christ.

The Anglican and Catholic members of ARCIC II in 1994 proposed this as a correct common formulation of the moral doctrine accepted by both communions. No wonder, then, that the ordination of a bishop in a homosexual partnership in New Hampshire, with subsequent approval by the General Convention of the Episcopal Church (USA) in 2003, and the authorization of rituals for the blessing of gay unions and marriages by the Anglican Church in Canada have caused an enormous upheaval within the Anglican Communion.

The fundamental issue here, as many have noted, is the question of authority. This may be briefly summed up in the following two points: Does the revelation of God, in Jesus Christ and in Scripture, intend to let us know God's will in a way that requires our obedience (i.e. the imitation of Christ, the Ten Commandments)? Has God in Christ left his Church, founded on the Apostles, an authority by which it can assure that we know the correct meaning of the revelation amid sometimes varying human interpretations (i.e. the *sensus fidei*, the ecumenical councils, the Magisterium of the Pope and Bishops)?

Notwithstanding the tensions created, not only within the Anglican Communion but also for ecumenical relations with the Catholic Church, by the above-mentioned issues of women's ordination and homosexuality, last November – on the occasion of the visit of the Archbishop of Canterbury, Dr Rowan Williams, to the Holy Father – Pope Benedict XVI approved the establishment of ARCIC III, which has for its mandate to continue the bilateral dialogue (with the theme 'Church as Communion: Local and Universal', including the discernment of ethical questions on these two levels and the interaction between them). Such a step is a sign of hope and a commitment to pursuing the path to full corporate union on the part of our two communions.

I think mention should also be made of the *Catechism of the Catholic Church* as an ecumenical initiative. It was promulgated by Pope John Paul II in 1992, and prepared by a commission headed by Cardinal Ratzinger, then prefect of the CDF. I served on the editorial committee of seven bishops which had the task of preparing and presenting the various drafts of the *Catechism* to the commission over a period of some six years. I personally witnessed the commitment of time, and of his own theological resources, on the part of Cardinal Ratzinger to this important task – a task proposed by the Synod of Bishops of 1985, in which the presidents of all the conferences of bishops participated to review the implementation of Vatican II.

Pope John Paul II's Apostolic Constitution *Fidei depositum* promulgating the *Catechism* points out that 'it is meant to support ecumenical efforts that are moved by the holy desire for the unity of all Christians, showing carefully the content and wondrous harmony of the catholic faith'.[2] As we met with Anglican consultants in the preparation of *Anglicanorum coetibus*, these bishops and theologians themselves proposed the *Catechism of the*

Catholic Church as the norm of faith for the corporate groups of Anglicans who might avail themselves of this new instrument for full corporate union with the Catholic Church. Thus I would also characterize the *Catechism* as an important ecumenical 'initiative' of both Pope Benedict XVI and of his predecessor.

To conclude this first section of my talk, I want to introduce the musical image I will use subsequently: in speaking of the extensive consultation of bishops, synods and episcopal conferences by which the *Catechism* was enriched, Pope John Paul said, 'This response elicits in me a deep feeling of joy, because the harmony of so many voices truly expresses what could be called the "symphony" of the faith.'[3]

The logic of *Anglicanorum coetibus*

We turn our attention now to the most recent of the Holy Fathers' initiatives, the Apostolic Constitution *Anglicanorum coetibus*, which is itself in continuity with the serious and long-standing engagement with Anglicans exemplified by the ARCIC process. The Apostolic Constitution provides for the reception, into the Catholic Church of communities, of Anglican faithful who can retain distinctive features of their Anglican spiritual, liturgical and disciplinary heritage.

Union with the Catholic Church *is* the goal of ecumenism, yet the very process of moving towards union works a change in churches and ecclesial communities that engage one another in dialogue, and actual instances of entering into communion, do indeed transform the Catholic Church by way of enrichment. Let me add right away that when I say *enrichment*, I am referring not to any addition of essential elements of sanctification and truth to the Catholic Church – Christ has endowed her with all the essential elements. I am referring to the addition of modes of expression of these essential elements, modes which enhance everyone's appreciation of the inexhaustible treasures bestowed on the Church by her divine founder. The 'new reality' of visible unity among Christians should not be thought of as the coming together of disparate elements that previously had not existed in any one community: the Second Vatican Council clearly teaches that all the elements of sanctification and truth which Christ bestowed on the Church are found in the Catholic Church.[4] What is new, then, is not the acquisition of something essential that had hitherto been absent. Instead, what is new is that perennial truths and elements of holiness already to be found in the Catholic Church are given new focus or a different stress by the way they are lived by various groups of the faithful who are called by Christ to come together in perfect communion with one another, enjoying the bonds of creed, code, cult and charity in diverse ways that blend harmoniously.

Since the Church is like a sacrament, she bears within herself the truth and grace of Christ. When we say that Christ reveals God, and that the Church bears the truths of Christ's revelation in the world, we are admitting that the unenlightened human intellect is not up to the task of knowing God's ways perfectly. We humans need revelation and enlightenment. Baptism, as the foundational sacrament of Christian faith, is the normal means for that enlightenment to begin to penetrate our intellects. Even so, while God in Christ has revealed as much about himself and about our relationship to him as we need, revealed truths about the infinite God still exceed our finite intelligence. There is always an element of mystery in our knowledge of God and God's work.

Therefore, we fully expect that while we may accurately know what can be truthfully said, the full knowledge of what that means is enhanced by the contemplation of many groups of people on the same mystery. This contemplation is not just an academic exercise; it also, and necessarily, entails worship.[5] That is why the Second Vatican Council's Dogmatic Constitution on the Church, *Lumen gentium*, closely associates elements of truth with elements of sanctification: worship enables one to penetrate divine truth with the clarity of lovers who have gotten to know their beloved through His love of them, and worship thus impels believers to study, just as their study strengthens their love of the God whose goodness they come to learn.

Visible union with the Catholic Church does not mean absorption into a monolith, with the absorbed body being lost in the greater whole, the way a teaspoon of sugar would be lost if dissolved in a gallon of coffee. Rather, visible union with the Catholic Church can be compared to an orchestral ensemble. Some instruments can play all the notes, like a piano. There is no note that the piano has that a violin or a harp or a flute or a tuba does not have. But when all these instruments play the notes that the piano has, the notes are enriched and enhanced. The result is symphonic: full communion. One can perhaps say that the ecumenical movement wishes to move from cacophony to symphony, with all playing the same notes of doctrinal clarity, the same euphonic chords of sanctifying activity, observing the rhythm of Christian conduct and charity and filling the world with the beautiful and inviting sound of the Word of God. While the other instruments may tune themselves according to the piano, when playing in concert there is no mistaking them for the piano.

It is God's will that those to whom the Word of God is addressed – the world, that is – should hear one pleasing melody made splendid by the contributions of many different instruments.

The Catholic Church approaches ecumenical dialogue convinced, as the Second Vatican Council's Decree on Ecumenism states that 'our Lord has entrusted all the blessings of the new covenant to the one apostolic college of which Peter is the head, in order to establish the one Body of Christ on earth into which all should be fully incorporated who belong in any way to the People of God'.[6] She believes that she is the Mystical Body of Christ,[7] and she is convinced that the Church of Christ *subsists* in her[8] because she recognizes that while she is like the piano that has all the notes – that is, all the elements of sanctification and truth – many of those notes are shared with other communities, and those communities often have beautiful ways of sounding those notes that can lead to a heightened appreciation of truth and holiness both within the Catholic Church and within her partners in the ecumenical endeavor.

Many Orthodox and Eastern Catholic Churches, for example, design their church buildings and the liturgies that are celebrated in them with an accent on the *eschaton*. One who walks into a building shaped like a Greek cross and surmounted by a dome, covered in mosaics and filled with icons that depict our brothers and sisters in heaven, and who breathes in the incense – a heavenly air – and listens to the chants, is expected to think that he or she is already experiencing the kingdom of heaven. No wonder Pope John Paul used the image of the Church 'breathing with two lungs'. For Latin Catholics, the Eastern Church liturgies can seem to provide a rich new timbre to the notes in which our common praise of God is lifted up.

Other ecclesial communities formed from the Reformation encourage their members to base their prayer lives on the written Word of God. This biblical focus – here I am not referring to the errors that underlie the Protestant phrase *sola scriptura* – is perhaps more intense outside the visible confines of the Church. The Catholic

Church plays the right note, but other communities give it more volume.

Turning to the Anglican Communion, we can see many elements that impel towards full unity: regard for the unifying role of the episcopate, an esteem for the sacramental life, a similar sense of catholicity as a mark of the Church and a vibrant missionary impulse to name but a few. These are by no means absent from the Catholic Church, but the particular manner in which they are found in Anglicanism adds to the Catholic understanding of a common gift.

These considerations help us appreciate the Catholic Church's insistence that there is 'no opposition' between ecumenical action and the preparation of people for reception into full Catholic communion.[9] Indeed, the first – ecumenical action – logically leads to the second – reception into full communion. *Unitatis redintegratio* asserts that almost all people 'long for the one visible Church of God, that truly universal Church whose mission is to convert the whole world to the Gospel, so that the world may be saved, to the glory of God'.[10]

To return to our earlier metaphor, people long for discordant tones and voices to be harmonized, united, and when an individual or, indeed, a community is ready for unity with the Church of Christ that subsists in the Catholic Church, it would be a betrayal of Catholic ecumenical principles and goals to refuse to embrace them, and to embrace them with all the distinctive gifts that enrich the Church, that help her approach the world *sym-phonically – sounding together* or united. Just as there is one Saviour, so there is one universal sacrament of salvation, the Church.

The Eastern Churches that are united to Rome are enjoined to preserve their distinct institutions, liturgical rites, ecclesiastical traditions and way of Christian life.[11] By so doing, the Second Vatican Council teaches, they do not harm the Church's unity, but rather make it manifest.[12] The experience we are embarking on with *Anglicanorum coetibus* promises also to make the Church's fundamental unity manifest by adding to her life distinctive expressions of Christ's gifts of holiness and truth. Nevertheless, a strict comparison between the Anglicans and the Eastern Catholic Churches would not be correct.

The Eastern Churches – like the Ukrainian Catholic Church so numerous in Canada – are in the fullest sense of the term *churches*, since they have valid apostolic succession and, thus, valid Eucharist.

They, therefore, are called Churches *sui iuris* because they have their own legal structures of governance, all the while maintaining bonds of hierarchical communion with the Bishop of Rome. The term *church* is applied differently to the Anglican Communion for reasons rehearsed over a century ago by Pope Leo XIII in *Apostolicae cura*. So the legal framework for Anglican communities seeking full communion precisely *as* communities has to be different from that of the Eastern Churches. They remain part of the Western Latin Church tradition. That is why the Holy Father has decided to erect 'personal ordinariates', in order to provide pastoral care for such groups who wish to share their gifts corporately with their Catholic sisters and brothers, and with whom they have shared a long history before the Reformation in the sixteenth century.

The Apostolic Constitution of Pope Benedict XVI is a courageous way of seeking to ensure that distinctive elements in the Anglican world which foster Catholic unity can remain distinctive when groups of Anglicans enter full communion. This is to the enrichment of everyone, even though these distinctive elements are to be lived ordinarily by those who come from an Anglican background.

Already in 2003, *The Book of Divine Worship: Being Elements of the Book of Common Prayer Revised and Adapted According to the Roman Rite for Use by Roman Catholics Coming from the Anglican Tradition* was published with the approval of the National Conference of Catholic Bishops of the United States of America and confirmation by the Apostolic See.[13]

Anglicanorum coetibus envisages not only the inclusion of significant elements of Anglican ritual for Anglican groups coming into full communion, but also certain pastoral practices that are part of their heritage in order to provide a greater continuity for enriching their spiritual and ecclesial life in the future. Moreover, among the distinctive elements of Anglican heritage should be included the spiritual and intellectual gifts of the Oxford Movement in the nineteenth century. The then Anglican cleric Newman, together with his fellow Tractarians, has left a legacy that still enriches a common Catholic patrimony.

This is the first time that the Catholic Church has reached out, in response to men and women of Western Christianity who desire full communion, and accorded them a distinctive place in the path toward full communion. This is not surprising. Twenty-eight years ago, the great historian of ecumenism Yves Congar wrote that if we take seriously that the Holy Spirit has been working among our fellow Christians, we have to take seriously the ways they express their beliefs.[14] When their particular expression of faith adds harmony to ours, and ours add harmony to theirs, the logical step is to pass from talking longingly *about* unity to living *in* unity – a unity whose essence is revealed in harmonious diversity.

The unity Christ desires is visible. It is not elusive or even unreachable. Likewise, the totality that Christ desires is visible. These assertions lie behind the famous teaching of *Lumen gentium* that the Church of Christ subsists in the Catholic Church. But it is equally true to say that the unity Christ desires for his Church can always be added to, just as there is room for another instrument in the orchestra. The totality that Christ desires does exist in terms of the elements of sanctification and truth that the Church possesses. But the sharing of those elements, and the manner of celebrating them, is still far from complete. We sometimes do not know the value of what we possess, and we need the Spirit-filled insights of others to recognize the treasures we have.

Conclusion

The Eucharist is the summit and the source of Christian life. It is celebrated in notably different ways in the various Churches that make up the Catholic world. Each liturgical rite sheds light on the mystery of the Eucharist – its re-presentation of the sacrifice of Calvary; its strengthening of the Mystical Body, the church; the real presence of our Saviour; the foretaste of the heavenly banquet and so on. May the diversity in unity that is the Eucharist – Joseph Ratzinger has said there is really just one Eucharist with many altars – be a model for the Christian unity to which we are all committed.

Notes

This text was originally given as an address by His Eminence William Cardinal Levada, Prefect of the Congregation for the Doctrine of the Faith, St John Fisher Visitor Lecture Series, Saturday, 6 March 2010, Queens University, Kingston, Ontario.

1 Cf. #1577.
2 Pope John Paul II, Apostolic Constitution *Fidei depositum*, no. 3.

3 Ibid., no. 1.
4 *Unitatis redintegratio*, 3: 'It is only through Christ's Catholic Church, which is the all-embracing means of salvation, that the fullness of the means of salvation can be attained.' Cf. *Lumen Gentium*, 8.
5 Thomas Aquinas, *Summa Theologiae* II-II, Q. 180, A. 3 *ad* 4.
6 *Unitatis redintegratio*, 3.
7 *Orientalium ecclesiarum*, 2.
8 *Lumen gentium*, 8.
9 *Unitatis redintegratio*, 4.
10 Ibid., 1.
11 *Orientalium Ecclesiarum*, 1; cf. Congregation for Oriental Churches, *Instruction for Applying the Liturgical Prescriptions of the Code of Canons of the Eastern Churches* (Città del Vaticano: Libreria Editrice Vaticana, 1996), par. 21.
12 *Orientalium Ecclesiarum*, 2.
13 National Conference of Catholic Bishops, *The Book of Divine Worship: Being Elements of the Book of Common Prayer Revised and Adapted According to the Roman Rite for Use by Roman Catholics Coming from the Anglican Tradition* (Mt Pocono, Pennsylvania: Newman House Press, 2003).
14 Yves Congar, *Diversités et communion* (Paris: Éditions du Cerf, 1982), pp. 241–2.

2

The Anglican patrimony in *Anglicanorum coetibus* and the Complementary Norms

Rev. Richard Waddell

On 4 November 2009, by the Apostolic Constitution *Anglicanorum coetibus* (*AC*),[1] Pope Benedict XVI established the ecclesial structure of the Personal Ordinariate for 'groups of Anglicans' entering into full communion with the Catholic Church. On the same day, the Congregation for the Doctrine of the Faith (CDF) issued Complementary Norms for the Apostolic Constitution, defining more precisely the manner of its application.[2] Since *Anglicanorum coetibus*, three Personal Ordinariates have been erected by the CDF in England and Wales, the United States of America and Australia.[3]

The purposes of the Holy See were set out in the documents themselves and in a number of official statements made at the time they were promulgated.[4] They may be summarized as follows:

- To recognize, respect and preserve, as was appropriate, the existing pastoral practices and structures of the groups of Anglicans with their bishops, priests and faithful, by establishing a Particular Church in an enduring canonical

structure which would recognize, respect and preserve, as was and is appropriate, these existing pastoral practices and structures;
- To ensure the integration of these groups in their new ecclesial structures into the life of the Catholic Church at every level – the universal, the regional and the local;
- To ensure the preservation of the elements of the Anglican patrimony consonant with Catholic faith, especially of its liturgical, spiritual and pastoral traditions, as something to continue to nourish the faith of the members of the Ordinariate and as a treasure to be shared.[5]

The means by which these purposes were to be carried was the establishment of Personal Ordinariates as Particular Churches with an especially close relationship to the Roman Pontiff and the Holy See which itself has two interdependent objectives, the maintenance of the separate identity and Anglican patrimony:

- A degree of independence from the local churches in order to avoid being overwhelmed by the different culture and traditions of the local church;
- The opportunity to ensure that the aspects of the Anglican tradition retained by the Ordinariates are in full harmony with Catholic tradition.

Thus, while the Personal Ordinariate is a Particular Church, it has a level of autonomy in relation to the Holy See which is less than that of a diocese and more like that of a vicariate or prefecture apostolic – a diocese in formation.

Finally, the Holy See intended the establishment of the Personal Ordinariate to have a positive ecumenical effect. The development of the Ordinariate was recognized by both Catholic and Anglican leaders as a fruit of ecumenical endeavour. The Holy See did not want the provision of the Ordinariate for Anglicans seeking union with the Catholic Church to be an impediment to continuing ecumenical relations with the Anglican Communion.

This was a response to a situation which had presented itself in the period immediately prior to the establishment of the Personal Ordinariates and which itself was part of a long history over a period of nearly five hundred years.

A pastoral response

In the *Adnotatio* published by the CDF, it was stated that in the period immediately before the promulgation of *Anglicanorum coetibus* and the Complementary Norms, 'many requests [had] been submitted to the Holy See from groups of Anglican clergy and faithful in different parts of the world who wish[ed] to enter into full visible communion with the Catholic Church'.[6] These involved some definite overtures from the Traditional Anglican Communion since the mid-1990s, some contacts with Forward in Faith over the same period and, in the previous eighteen months, some discussions with some bishops and theologians from the Church of England.[7] Thus, in the *Adnotatio*, the CDF described *Anglicanorum coetibus* as a 'reasonable and even necessary response to a worldwide phenomenon'.[8]

The preamble to *Anglicanorum coetibus* puts the situation in a spiritual context:

> In recent times the Holy Spirit has moved groups of Anglicans [*Anglicanorum coetibus*] to petition repeatedly and insistently to be received into full Catholic communion individually as well as corporately. The Apostolic See has responded favorably to such petitions. Indeed, the successor of Peter, mandated by the Lord Jesus to guarantee the unity of the episcopate and to preside over and safeguard the universal communion of the Churches, could not fail to make available the means necessary to bring this desire to realization.[9]

Essentially, it was a pastoral response.

Corporate reunion

The principal novelty of the situation to which the Holy See was called upon to respond was that the request for full communion was coming from what seemed to be large groups of Anglicans, some of which were part of continuing Anglican churches.

This was not, of course, the first time that Anglicans had joined the Church as groups. At the beginning of the twentieth century, two religious communities had entered full communion with the

Church.[10] More recently, since 1980, the Pastoral Provision had been implemented in the United States providing for groups of Anglicans to form 'personal parishes' within current diocesan structures.[11]

The situation that presented itself this time seemed to involve more people in more places than previously,[12] but, more importantly, many of the groups had an ecclesial configuration; the churches of the Traditional Anglican Communion had a hierarchical structure with bishops, priests and lay faithful. They were ecclesial communities with structures resembling those of a Particular Church as understood in Catholic ecclesiology. All they lacked, from the Catholic point of view, was a valid ministry that would make their communities 'hierarchically vertebrate'.[13]

So, in the press statement released by the Holy See Press Office on 4 November 2009, it was stated that the Apostolic Constitution *Anglicanorum coetibus* would provide for corporate reunion for groups of Anglican clergy and laity.[14]

Anglican patrimony: Its preservation and maintenance

The recognition and maintenance of a distinct Anglican patrimony containing elements of Catholic faith and practice in a model of organic unity had been a theme in ecumenical discussions for almost four hundred years.[15] In discussions in the seventeenth century, some reformed aspects of Anglicanism were considered by the Holy See to be acceptable in a form of corporate reunion.[16] In the Malines Conversations, the aspiration for unity on a basis of 'united not absorbed' – first proposed during the reign of Charles II – was revived.[17] The Second Vatican Council acknowledged that 'elements impelling towards Catholic unity' existed in non-Catholic churches and ecclesial communities[18] and that the Anglican Communion had 'a special place having retained in part many Catholic traditions and institutions'.[19] In 1970, at the Canonization of the Forty English Martyrs, Pope St Paul VI acknowledged 'the legitimate prestige and the worthy patrimony of piety and usage proper to the Anglican Church'.[20] In 1996, Pope St John Paul II, in a letter to Cardinal Cassidy to mark the seventy-fifth anniversary of the Malines Conversations, specifically referred to the ecumenical model of 'the Anglican Church united not absorbed'.[21]

Two theological principles have come into play. The first which is the basis of the Holy See's desire for the preservation,[22] maintenance,[23] sharing[24] and transmitting[25] of Anglican traditions precious to the groups of Anglicans and consistent with the Catholic faith,[26] is found in *Lumen gentium* at n. 8:

> This Church constituted and organized in the world as a society, subsists in the Catholic Church, which is governed by the successor of Peter and by the Bishops in communion with him. Nevertheless, many elements of sanctification and of truth are found outside her visible confines. Since these are gifts properly belonging to the Church of Christ, they are forces impelling towards Catholic unity.

The second theological principle is that the unity of the Church does not require a uniformity that ignores cultural diversity.[27] The many diverse traditions present in the Catholic Church today are sustained by the commitment to unity expressed by St Paul in the letter to the Ephesians: 'There is one Lord, one faith, one baptism' (Eph. 4.5).[28]

Thus, the primary purpose of the Holy See in establishing the ecclesial structure of the Personal Ordinariate for the groups of Anglicans coming into the Church was the preservation of 'elements of the distinctive Anglican and spiritual patrimony'.[29] In the *Adnotatio*, it was stated that the canonical structure would 'allow former Anglicans to enter full communion with the Catholic Church while preserving elements of the distinctive Anglican spiritual and liturgical patrimony'. The concern was 'to preserve the worthy Anglican liturgical and spiritual patrimony' while also ensuring the full integration of the groups and their clergy into the Catholic Church.[30]

Ecumenical foundations

The establishment of the Personal Ordinariate was, in many ways, a fruit of the modern ecumenical movement. It was described by the CDF as within the 'framework' of the work of the Anglican–Roman Catholic International Commission (ARCIC) in providing statements in which a common expression of faith could be recognized.[31] In the 'Joint Statement of the Archbishops of

Westminster and Canterbury', it was accepted that *Anglicanorum coetibus* 'is one consequence of ecumenical dialogue between the Catholic Church and the Anglican Communion'.[32] The *Holy See Press Office Release* stated, 'The provision of this new structure is consistent with the commitment to ecumenical dialogue, which continues to be a priority for the Catholic Church.' It described *Anglicanorum coetibus* as 'a new avenue for promotion of Christian unity while, at the same time, granting legitimate diversity in the expression of our common faith'.[33] The Personal Ordinariates were seen by the Holy See as 'another step toward the realization of the aspiration for full, visible union in the Church of Christ, one of the principal goals of the ecumenical movement'.[34]

The 'Anglican patrimony'

The phrase 'Anglican patrimony' is used in the *Adnotatio*, in *Anglicanorum coetibus* and in the Complementary Norms. The Anglican patrimony is to be preserved, maintained, shared and transmitted,[35] having regard to the content of the patrimony and in accordance with the relevant canonical provisions.[36]

The content of the Anglican patrimony

Ascertaining the precise content of the Anglican patrimony is a task for theologians and liturgists rather than canonists. There is no definition provided in any of the foundation documents. Broad references are found in the *Adnotatio* to 'those Anglican traditions which are precious' to Anglicans, to the Church of England's 'own doctrinal confessions, liturgical books, and pastoral practices, often incorporating ideas from the Reformation on the European continent', to 'the Catholic aspects of Anglicanism' included in the reference in *Unitatis redintegratio* (n. 13), to 'Catholic traditions and institutions in part' and to the ARCIC statements in which 'a common expression of faith could be recognized'.[37] Thus, it would seem that the Anglican patrimony may encompass more than just 'liturgical, spiritual, and pastoral' traditions and may also include elements of the theological tradition.[38]

While the content of the Anglican tradition is broad, that which may be taken from it must be consonant with Catholic faith and practice. It is envisaged, therefore, that only 'aspects' will be 'of particular value' and in 'full harmony with Catholic tradition'[39] or that only some 'elements' may be 'worthy'[40] or 'consistent with the Catholic faith'.[41] Nevertheless, 'insofar as they express in a distinctive way the faith that is held in common, they are a gift to be shared in the wider Church'.[42]

Just autonomy: The structure of the Personal Ordinariate

There were two objectives guiding the thinking of the Holy See in determining a canonical structure for the groups of Anglicans entering the Church. First, it was necessary that the communities of former Anglicans in the Catholic Church have a level of autonomy which would ensure that they would be able to preserve a distinct identity and to flourish as an example of the rich diversity to be found within the Church. Secondly, it was necessary to provide for a level of pastoral supervision by the Holy See which would ensure both the complete integration of these communities into the wider Church and the conformity with Catholic tradition of the relevant elements of the Anglican patrimony brought into the wider Church.

The question was, what kind of canonical structure would be best for carrying out these purposes? Since 1912, a canonical structure other than a diocese or the other ecclesial structures mentioned in Codes of 1917 or 1983 has existed in the Catholic Church for groups of the faithful who have special pastoral needs. This canonical structure has been the 'Ordinariate'. For over one hundred years, the canonical structure of the Ordinariate has shown itself adaptable to a wide range of situations requiring flexible pastoral responses.[43]

An Ordinariate is composed of a portion of God's people forming a hierarchical community with a head, a clergy and lay faithful. Unlike a territorial diocese, where membership is determined by reference to domicile or quasi-domicile in a particular place, the membership of an Ordinariate is determined by reference to an objective criteria pertaining to individual persons – for example, ethnicity, rite or occupation. Thus, an Ordinariate may be called a 'Personal Ordinariate' and the jurisdiction of an Ordinariate is called a 'personal jurisdiction'. Apart from these fundamental and therefore common characteristics, each Ordinariate has different arrangements appropriate to its situation with respect to the nature of its ordinary's jurisdiction (whether it is proper, vicarious, exclusive or cumulative) and the relationship of the Ordinariate with the local church.

In due course, the Holy See decided the canonical structure of the personal ordinariate, erected as a Particular Church by the Roman Pontiff, was the most suitable means of responding to the requests of the groups of Anglicans seeking full communion with the Church. There is specific reference in the footnote to Article 1 of the Decrees of Erection of each of the three Ordinariates to canon 372 §2, which states the power by which each Personal Ordinariate has been established as a Particular Church.

The Personal Ordinariate is, therefore, a Particular Church. It is like a diocese ('juridically assimilated to a diocese') but unlike a diocese in two important respects concerning its relationship to the Holy See. An Ordinary of a Personal Ordinatiate exercises jurisdiction *on behalf of* the Roman Pontiff. Unlike a diocesan bishop whose jurisdiction is 'proper' to himself, a Personal Ordinary's jurisdiction is 'vicarious'. Secondly, the Ordinariate is 'subject to' the CDF and other dicasteries of the Roman Curia. A diocese has greater autonomy than this. Nevertheless, with respect to the Ordinariate's internal government and in its external relations with the local bishops' conference and other dioceses, the Ordinary is the equivalent of a diocesan bishop. It is interesting to note that some of the provisions for the internal ordering and government of the Personal Ordinariates reflect the synodal traditions of Anglican diocesan polity.[44]

Eligibility for membership of the Ordinariate

The qualifications for membership of the Personal Ordinariate are intended to preserve its Anglican character.[45] *Anglicanorum coetibus* and the Complementary Norms are not, however, entirely consistent as to their definitions of the personal criteria required and, in any case, the qualifications for membership have since been expanded to include members of ecclesial communities in the Methodist tradition.[46]

Article I §4 of *Anglicanorum coetibus* provides as follows:

> The Ordinariate is composed of lay faithful, clerics and members of Institutes of Consecrated Life and Societies of Apostolic Life, originally belonging to the Anglican Communion and now in full communion with the Catholic Church, or those who receive the Sacraments of Initiation within the jurisdiction of the Ordinariate.

Thus, there are essentially two categories of persons eligible for membership of the Ordinariate:

- Anglicans or former Anglicans; and
- persons unbaptized or baptized in a church other than an Anglican church.

With respect to the first category, in *Anglicanorum coetibus* the qualification for membership is restricted to persons originally belonging to 'the Anglican Communion'.[47] The Complementary Norms refer more broadly to the 'the lay faithful originally of the Anglican *tradition* who wish to belong to the Ordinariate' (my emphasis).[48]

In the second category – persons who receive all or some of the Sacraments of Initiation within the jurisdiction of the Ordinariate – there are three types of persons who may enter the Church through the Ordinariate:

- A person who is not baptized;[49]
- A person baptized in a non-Anglican church other than the Catholic Church;[50]
- A person baptized in the Catholic Church but only in two specific situations.

The two situations in which a baptized Catholic may become a member of an Ordinariate are as follows:

- A person who has been baptized in the Catholic Church but has not completed the Sacraments of Initiation and subsequently returns to the faith and practice of the Church as a result of the evangelizing mission of the Ordinariate,

may be admitted to membership in the Ordinariate and receive the Sacrament of Confirmation or the Sacrament of the Eucharist or both.[51]
- A person who is Catholic is eligible for membership if he is a 'member of a family belonging to the Ordinariate'[52] or 'part of a family belonging to the Ordinariate'[53] even if he has received all of the Sacraments of Initiation outside the Ordinariate.

More precision has been urged in relation to the second situation, one suggestion being that relevant degrees of consanguinity and affinity within the family should be prescribed.[54] In canonical practice, an ambiguity in specific legislation may be resolved by reference to similar legislation elsewhere.[55] In this case, the law governing privileges is helpful and suggests that the criterion should be interpreted broadly.[56] This is consistent with the traditional rule for interpretation of the law – *favorabilia amplianda odiosa restringenda*.

A Catholic cleric, who came originally from the Anglican Communion and is already incardinated in a diocese, may be incardinated in the Ordinariate in accordance with canon 267.[57]

Formation of the clergy in the Anglican tradition

In both *Anglicanorum coetibus* and the Complementary Norms, the phrase 'Anglican patrimony' is frequently used in the context of the training of priests. *Anglicanorum coetibus* refers to their 'formation in Anglican patrimony' in relation to their preparation 'in the areas of doctrinal and pastoral formation'.[58] The Complementary Norms provide that candidates for the ministry should receive 'formation, in full harmony with Catholic tradition, in those aspects of Anglican patrimony which are of particular value'[59] (and may receive aspects of priestly formation at a seminary program or house of formation established 'expressly for the purpose of transmitting Anglican patrimony').[60] The ongoing formation of Ordinariate clergy is to take place in programs provided by the relevant Episcopal Conference and Diocesan Bishop 'as well as in their own programs of ongoing formation'.[61]

The Anglican liturgical patrimony

For the purpose of compiling and approving of the 'liturgical books proper to the Anglican tradition' as required by Article III of *Anglicanorum coetibus*, it became necessary to develop a specific working definition of 'the Anglican liturgical patrimony'. This was done by the CDF, the Congregation of Divine Worship and the Discipline of the Sacraments through the *Anglicanæ traditiones* Commission mandated by *Anglicanorum coetibus* and established in 2011.[62] The working definition employed by the *Anglicanæ traditiones* Commission was:

> That liturgical expression which has maintained and nourished Catholic faith among Anglicans through the period of ecclesiastical separation and which in these days has given rise to aspirations of full communion with the Catholic Church.[63]

The principal sources were identified in the classic Prayer Book heritage: England, 1549, 1662, 1928; the United States, 1929; Scotland, 1929; South Africa, 1954; Canada, 1962; the English Missal, 1958; and the Anglican Missal, 1961.[64]

The liturgical books

On 22 June 2012, the first liturgies for the Order of Funerals[65] and the Celebration of Matrimony[66] were approved by the Congregation of Divine Worship for use in each of the Personal Ordinariates. In April 2014, these liturgies were published in the book *Divine Worship: Occasional Services*. This book also contains the Order of Holy Baptism and Confirmation for Adults and Older Children, the Order of Baptism for Infants and associated rites, the Order of Solemnization of Marriage and the Order of Funerals. These all draw on traditional Anglican sources and are in the language of the Book of Common Prayer.[67]

On 27 May 2015, the liturgy for the Order of the Mass was approved by the Congregation of Divine Worship.[68] On 22 June 2015, a decree was issued by each Ordinary authorizing the publication of *Divine Worship: The Missal* and authorizing its use from the First Sunday in Advent, 29 November 2015.[69]

In 2015, a 'study edition' of *Divine Worship: The Missal – in accordance with the Roman Rite* was published by the Catholic Truth Society. In 2018, *The CTS Divine Worship Sunday Missal – Peoples' Edition* was published by the CTS. On 20 February 2019, the *St Gregory's Prayer Book* was published by the American Ordinariate.

On 11 November 2019, orders for the Visitation of the Sick, the Blessing of a Sick Child, Communion of the Sick (in an 'ordinary rite' and a 'shorter rite'), Anointing of the Sick Outside of Mass, Penance, Anointing, and Viaticum, Supplication for the Dying and Commendation of a Soul, Additional Prayers and Sacramental and Other Forumulas, were approved by a decree of the CDF.[70] On 11 February 2020, a decree was issued by each Ordinary authorizing the publication of *Divine Worship: Pastoral Care of the Sick and Dying* and its use from 12 April 2020.[71]

With respect to the Daily Offices of Morning and Evening Prayer, many members of the Ordinariates have been using the orders found in one or other of the 1662 Book of Common Prayer, the 1928 Prayer Book or the American prayer books.[72] In the UK, *The Customary of Our Lady of Walsingham* was published in 2012.[73] It was edited by Mgr Andrew Burnham and Fr Aiden Nichols OP and contains forms of the daily offices and other devotions drawn primarily from the English strand of the Anglican tradition. The intention was to bring into the discussion leading to the compilation of liturgical books for the Ordinariates something of the experience of England and Wales. In the introduction, it is stated that the effect of the *Imprimatur* was to authorize the materials in the collection for use in daily devotion and worship. *The Customary* was, however, only intended as an interim liturgical resource for the daily office.[74]

The publication of an office book for use by the English and Australian Ordinariates is planned for Advent 2021. The proposed office book will contain Morning and Evening Prayer from the 'prayer book tradition', together with optional office hymns and antiphons for use with the Benedictus and Magnificat. The 'book ends' of Matins and Evensong will be enriched by the Lesser Hours of Prime, Terce, Sext, None and Compline. It will be called *Divine Worship: Daily Office* (Commonwealth Edition).[75]

The Ordinariate of the Chair of St Peter is expected to publish its own Daily Office book, based principally on the Anglican tradition as developed in the United States. No publication date has yet been announced.[76]

In the Ordinariates, the Roman Rite in both the Ordinary and the Extraordinary Forms and, now, as it is expressed in *Divine Worship: Occasional Services*, *Divine Worship: The Missal* and *Divine Worship: The Pastoral Care of the Sick and Dying* may be used. Public celebration of Divine Worship liturgies is restricted to the Personal Ordinariates.[77] Specifically with respect to the Mass, a priest incardinated in an Ordinariate may celebrate the Mass according to Divine Worship outside the parishes of the Ordinariate when celebrating Mass without a congregation or publicly (for members of an Ordinariate) with the permission of the pastor of the relevant church or parish.[78] In cases of pastoral necessity or in the absence of an Ordinariate priest, any priest may celebrate Mass according to Divine Worship for members of an Ordinariate who request it. Any priest may concelebrate the Mass according to Divine Worship.[79]

The preservation of the Anglican patrimony in the liturgy

By the recent changes to the Complementary Norms (on 8 March 2019), Article 15 was added under the heading 'The Celebration of Divine Worship'. Article 15 §1 incorporates a statement made in the Introduction to the *Rubrical Directory*,[80] providing that

> *Divine Worship*, the liturgical form approved by the Holy See for use in the Ordinariate, gives expression to and preserves for Catholic worship the worthy Anglican liturgical patrimony, understood as that which has nourished the Catholic faith throughout the history of the Anglican tradition and prompted aspirations towards ecclesial unity.

The relationship between Ordinariate Missal and the Anglican patrimony is described in several other passages in the introduction to the *Rubrical Directory*. For example, 'It is a liturgical provision for the sanctification of the faithful who come to the Catholic Church from the Anglican tradition [and] preserves such features and elements that are representative of the historic Anglican Books of Common Prayer and Anglican Missals, in conformity with Catholic doctrinal and liturgical norms.'[81]

Further:

> The celebration of the Holy Eucharist expressed by Divine Worship is therefore at once distinctively and traditionally Anglican in character, linguistic register, and structure, while also being clearly and recognizably an expression of the Roman Rite.[82]

In relation to the texts of the liturgy, under the heading 'General Norms', it is stated that:

> Insofar as *Divine Worship* respects received texts in their integrity, variations of idiom and linguistic register have been harmonized so that the texts chosen are broadly representative of the classic Prayer Book tradition while also attempting to avoid undue preference for wordings distinctive to any particular country.[83]

In relation to the rubrics, it is explained that the rubrics of the *Divine Worship* Order of Mass 'aim to preserve traditional customs of Anglican Eucharistic worship with respect to orientation, postures, gestures, and manual acts'.[84] The texts of the chants (Introit, Gradual, Alleluia, Tract, Offertory and Communion) come from 'the musical patrimony of the Anglican tradition' as well as the 'Coverdale translations of Psalm texts in the chants [which] are common to the Anglican Missals and Anglican translations of the *Graduale Romanum*'.[85]

Finally, both the *Occasional Services* and *The Missal* draw upon Anglican patrimony in the visual arts. Each is illustrated with black and white illustrations by the English artist Martin Travers, whose work was originally commissioned by the Anglican Society of St Peter and St Paul in 1939 for their publication of the first edition of *The Anglican Missal*.[86]

For the Eucharistic Lectionary, the use of the Revised Standard Version of the Bible (the second Catholic edition) and the Coverdale translation of the Psalms from the Book of Common Prayer maintains an Anglican linguistic flavour.[87] The Liturgical Calendar for all of the Ordinariates is the General Roman with the addition of certain commemorations of English saints.[88] In addition, each Ordinariate has its own Calendar and Propers of Masses, as well as any National Calendar drawn up by the local Episcopal Conference.[89]

The Temporal Cycle follows that of the older Anglican tradition, preserving Sundays 'after Epiphany', Septuagesima, Sexagesima and Quinquagesima Sundays before Lent, and numbering the Sundays after Pentecost as Sundays 'after Trinity'.

Thus, the work of promulgating the proper liturgical books of the Ordinariates has been substantially completed, and the implementation of Pope Benedict XVI's desire that the liturgical patrimony of the Anglican tradition be shared with the wider Catholic Church is underway. This is the first time in history that distinctive elements of an ecclesial community established at the Reformation have found an honoured place in the life of the Catholic Church.

Conclusion

The Holy See has given the groups of Anglicans who have been received into full communion with the Catholic Church a canonical structure – the Personal Ordinariate – which has the theological nature and canonical status of a Particular Church but which differs from a diocese by reason of its dependent relationship with the Roman Pontiff and with the Holy See, in particular the CDF and the Congregation for Divine Worship. By these two means, the Holy See intends to ensure both the preservation and maintenance of those elements of the Anglican patrimony – liturgical, spiritual, pastoral and theological – which are consonant with Catholic faith and practice.

In this Anglican patrimony, the Personal Ordinariates in England, Australia and the United States have a treasure to be shared with the whole of the Catholic Church, which will add to the richness of its diversity and which will also maintain that inner dynamic towards Catholic unity which has brought these groups of Anglicans into full communion with the Church and which will further advance the cause of ecumenism and the realization of the prayer, 'Ut unum sint'.

Notes

1   Benedict XVI, Apostolic Constitution *Anglicanorum coetibus* (AC), *AAS* 101 (4 November 2009), pp. 985–90.

2   As amended on 19 March 2019, https://press.vatican.va/content/salastampa/en/bollettino/pubblico/2019/04/09/190409a.html (accessed: 13 December 2020); *Code of Canon Law* 1983 (CIC 1983), canons 31–3.

3   On 15 January 2011, by a decree of the CDF, the Personal Ordinariate of Our Lady of Walsingham was erected for the territory of the Bishops' Conferences of England and Wales and of Scotland. On 1 January 2012, by a decree of the CDF, the Personal Ordinariate of the Chair of St Peter was erected for the territory of the Bishops' Conference of the United States of America. In December 2012, the territory of the Ordinariate was extended into Canada (with the deanery of St John the Baptist). On 15 June 2012, by a decree of the CDF, the Personal Ordinariate of Our Lady of the Southern Cross was erected for the territory of the Bishops' Conference of Australia.

4   CDF, *Adnotatio circa Ordinariatum Personalem pro Anglicanis Catholicam Ecclesiam ingredientibus*, *AAS* 101 (20 October 2009), pp. 939–42; *Holy See Press Office Release*, in Canon Law Society of Great Britain and Ireland, *Newsletter* 160 (4 November 2009), p. 16.

5   Cf. *AC* III.

6   CDF, *Adnotatio*, pp. 939–42.

7   G. Ghirlanda, 'La Costituzione Apostolica *Anglicanorum coetibus*' in *Periodica* 99 (2101), pp. 373–430; G. Read, '"Commentary" in Canon Law Society of Great Britain and Ireland', *Newsletter* 160 (2009), pp. 24–35; W. Tighe, 'The Genesis of *Anglicanorum Coetibus*', a paper presented at the 2011 Anglican Use Conference, Arlington, Texas, the United Sates, available at https://ordinariateportal.wordpress.com/2011/07/19/william-tighe-the-genesis-of-anglicanorum-coetibus/ (accessed: 11 December 2020); J. Wynne-Jones, 'Anglican bishops in secret Vatican summit', *The Telegraph*, 5 July 2008, http://www.telegraph.co.uk/news/uknews/2254269/Anglican-bishops-in-secret-Vatican-summit.html (accessed: 7 January 2016).

8   CDF, *Adnotatio*, p. 939.

9   *AC, Proemio*.

10 Two examples are the Anglican Benedictine Abbey of Caldey Island: P. Anson, *Abbot Extraordinary: A Memoir of Aelred Carlyle, Monk and Missionary* (London: Faith Press, 1958); and the Franciscan Friars and Sisters of the Atonement, New York: Wikipedia, 'Society of the Atonement', available at https://en.wikipedia.org/wiki/Society_of_the_Atonement; Read, 'Commentary', pp. 14–15.

11 Wikipedia, 'The Pastoral Provision', available at https://en.wikipedia.org/wiki/Pastoral_Provision (accessed: 24 April 2019); Ghirlanda, 'La Costituzione Apostolica', p. 379.
12 Ghirlanda, 'La Costituzione Apostolica', p. 381.
13 J. Arrieta, 'Gli ordinariati personali', *Ius ecclesiae* 22 (2010), pp. 151, 154.
14 *Holy See Press Office Release*, 16.
15 B. Pawley and M. Pawley, *Rome and Canterbury through Four Centuries: A Study of the Relations between the Church of Rome and the Anglican Churches 1530-1981* (Mowbray: London and Oxford, 1981).
16 F. Bliss, *Anglicans in Rome: A History* (Norwich: Canterbury Press, 2006), p. 15; Ghirlanda, 'La Costituzione Apostolica', p. 374; B. Pawley and M. Pawley, *Rome and Canterbury*, pp. 7, 25–7; Read, 'Commentary', p. 24; M. Rear, 'A new and living way' in *The Messenger of the Catholic League* 292 (April–August 2010) pp. 51–2.
17 The Malines Conversations were 'quasi-official' on the Anglican side by the time of the second conversation on 14–15 March 1923 and Rome 'approved and encouraged' them: H. McAdoo, 'Anglican/Roman Catholic Relations', in J. Aveling et al. (eds), *Rome and the Anglicans: Historical and Doctrinal Aspects of Anglican – Roman Catholic Relations* (Berlin: De Gruyter, 1982), pp. 199, 202; Ghirlanda, 'La Costituzione Apostolica', p. 375; B. Pawley and M. Pawley, *Rome and Canterbury*, pp. 261–77; Read, 'Commentary', p. 26; M. Reath, *Rome and Canterbury: The Elusive Search for Unity* (Lanham: Rowman and Littlefield, 2007), pp. 33–4; M. Yelton, *Anglican Papalism: A History 1900–1960* (Norwich: Canterbury Press, 2005), 35–7.
18 *Lumen gentium* (LG), 8, '*ad unitatem catholicam impellunt*'. Perhaps the sense of the Latin is better expressed in English by 'having an inner dynamic towards Catholic unity'.
19 *Unitatis redintegratio*, 13, 21 November 1964: *Enchiridion Vaticanum* 1/494–572.
20 St Paul VI, *Homily*, 25 October 1970, available at https://w2.vatican.va/content/paul-vi/it/homilies/1970/documents/hf_p-vi_hom_19701025.html (accessed: 24 April 2019).
21 R. Donohoe, *Continuity or discontinuity? Apostolicae curae* to *Anglicorum coetibus*, Rome 2014; Doctoral thesis at the Pontifical Gregorian University: n. 416590, p. 269.
22 CDF, *Adnotatio*, p. 939.
23 AC III.

24 CDF, *Adnotatio*, p. 940; AC III.
25 CN 10 §2
26 AC III; CDF, *Adnotatio*, p. 940.,
27 LG, 13c.
28 CDF, *Adnotatio*, pp. 940–1.
29 *Holy See Press Office Release*, p. 16.
30 CDF, *Adnotatio*, pp. 939–40.
31 Ibid., p. 941.
32 Archbishops of Westminster and Canterbury, 'Joint Statement by the Archbishop of Westminster and the Archbishop of Canterbury', 20 October 2009, in *The Messenger of the Catholic League* 292 (2010), April–August, p. 260.
33 *Holy See Press Office Release*, 16.
34 CDF, *Adnotatio*, p. 942.
35 See endnotes 20–23.
36 For a more complete list, see Ghirlanda, 'La Costituzione Apostolica', pp. 415–17.
37 CDF, *Adnotatio*, pp. 940–1.
38 Ghirlanda, 'La Costituzione Apostolica', pp. 386–9; Archbishop J. Augustine Di Noia put it as follows: 'The tradition was still there, even after the break, preserving the substance of the faith: zeal for sacred beauty, parochial experience of the divine office; robust devotional life; robust biblical faith; sacred music; Anglican divines and writers', in *Antiphon* 19.2 (2015), pp. 109–15.
39 CN 10 §1 (2).
40 CDF, *Adnotatio*, p. 939.
41 Ibid., p. 940.
42 Ibid.
43 In 1912, the first Ordinariate was established in Canada for the faithful of the Ukrainian Catholic Church by Pius X in 'Apostolic Letter *Officium supremi Apostolatus*', 15 July 1912, *AAS* 4 (1912), pp. 555–6; J. Arrieta, *Governance Structures within the Catholic Church* (Montreal: Midwest Theological Forum, 2000), pp. 187–9. At the time of Second Vatican Council, apostolic Ordinariates for Eastern Catholics had been erected in Greece (1923), Romania (1930), Brazil (1951), France (1954), Austria (1956) and Argentina (1959). In 1991 one was erected in Poland and another for Armenia, Georgia, Russia and Ukraine; Secretary of State, *Annuario Pontifico* (Città del Vaticano, 2015), pp. 1029–33. Each is adapted to its own

circumstances and there is no general norm regarding this kind of Ordinariate; S. Congregation for the Oriental Churches, Decree *Nobilis Galliæ natio*, 27 July 1954, *AAS* 47 (1955) pp. 612–13; E. Baura, 'Personal Ecclesiastical Circumscriptions', in *Philippine Canonical Forum* 12 (2010), pp. 103–30, 121. The Ordinariate structure also has a long history in relation to the pastoral care of members of the armed forces. In 1940, the first military Ordinariate was established in Italy by the Decree *L'ordinario militare*; S. Congregation of the S. Consistory (CSC), Decree *Circa la giurisdizione dell'ordinario militare in italia*, 13 April 1940, *AAS* 32 (1940), pp. 280–1. In 1951, a further Instruction *Sollemne semper* which applied to all the military vicariates was promulgated: cf. CSC, Instruction *Solemne semper*, 24 April 1951, *AAS* 45 (1951), pp. 562–5. The existence of 'special laws' for chaplains to the armed forces was recognized in canon 569 of the 1983 Code. In 1986, by the Apostolic Constitution *Spirituali militum curæ*, 24 April 1986, *AAS* 78 (1986), pp. 481–6, Pope St John Paul II erected the military Ordinariates that now exist in many countries. In the *Adnotatio*, it was noted that the structure of the Personal Ordinariate is similar to that of the Military Ordinariates: *Adnotatio*, 940. In AC there is a footnote reference to *Spirituali militum curæ* in the context of the juridical comparability of the Personal Ordinariate to a diocese: *AC* I §3; St John Paul II, *Spirituali militum curæ*, I §1.

44 CN, 12.

45 Domicile or quasi-domicile (canons 102, 107§1) is only relevant to members of the Ordinariate in relation to Ordinariate clerical assistance to the local diocese (CN 9 §1), to the jurisdiction of an ecclesiastical tribunal (*AC* XII; *DE* 8); canons 1408, 1409, 1413 2°; 1472, or to the territorial jurisdiction to which a member who leaves the Ordinariate automatically belongs (*DE* 10).

46 Website of the Personal Ordinariate of St Peter's Chair, available at https://ordinariate.net/join (accessed: 25 April 2019).

47 http://www.anglicancommunion.org/identity/about.aspx (accessed: 6 February 2016). For a list of member churches of the Anglican Communion see http://www.anglicancommunion.org/structures/member-churches.aspx (accessed: 6 February 2016).

48 CN 5 §1.

49 *AC* I §4.

50 *AC* I §4; CN 5 §3.

51 CN 5 §2.

52 CN 5 §1.

53 Decree of establishment (DE), 1.
54 J. Renken suggests that family members be persons in the first degree of the direct line and the second degree of the collateral line: J. Renken, 'The Personal Ordinariate of the Chair of St Peter: Some Canonical Reflections' in *Studia Canonica* 46 (2012), pp. 5, 21.
55 Cf. canon 17.
56 Cf. canon 77.
57 *DE* 7; CN 4 §2.
58 *AC* VI §5.
59 CN 10 §1 (2).
60 CN 10 §2.
61 CN 10 §5.
62 *AC* III; 'The Personal Ordinariate of the Chair of St Peter', available at http://ordinariate.net/divine-worship-missal (accessed: 5 March 2016).
63 S. Lopes, '"Divine Worship: Occasional Services": A Presentation', in *The Jurist* 74 (2014), pp. 79 at 81.
64 Ibid., p. 81.
65 CDF, Prot. N. 357/12/L (for the Person Ordinariate of Our Lady of the Southern Cross Australia), 22 June 2012.
66 Ibid.
67 R. Williams, 'Radical Ecumenism: New Missal for Anglican Ordinariate' in *The Catholic Weekly*, 15 October 2015, available at https://www.catholicweekly.com.au/radical-ecumenism-a-new-catholic-missal/ (accessed: 24 April 2019). See also Steven Lopes's summaries of their contents in 'Divine Worship'.
68 Congregation for Divine Worship and the Discipline of the Sacraments (CDW), Prot. N. 160/15; Ordinariates, *Divine Worship: The Missal*, 5. The text for the Ordinariate Mass is stated to have been drawn from 'various Anglican sources and from the current Roman Missal and approved as "a legitimate adaptation of the Rome Rite"'.
69 Ibid., pp. 7–9; Williams, 'Radical Ecumenism'.
70 CDF, Prot. N. 5362012; *Divine Worship: Pastoral Care of the Sick and Dying* (London: Catholic Truth Society, 2020), pp. 4–5).
71 *Divine Worship: Pastoral Care of the Sick and Dying* (London: Catholic Truth Society, 2020), pp. 6–7.
72 Each of the three Ordinariates publishes its own daily *Ordo* containing the Calendar, the Eucharistic Lectionary and the Proper

Psalms and Lectionary for the Daily Offices of Morning and Evening Prayer.

73 The Personal Ordinariate of Our Lady of Walsingham, *The Customary of Our Lady of Walsingham* (London: Canterbury Press, 2012).

74 Ibid., pp. ii–iii.

75 Personal Ordinariate of Our Lady of Walsingham, *Bulletin on Divine Worship: Personal Ordinariate of Our Lady of Walsingham*, vol. 1, n.1 (September 2020); https://www.ordinariate.org.uk/cmsAdmin/uploads/2020-1-olw-liturgy-bulletin_compressed.pdf (accessed: 11 December 2020).

76 Anglicanorum Coetibus Society, 'Coming Soon: Ordinariate Daily Office "Commonwealth Edition" Expected Advent 2021', 7 October 2020, available at https://acsociety.org/news/coming-soon-ordinariate-daily-office-commonwealth-edition-expected-advent-2021 (accessed: 11 December 2020).

77 *AC*, Art. III; Introduction to the Order of Holy Baptism, n. 2; Introduction to the Order of Solemnisation of Holy Matrimony, n. 2; Introduction to the Pastoral Care of the Sick and Dying, n. 2; Introduction to the Order of Funerals, n. 2.

78 'Rubrical Directory' (RD), 4, in Ordinariates, *Divine Worship: The Missal*, 120; *AC* III; CN 15 §2.

79 RD 5; CN 15 §3. They are not the equivalent of priests having their own rite (canon 846 §2). The liturgical books of the Ordinary Form are, therefore, the Roman Missal (third edition), the Liturgy of the Hours, the Roman Ritual, the Pontifical, the liturgical books of the Extraordinary Form, the 1962 editions of the Roman Missal, the Breviary, the Ritual, the Pontifical and the liturgical books of the Ordinariate liturgies – *Divine Worship: Occasional Services*, *Divine Worship: The Missal* and *Divine Worship: Pastoral Care of the Sick and the Dying*.

80 RD 3, in Ordinariates, *Divine Worship: The Missal*, p. 120.

81 Ibid., p. 121.

82 Ibid. Second Vatican Council, Constitution *Sacrosantcum consilium*, 38.

83 Ordinariates, *Divine Worship: The Missal*, p. 122.

84 RD 10, Ordinariates, *Divine Worship: The Missal*, p. 122.

85 RD 13, Ordinariates, *Divine Worship: The Missal*, p. 123.

86 Ibid., the title pages.

87 Williams, 'Radical Ecumenism'.

88 Such as St Alban the first English martyr, St Thomas of Hereford, St Edward the Confessor, St Frideswide of Oxford, St Aidan of Lindisfarne and various canonized Archbishops of Canterbury, including, of course, St Augustine of Canterbury. More recently recognized holy persons, such as St Elizabeth Seton and Blessed John Henry Newman, both converts from Anglicanism, are also found in the Ordinariate calendar: Ordinariates, *Divine Worship: The Missal*, pp. 135–48.

89 Ordinariates, *Divine Worship: The Missal*, 'General Instruction', p. 394.

3

The worship of God in the beauty of holiness: A presentation of *Divine Worship*

Most Rev. Steven J. Lopes, STD

The proper liturgy of the Personal Ordinariates established under the 2009 Apostolic Constitution *Anglicanorum coetibus* provide a new occasion for theological reflection on the worship of God in the beauty of holiness. Known collectively as *Divine Worship*, texts for the celebration of the Eucharist and other sacraments were approved by the Holy See specifically for those communities who have come into full Catholic communion from various Anglican and Episcopal traditions. Simply put, the Ordinariates spring from the ecumenical vision of Pope Benedict XVI as a concrete way for inviting formerly Anglican parishes and communities into full communion with the Catholic Church. The Apostolic Constitution itself revolves around a very clear and important ecumenical principle: the unity of faith allows for a vibrant diversity in the expression of that same faith. Three Ordinariates have thus far been established in England, in North America and in Australia, and, over the course of the last ten years, we have worked to develop our own ecclesial life and structures even as we continue to invite new persons and communities to join us in the adventure of Catholic communion.

Pope Francis has taken the principle of the unity of faith allowing for a diversity of expression and given it even more concrete parameters. It is Pope Francis who promulgated *Divine Worship: The Missal* for the celebration of Holy Mass for the Ordinariate communities. During the same week in 2015 in which the *Divine Worship* Missal was first authorized for use, the Holy Father appointed me Bishop of the Ordinariate of the Chair of Saint Peter in the United States and Canada, thereby demonstrating that the Ordinariates are truly Particular Churches, equivalent to dioceses, although organized on the canonical principle of personality rather than territory. It is my privilege to present the Missal to you today and, in so doing, highlight the particular liturgical patrimony of the Ordinariates, a beautiful example of the realization of the ecumenical vision of Pope Saint John Paul II, Pope Benedict and Pope Francis.

At the outset of this reflection, I find it necessary to articulate something of a thesis statement, arising out of my experience, that Ordinariate liturgy is often misunderstood and, therefore, not described correctly. Because *Divine Worship* liturgy shares many traditional elements and gestures in common with the Extraordinary Form of the Roman Rite, it is thought to be a type of 'subset' of that form: 'the Extraordinary Form in English' as it is sometimes called. But this is neither accurate nor, honestly, helpful. For one thing, the 1549 *Book of Common Prayer*, a principal source for the Ordinariate Missal, is *older* than the Missal of Saint Pius V and has its own origins in the Sarum Missal, a variant of the Roman Rite going back to the eleventh century. The first goal should be to understand *Divine Worship* on its own terms, to see the historical and ritual context out of which it develops, and in that light to recognize how it might contribute to the ongoing renewal and development of the Roman Rite.

And so the thesis *Divine Worship* is more than a collection of liturgical texts and ritual gestures. It is the organic expression of the Church's own *lex orandi* as it was taken up and developed in an Anglican context over the course of nearly five hundred years of ecclesial separation, and is now reintegrated into Catholic worship as the authoritative expression of a noble patrimony to be shared with the whole Church. As such, it is to be understood as a distinct form of the Roman Rite. Further, while *Divine Worship* preserves some external elements more often associated with the Extraordinary Form, its theological and rubrical context is clearly the Ordinary Form of the Roman Rite. That I situate *Divine Worship* within the context of the Ordinary Form becomes a fact more discernable when one considers the dual hermeneutic of continuity and reform, which informs the project.

A preliminary consideration: What is patrimony?

Divine Worship – expressed in the Missal, in a ritual book called Occasional Services and in the Divine Office – is the concrete realization in Catholic worship of the liturgical and spiritual patrimony of Anglicanism. In making provision for the incorporation of this patrimony into Catholic life, the Apostolic Constitution *Anglicanorum coetibus* specifies:

> the Ordinariate has the faculty to celebrate the Holy Eucharist and the other Sacraments, the Liturgy of the Hours and other liturgical celebrations according to the liturgical books proper to the Anglican tradition, which have been approved by the Holy See, so as to maintain the liturgical, spiritual and pastoral traditions of the Anglican Communion within the Catholic Church, as a precious gift nourishing the faith of the members of the Ordinariate and as a treasure to be shared.[1]

Understanding what patrimony is and how it 'works' is a necessary first step before we are able to articulate something more about the liturgical expression of that patrimony. From the outset, the Constitution itself articulates the necessity of the approval by the Holy See for any liturgical provision. This fact itself indicates that the Church is the ultimate arbiter of what is or is not to be considered patrimony. This can be considered the *first key* to unlocking the concept of patrimony. It is not what you or I, or this scholar or that community says it is but involves discernment by the Church, which is then confirmed by the exercise of ecclesiastical authority.

In this age in which liturgical matters are more likely to be debated on blogs rather than in scholarly journals, the judgement of legitimate ecclesiastical authority becomes increasingly important. Indeed, the very affirmation that there is such a thing as an Anglican liturgical and spiritual patrimony, which enriches the whole Church as 'a treasure to be shared', enters the Catholic lexicon in 1970. On October 25 of that year, Pope Paul VI canonized forty English and Welsh martyrs. In his homily, the Holy Father praised 'the legitimate prestige and worthy patrimony of piety and usage proper to the Anglican' Communion, words that were viewed both as a crucial validation of the special relationship between Catholics and Anglicans and as a confirmation of the existence of an Anglican patrimony worthy of preservation.[2] By his authority, Pope Paul articulated a principle: for whatever other ecclesial deficits resulting from the lack of full communion between the Catholic Church and the Anglican Communion, the Catholic Church acknowledges the work of the Holy Spirit in this body of separated brothers and sisters so as to be able to say that the manner in which the faith was nourished, proclaimed and celebrated in the Anglican Communion these past five hundred years adds to the vitality of the Church and enriches the body Catholic.

In *Anglicanorum coetibus*, we see Pope Paul's insight framed in Pope Benedict's concern 'to maintain the liturgical, spiritual and pastoral traditions of the Anglican Communion within the Catholic Church' not only 'as a precious gift nourishing the faith of the members of the Ordinariate', but also importantly 'as a treasure to be shared'. Concretely, then, the Interdicasterial Commission charged with preparing the *Divine Worship* was not given the task of composing a new liturgical text or devising new liturgical forms, but rather of identifying the patrimony from 'the liturgical books proper to the Anglican tradition'.

This mention of Anglican liturgical books naturally invites the question: which books? Liturgy is one of the most tangible forms of patrimony, one expressed in a variety of texts, rituals, devotions and customs over the course of the near five-hundred-year history of Anglicanism – and that history has not always been serene in its unfolding! To summarize briefly:

- Though Henry VIII will always be known for the break with Rome, there was actually little doctrinal and liturgical alteration in the English Church during his reign. The rest of the Tudor period is marked by the introduction of more clearly Protestant theology and liturgy under Edward VI (1547–53), a brief Catholic restoration under Queen Mary (1553–8) and the settlement of the long reign of Elizabeth I (1558–1603), during which time Calvinist accents and emphases came to the fore, even as these coexisted uneasily with of Catholic habits of worship that has also been retained.[3]

- The pendulum swings widely during the period of the Stuart kings (1603–88), beginning with both James I and Charles I gesturing toward the possibility of reunion with the Holy See and ending with an eleven-year Puritan Protectorate after the civil war in which the Church of England and its liturgy were outlawed.[4] Not only does the political situation have enormous ramifications for Anglican worship, but this is also the period of the 'Caroline Divines' who sought to provide an authoritative foundation for the teaching of the Church of England based on patristic sources for Catholic traditions and institutions. They ensured, for example, that the *Book of Common Prayer* retained elements such as an ordered liturgy, the liturgical calendar, the indissolubility of marriage, the sacramental character of priestly absolution and confession and the retention of a three-fold sacrament of Orders.

- From 1688 to 1833, different 'streams' or parties form within the Church of England – 'latitudinarian' broad church, an evangelical low church and a mildly Catholic high church – each bringing different emphases and approaches to the celebration of the liturgy, at times so distinct one from the other that it would be difficult to see them as expressions of the same ecclesial communion.[5]

- The mid-nineteenth century sees the revival of Catholic faith in Anglicanism, notably with the conversion of Blessed John Henry Newman and others, the Oxford Movement and the parallel development of Victorian ritualism.[6] In the early twentieth century, another small group emerged who styled themselves as Anglo-Papalists who understood themselves as working for the corporate unification of the Church of England with the Holy See.[7] These would adopt many of the ritual gestures, observances and practices of the Roman Rite (prior to the reforms of the Second Vatican Council, of course). The Anglican or English Missal tradition has its beginning here.

In all of this, the *Book of Common Prayer* is the point of departure for any understanding of Anglican worship. The Prayer Book itself has experienced several revisions since its first appearance in 1549, some of these quite notable. Given the historical arc and development of Anglican liturgical worship, both in its more Protestantizing reforms and its more conservative tendencies to retain Catholic elements, how does ecclesiastical authority – in this case the Holy See – identify what truly constitutes patrimony? Put another way, when faced with the great variety of forms and texts in Anglican worship, how is the Church to discern what might be incorporated into Catholic worship?

We need, it seems, more keys to unlock the concept of patrimony. A *second key* has been articulated by Archbishop J. Augustine DiNoia, OP, who was intimately involved both in the process that led to *Anglicanorum coetibus* and in his leadership of the commission which produced *Divine Worship* for the Ordinariates. He offers the following definition of patrimony:

> The liturgical books comprised by *Divine Worship* arise from an exercise of Peter's authority over the churches that recognizes the authentic faith of the Church expressed in Anglican forms of worship and confirms that expression as a treasure or patrimony for the whole Church. In other words, the Church recognizes the faith that is *already hers* expressed in a new idiom or felicitous manner. The elements of sanctification and truth that are present in the patrimony are recognized as properly belonging to the Church of Christ and thus as instruments of grace that move the communities where they are employed towards the visible unity of the Church of Christ subsisting in the Catholic Church.[8]

If the first key is the external authority of the Holy See which chooses and confirms liturgical texts, the second key is the internal authority of Catholic truth to which these liturgical forms give voice; elements of sanctification and truth which ultimately impel towards the fullness of Catholic communion.

There was – and perhaps continues to be – great confusion caused by the tremendous variety of liturgical forms in the Anglican world, each of which advances a competing claim to patrimony and to authority as 'Anglican use'. Even following the publication of *Anglicanorum coetibus*, no less than six different liturgical books were being used for the celebration of the Eucharist by Ordinariate communities at the time the Liturgical Commission began its work. The task of the Holy See's Commission was to extract out of this disorientating variety a *lex orandi*, the systematic presentation of Christian faith, nourished and preserved in the classical Prayer Books and Anglican Missals, in order to provide the sure doctrinal foundation that makes a diversity of liturgical expression possible. The search for the authentic faith of the Church within Anglican worship allows us to situate *Divine Worship* firmly within the shape and context of the Roman Rite so that it might be approached in a manner that respects its own integrity and authority.

A *third key* is pastoral in nature as evidenced by the Holy See's concern for those parishes and communities entering into the Ordinariate. What was their formative liturgical experience? How has the manner of their worship and prayer sustained and nurtured their faith, prompting them towards Catholic unity? If there are rituals, liturgical postures, gestures and vesture common to all of the Ordinariate communities, then the pastoral good of leading these communities into full communion should respect that insight, and the liturgical provision make allowance for continuity in those practices which, consonant with the Catholic faith and sacramental understanding, impel towards Catholic unity (the allusion to *Lumen gentium* number 8 is fully intended: *Elementa ... ad unitatem catholicam impellunt*). Entrance into full communion involves an act of the will, but it is not merely an intellectual exercise.

An example may help: in the United States and Canada, all but a very small handful of our communities celebrated Mass *ad orientem* as Anglicans and desire to continue doing so as Catholics. This is certainly consistent with the faith of the Church! Further, forcing these communities to adopt an entirely foreign orientation in prayer during that vulnerable time of coming into full communion is, to say the least, pastorally unnecessary and disadvantageous. And so Mass according to *Divine Worship* is normally celebrated *ad orientem*, with allowance made in the proper rubrics for *versus populum* celebration if the architecture or a parish's particular experience suggests that it is more appropriate.

To conclude this preliminary reflection on patrimony, let me offer that these three keys to 'patrimony' as enunciated here are not meant as an exclusive list. To these, one might rightly add an evangelistic key or the interiorization of the mission to spread the Gospel. Nevertheless, the dual dynamic of authority and right concern for the pastoral good of people are absolutely foundational for the incorporation of this form of worship in the Catholic Church. In an Ecclesial Communion that eschewed both a Magisterium and the exercise of papal authority, one can argue that it was the *Book of Common Prayer* itself that ensured a *lex orandi*, the systematic presentation through liturgical expression of the Christian faith. With the establishment of the Ordinariates, it is an exercise of Peter's authority over the Churches which *recognizes* the authentic faith of the Church expressed in Anglican forms of worship, which *confirms* that expression as a treasure or patrimony for the whole Church and which *orders* that expression in such a way as to favour the forms and rituals that have given rise to the desire for *communio*. In the movement into full communion, this liturgical treasure is further enriched by access to the Magisterium, which authentically interprets the Word of God, preserves Christian teaching from error and assists the faithful and their pastors in the delicate task of expressing timeless truths in a way that is fresh, beautiful and attractive. This is not to impose a Roman perspective on this liturgical prayer, but to draw out of these rich sources an authentic expression of the faith so that they might continue to provide the *lex orandi* to the nourishment of this and future generations.

Divine Worship: The Ordinariate Form of the Roman Rite

We can now move beyond the background of patrimony to a more specific consideration of *Divine Worship* understood as a distinct form of the Roman Rite – an Ordinariate Form, if you will. Tracing its relationship to the other two Forms of the Roman Rite is not at first glance obvious. Although *Divine Worship* preserves some ritual elements and traditional gestures associated with the Extraordinary Form, its theological and rubrical context is the Ordinary Form of the Roman Rite. This is demonstrated by the fact that the *General Instruction of the Roman Missal* is printed in its entirety at the beginning of the *Divine Worship* Missal. Further, the particular Rubrical Directory of *Divine Worship: The Missal* states:

> The liturgical norms and principles of the *General Instruction of the Roman Missal* are normative for this expression of the

Roman Rite, except where otherwise stipulated in this Directory and in the particular rubrics of *Divine Worship*. This present Directory is intended to provide instructions for those areas in which *Divine Worship* diverges from the *Roman Missal*.[9]

Concretely, this means that those gestures and elements more associated with the Extraordinary Form are accounted for explicitly in the particular rubrics of *Divine Worship*. Where there are lacunae or when questions arise about pastoral practice, adaptations and so on, the celebrant has recourse to the *General Instruction* and not to other pre-conciliar sources.

On one hand, this is an understandable canonical framework, since the *General Instruction* is one of the highest expressions of law in the Church, ranked alongside the *Code of Canon Law*. The particular rubrics that govern *Divine Worship* are a derogation from that universal disposition (and hence it is called a Rubrical Directory). This also implies an understanding of the *General Instruction* as something more than a 'road map' of rubrics, but rather unfolding the shape and logic of Catholic worship. So even if there is divergence in some of the rubrical practices, there is a much more important theological unity of the Roman Rite that informs this Missal.

To understand the right relationship between *Divine Worship*, the Extraordinary Form and the Ordinary Form, it will be helpful to consider some of the hermeneutics that guided the development of this Missal. The hermeneutics of 'continuity' and 'reform' are familiar enough terms and I will use them here, though only to illustrate that the *pastoral hermeneutic* is the overarching structure determining when continuity is best preserved and when reform is best applied. When we hear 'hermeneutic of reform', most of us will immediately think of the reforms of the sacred liturgy that followed the Second Vatican Council, although these certainly had their antecedents in the reforms of previous Popes. In the case of *Divine Worship*, there is what might be called a dual hermeneutic of reform, one arising out of the reform of the Roman Rite undertaken in Anglicanism – especially by Archbishop Thomas Cranmer in the development of the first prayer books of 1549 and 1552 – and only then the reforms of the Roman Rite following the Second Vatican Council. Both of these have important implications for the structure and content of *Divine Worship*.

Here are two examples of the adaptation of the Roman Rite in Anglicanism, which were themselves guided by the theological emphases of the English Reformation:

1. *Emphasis on the proclamation and preaching of the Word of God.* This finds expression in certain Collects composed by Cranmer himself that petition for the efficacy of God's Word, as well as in ritual elements of the Mass, which favour the biblical formation of the assembly. According to *Divine Worship*, the Gospel is ordinarily proclaimed in the midst of the congregation (i.e. in the nave), which is itself evocative of the ecclesial context for the liturgical proclamation of Scripture. The Penitential Rite is transposed from its familiar Roman position as an introductory rite to the conclusion of the Liturgy of the Word just prior to the Offertory. It is the proclamation of the Word of God, in the Scriptural lessons, in preaching and in the response of faith that is the Creed and Prayers of the People, that convicts us of our sins and brings us to repentance and contrition prior to offering our gift on the Altar. The Penitential Act itself is one of Cranmer's longer compositions said by priest and people together in an attitude of penance (the people kneeling).

2. *Emphasis on liturgy as the prayer of the Church, head and body.* Cranmer apparently had a healthy disdain for the so-called 'secret' prayers of the Mass said silently by the priest alone, perhaps particularly the practice of the 'whispered Canon'. He eliminated secret prayers completely from the Prayer Book, replacing them with original compositions said by priest and people together. These too are preserved in the *Divine Worship* Missal and, at least from the experience of the worshipping faithful, are three of the most notable transitions in the Mass. We have already mentioned the Penitential Act. After the *Agnus Dei*, the priest's private prayers of preparation for receiving Holy Communion are replaced by a very public, corporate act of preparation in the Prayer of Humble Access. This prayer, said by all who will receive the sacrament, has long been noted for the richness of its Eucharistic theology as well as the beauty of its rhetoric. Finally, at the conclusion

of the Communion Rite, the Missal preserves the general thanksgiving, again said by priest and people together as a corporate act of thanksgiving for the gifts received. This prayer is concluded by the priest singing or saying the proper post-communion prayer for the given Mass.

If we were to set *Divine Worship* within the overall context of the development of the Roman Rite, these two 'Cranmerian' emphases, already expressed in the first Anglican Prayer Books, are the reason for the clearest ritual differences between *Divine Worship* and the Roman Missal. To these – again, along the lines of the reform/development of the Roman Rite – we must add the insights of the liturgical reform following the Second Vatican Council. These contemporary emphases can be seen in the *Divine Worship* Missal in terms of the structure and rubrics of the Sacred Triduum, the inclusion of proper Masses for 17–24 December, the Calendar of Saints, votive Masses and the inclusion of several Masses (sixteen in all) for various pastoral and spiritual necessities.

Thus far, I have mentioned several ways in which reforms of the Roman Rite, both historical and contemporary, have influenced the structure of the Missal. What about examples of continuity with the more ancient form of the Roman Rite? That is certainly present in the Missal too, although the line between the celebration of Mass prior to the English Reformation and its expression in the *Divine Worship* Missal is neither straight nor without interruption. This is where some of the history of Anglicanism described earlier becomes important. It is a history of tension between more Catholic sensibilities on one side, and more Protestant leanings on the other. It is a tension between the Caroline Divines and the Puritan Protectorate, between the Oxford Movement and broad-church liberalism.

The 1662 Book of Common Prayer, which, note, is still the authoritative version, contains vestiges of Catholic ritual and practice that were present in the 1549 Prayer Book, though to a lesser extent in the 1552 Book of Common Prayer. There is a clear rupture between what has become a clearly Protestant Prayer Book and its Catholic roots. It is not until the early twentieth century that the situation changes in substantive ways. The emergence of the Anglo-Papalists with their explicit desire for reunion with the Holy See prompts a significant liturgical renewal in at least that small portion of Anglicanism. Through the development of the English

Missal and the Anglican Missal, the form of worship takes on the outward appearance of what we would now call the Extraordinary Form of the Roman Rite, though with the Collects, prefaces and some other elements of the *Book of Common Prayer* folded in. To a great extent, this liturgical expression achieves its desired effect: Anglo-Catholics who worship according to the Missal *do* understand themselves as the Catholic party within Anglicanism, and it is many of these same clergy and faithful who sought full communion with the Holy See both before and after the publication of *Anglicanorum coetibus*.

So, with this in mind, let us turn to the recent work of the Commission tasked with developing the liturgy for the Ordinariates. One of that body's principal objectives was 'to propose an Order of Mass at once distinctively and traditionally Anglican in character, content, and structure, while also being clearly and recognizably an expression of the Roman Rite, in both its ordinary and extraordinary forms'.[10] Many of the parishes and communities coming into the Catholic Church (notably in North America and Australia) were indeed formed in the Anglican Missal tradition, and so things such as prayers at the foot of the Altar, the traditional form of the Offertory, communion at the rail, the Last Gospel were all familiar, regular aspects of their worship. Other parishes and communities (notably in England) did not share this experience, since their worship over the course of the last forty years as Anglicans mirrored the modern Roman Rite, and many of these Anglican communities would have even directly used the Roman *Sacramentary*.

The Commission was therefore faced with a dilemma. On the one hand, though there was tremendous agreement on the essential *content* of the Prayer Book, which should be preserved in the Catholic Church (collects, prefaces, hieratic English, etc.), there was simply not the liturgical uniformity *in practice* throughout the three Ordinariates that would allow one agreed-upon form or structure. It seemed counter-intuitive, even absurd, to apply a strict hermeneutic of reform, as conforming their liturgy to the reforms of the Second Vatican Council would, in effect, disallow the very traditional liturgical practices and gestures which sustained the Catholic faith of so many people and even prompted the desire for unity at the heart of *Anglicanorum coetibus*. At the same time, it seemed counter-intuitive, even absurd, to force more traditional rituals and gestures on communities which simply had no experience of them at all.

The Commission therefore decided for what at the time we called a 'flexible' approach. The Rubrical Directory of the Missal describes it this way:

> The rubrics of the *Divine Worship* Order of Mass aim to preserve traditional customs of Anglican Eucharistic worship with respect to orientation, postures, gestures, and manual acts, while also permitting the celebration of Mass in a manner similar to that of the *Roman Missal, Third Typical Edition*. This rubrical flexibility provides for the variety of liturgical traditions and experiences among the parishes and communities of the Personal Ordinariates.[11]

The aim, therefore, is pastoral accommodation. The Missal is structured in such a way so as to accommodate those communities who, professing the same Catholic faith, come from the Anglican Missal tradition, the Prayer Book tradition and even the tradition of using the Roman *Sacramentary*.

Structurally, this means that many traditional elements are given as options in *Divine Worship*, particularly through a series of appendices. Appendix one supplies the prayers of preparation (Psalm 43, *Confitior*, vesicles), which may be said in the sacristy or at the foot of the Altar. Appendix two has the forms of the *Asperges* and *Vidi aquam*. Appendix six is the Last Gospel, which may be used at the conclusion of Mass at the discretion of the priest and is even recommended in Christmastide. Two forms of the Offertory are given, the first drawn out of the Anglican Missal tradition while the second form reflects the *Roman Missal* as revised following the Second Vatican Council.

The particular rubrics of the *Ordo Missae* also reflect this pastoral accommodation of varying experiences. The rubrics both in the introductory rites and during the concluding rites make reference to the priest's location and actions at the Altar, but they are introduced by this general note: 'Where appropriate, [these rites] may take place at the sedilia, omitting in that case the rubrics hereafter referring to the Altar.'[12] Other traditional gestures are rubricated with the permissive 'may' rather than the prescriptive 'is'. In this way, allowance is made for particular custom, not in order that there be novelty or variety from week to week but out of respect of the custom which has arisen in the context of a particular parish or community of the Ordinariate.

Again, an example or two may help. In the parishes of the North American Ordinariate, all but two of our parishes celebrate Mass *ad orientem* – and this was really never a question but a simple reflection of the liturgical practice of these communities even prior to entering full communion with the Catholic Church. Consequently, though it is possible according to *Divine Worship* to preside from the sedilia as is common in the Ordinary Form, the vast majority of our priests preside from the Altar and go to the sedilia only for the readings. Of our forty-seven parishes, perhaps fifteen have the custom of the Prayers at the Foot of the Altar and the Last Gospel every Sunday. A dozen more would take a seasonal approach, using the Last Gospel during Christmastime, for example. Those who come from strongly Anglo-Catholic parishes that use the Prayers at the Foot of the Altar would also use Offertory Form One almost exclusively, or at least Form One on Sundays and Form Two during weekday Masses.

Again, the point is that *Divine Worship*, as a form of the Roman Rite, must be approached and considered in its own integrity. It is certainly possible to see the influences of the traditional Roman liturgy, as well as many insights of the reforms of the Second Vatican Council. Understanding the particular insights of Archbishop Cranmer and the English Reformation is important in order to visualize the overall structure of the Order of Mass. The generous accommodation of custom is intentional, and reflects a pastoral hermeneutic faithful to Pope Benedict XVI's principle of diversity in unity that is at the very heart of *Anglicanorum coetibus*.

Distinctive elements of *Divine Worship*

That we have considered some of the theological presuppositions of *Divine Worship* and looked at its overarching structure, a brief overview of some of the elements of the Missal would now be in order. These not only give a sense of the order and content of the celebration of Mass in the Ordinariate, but will illustrate some of the principles we have been considering.

The liturgical year

Generally speaking, the flow of the Proper of Time in the *Divine Worship* Missal is in harmony with the Roman Rite. The Calendar of Saints, for example, is identical to the General Roman Calendar, though it incorporates the national calendars of England, Wales, the United States, Canada and Australia, as well as celebrations of Saints special to the Ordinariate. One distinction between *Divine Worship* and the typical edition of the Roman Missal is that the category of 'Ordinary Time' does not have any resonance in our communities. Following Christmas, *Divine Worship* observes Time after Epiphany or Epiphanytide, which lasts until pre-Lent (the three so-called 'Gesima' Sundays). Whereas the Extraordinary Form counts Sundays after Pentecost, *Divine Worship* follows the traditional Anglican practice of numbering Sundays after Trinity Sunday. Trinitytide concludes with the celebration of Christ the King on the Sunday prior to the first Sunday of Advent.

Eucharistic Prayer

The Roman Canon is the privileged Eucharistic Prayer of the Missal. Its use is obligatory on all Sundays and solemnities. An Alternative Eucharistic Prayer, which corresponds to the second prayer of the Roman Missal, is also given for pastoral reasons. It may be used on weekdays or in Masses with children. Its use on Sunday is explicitly prohibited.

Advent, Ember days and Rogation Days

The typical edition of the *Roman Missal* focuses on Christ's second coming in glory and, during the days of 17–24 December, provides a more intense preparation of Christmas. The inclusion of these additional Masses has meant, at least in practice, the loss of the Ember days.[13] The Commission was faced with a two-fold desire: (1) to maintain the Ember days and their proper seasonal context as expressive of a venerable element of Anglican worship; (2) to appreciate and incorporate the richness of the proper Masses for 17–24 December in harmony with the Ordinary Form of the Roman Rite. The problem is that the two overlap, since the Advent Ember days have been celebrated beginning on the Wednesday 'following St. Lucy's Day' since the time of Pope St Gregory VII. The Advent context of the December Ember days was judged to be the factor of importance, not the location of the celebration in the third week of Advent. In the Missal, the Ember days have been located in the first week of Advent, and the proper Masses for

17–24 December have likewise been incorporated into the Missal. The other Ember days are maintained in their traditional locations in Lent, in conjunction with Pentecost and in September.

In light of what has just been said about the Ember days, a word about Rogation Days seems in order. These days had a particular resonance in medieval English piety, litanies and processions forming a principal expression of English spiritual life, notably the pilgrimage to the shrine of Our Lady at Walsingham. These expressions endured in Anglicanism, particularly in those communities that did not disdain their Catholic roots. In the *Divine Worship* Missal, the Rogation Days are in their traditional Roman location preceding Ascension.

The Paschal Triduum

By way of introducing the Paschal Triduum, it may be worth noting again that no less than six different liturgical books were being used by Ordinariate communities at the time the Commission began its work. When looking at Holy Week in particular, the variety was rather disorienting. I don't mind saying that this is a point where the Holy See 'steered' the work of the Commission in setting the parameters for the celebration of the Paschal Triduum within the Ordinariates. This is understandable if you approach liturgy not as the expression of personal preference or insights, but as a fundamentally ecclesial act.

The Missal attempts to achieve balance: balance between essential unity and legitimate diversity, between the universal and the particular and between Roman patrimony and Anglican patrimony. This desire for balance is reflected in Rome's decisions regarding the rites for the Paschal Triduum. On the one hand, it was decided that Catholic unity would be best expressed if the overall shape and structure of the Triduum is simply that of the normative Roman Rite. Ordinariate parishes and communities celebrate the central liturgy of the Passion, Death and Resurrection of the Lord *in communion* with the universal Church. On the other hand, diversity and patrimony is expressed in these rites in that the texts themselves are drawn from the Anglican sources and, therefore, enrich the celebration. The result is an integral whole and not simply a shuffling together of pieces from various sources. Most of the rubrics which guide the liturgies of Holy Thursday, Good Friday and the Easter

Vigil will be nearly identical to those of the *Roman Missal*, third typical edition. The sequence of scriptural readings, notably those of the Easter Vigil, have been harmonized with the lectionary. Some flexibility has been worked into the rubrics to take account for local traditions (musical options and vestment colour, for example). Great care was taken that there be an integrity and internal coherence to the shape of the celebration of the Paschal Triduum so that it exemplifies essential ecclesial unity, while allowing some legitimate diversity, in the fullness of Catholic communion.

Minor propers

For each celebration of Mass, the *Divine Worship* Missal provides full texts of the minor propers (Introit, Gradual, Alleluia/Tract, Offertory and Communion). As noted in the *Praenotanda*, these texts are provided in service to the musical patrimony of the Anglican tradition and so it is specified:

> The given texts of the chants may be substituted by the chants of the *Graduale Romanum* or by musical settings of the *Graduale* which rely on a different translation of the same texts. The Gradual and Alleluia may be substituted for the Responsorial Psalm and Alleluia of the Lectionary. In addition to, or in place of, the Introit, Offertory, and Communion, an appropriate hymn may also be sung. Likewise, the given text of a Sequence may be replaced by another translation of the text.[14]

The presence of the minor propers in the *Divine Worship* Missal is motivated by three factors:

1. This is clearly part of the Anglican liturgical tradition as the chants are present in so many of the sources. The Coverdale translations of Psalm texts in the chants are common to the Anglican Missals and Anglican translations of the *Graduale Romanum*.
2. Much like the King James version of the Bible, the Coverdale translation of the Psalms has played a formative role in English language, culture and religious imagination.
3. Again, authority is important. There are various hymnals, graduals, prayer books and ritual books out there that present

the same basic texts but with all sorts of little variations. The Missal, as a liturgical book promulgated by the Holy See, establishes *with authority* the texts of the minor propers on the basis of which other musical settings and books can be developed.

Consistently and from various sources both Anglican and Catholic, historical and contemporary, one finds the assertion that the Anglican liturgical tradition has been distinguished by the prominence it gives to Scripture in the conduct of public worship and in the promotion of biblical piety. Scriptural words and images are almost a default starting position, a fact that no doubt bears witness to the hallowed tradition of English monasticism, which informs so much of Anglican worship. The minor propers beautifully rendered in 'Prayer Book English' allow for a greater inclusion of Scripture in worship. It is about reading the Bible liturgically, allowing the words and poetic cadences to linger, penetrate, and take root in the soul as a sustained, communal *lectio*.

Conclusion

The famous and often-cited passage in the correspondence between Pope St Gregory the Great and St Augustine of Canterbury takes on new resonance in the liturgical project of the Ordinariates and offers not only a fitting conclusion to this discussion:

> *Augustine's Second Question:* Since we hold the same Faith, why do customs vary in different Churches? Why, for instance, does the method of saying Mass differ in the holy Roman Church and in the Churches of Gaul?
>
> *Pope Gregory answers:* My brother, you are familiar with the usage of the Roman Church, in which you were brought up. But if you have found customs, whether in the Roman, Gallican, or any other Churches that may be more acceptable to God, I wish you to make a careful selection of them, and teach the Church of the English, which is still young in the Faith, whatever you can profitably learn from the various Churches ... Therefore select from each of the Churches whatever things are devout, religious, and right [*quae pia, quae religiosa, quae recta*]; and

when you have arranged them into a unified rite, let the minds of the English grow accustomed to it.[15]

From the first evangelization of England down to the present day and the publication of *Anglicanorum coetibus*, there is an overarching concern of the Church to place sacramental formulae and traditions of worship at the pastoral service of the People of God. Such liturgical 'inculturation' is only good if, as Pope Gregory says, it nurtures faith and results in something devout, religious and right. This is the context in which to situate the *Divine Worship* Missal and ritual books. Again, Archbishop Augustine Di Noia says, '*Divine Worship* is not a museum piece, but rather the Holy See's prudent grafting of proven Anglican shoots on the rooted, living trunk of the Roman Rite to promote new and healthier growth.'[16] That is ultimately the point. The beautiful expression of these prayers, the rich tapestry of the English language they preserve and even the emphasis on transcendence in worship is not really worth preserving *in itself*. Rather, the pastoral contribution to the vitality of Catholic life is the goal. This is expressed in the growth of Ordinariate communities, both through inviting other people to enter into full communion and by inviting other Catholics to re-engage with their faith and their Church at a deeper level. It is also expressed in the ongoing, ever-deepening conversion, which is the hallmark of true discipleship. In other words, the value of *Divine Worship* is measured to the degree it positively contributes to making more Catholics and better Catholics.

Notes

This text was originally given as the Hillenbrand Lecture on 21 June 2017, at the Liturgical Institute, University of St Mary of the Lake, Mundelein, Illinois.

1 Pope Benedict XVI, Apostolic Constitution *Anglicanorum coetibus*, Art. III.
2 Pope Paul VI, Homily at the Canonization of Forty Martyrs of England and Wales, St Peter's Square, 25 October 1970. The homily was spoken largely in Italian, though the words quoted here were pronounced at the conclusion of the homily in English as part of Pope Paul's prayer for the unity of Christians. A full text is available

at http://www.vatican.va/content/paul-vi/it/homilies/1970/documents/hf_p-vi_hom_19701025.html.

3   For a fuller treatment of the Tudor Reformation, see S. Neill, *Anglicanism* (London: Pelican, [1958] 1977), pp. 34–133.

4   Cf. Neill, *Anglicanism*, 133–68.

5   A robust treatment of the development of these three movements or parties within Anglicanism is given by Aiden Nichols in his book *The Panther and the Hind: A Theological History of Anglicanism* (Edinburgh: T&T Clark, 1993).

6   Cf. Neill, *Anglicanism*, 254–61.

7   Few Anglicans actually espoused the claim to papal authority. Much more prevalent was the so-called 'branch theory' which proposes that Rome and England were parts or branches of the one Catholic Church. See, for example, A. Nichols, 'Anglican Unitism: A Personal View', *The Messenger of the Catholic League* 292 (2010), pp. 13–20. This theory even enters official Anglican parlance, as three Lambeth Conference resolutions (in 1867, 1920 and 1930) refer to the Anglican branch of the Catholic Church.

8   J. Augustine Di Noia, '*Divine Worship* and the Liturgical Vitality of the Church', *Antiphon* 19 (2015), p. 113. Cf., also, Second Vatican Ecumenical Council, Dogmatic Constitution on the Church *Lumen gentium* (21 November 1964), 8.

9   *Divine Worship: The Missal*, Rubrical Directory, no. 7.

10 For a detailed presentation of the objectives and work of the commission, see my article 'A Missal for the Ordinariates: The Work of the Anglicanae Traditiones Interdicasterial Commission', *Antiphon* 19 (2015), pp. 116–31.

11 *Divine Worship: The Missal*, Rubrical Directory, no. 10.

12 Cf. *Divine Worship: The Missal*, pp. 560, 656.

13 Though, as the *General Instruction on the Roman Missal* makes clear in nos. 394 and 397, there was never an intention to disregard the tradition of Ember days entirely.

14 *Divine Worship: The Missal*, Rubrical Directory, no. 13.

15 Saint Bede the Venerable, *Ecclesiastical History of the English People*, trans. Leo Sherley-Price (London: Penguin Books, 1990) I, p. 27.

16 Di Noia, '*Divine Worship* and the Liturgical Vitality of the Church', p. 112.

4

The evangelizing mission of the Ordinariate

Very Rev. Timothy P. Perkins

Since the promulgation of the Apostolic Constitution *Anglicanorum coetibus* by Pope Benedict XVI in 2009, the character of the parochial communities established in the Ordinariate has largely been responsive. Just as the Constitution was written in response to requests received by the Holy See from various groups of Anglicans, those groups, having now been incorporated into full communion within the life of the Church, have themselves become responsive in disposition, welcoming others who have come to them out of either curiosity or informed interest. This is in itself a good thing. In some instances, the friendly welcoming response to inquirers has become the means through which interested persons have been led into full communion with the Church. But membership growth of this kind is limited, and many of the parochial communities of the Ordinariate have not yet achieved the sufficient size and stability necessary for long-term sustainability. The future well-being of many Ordinariate communities and, thus, the foundational strength of the Ordinariate depend on attracting others by intentional evangelization.

The evangelical character that undergirds such intentionality is a Gospel mandate. The oft-quoted commission to 'make disciples of all nations' at the conclusion of Matthew's Gospel established an evangelical world view in the life of the Church. It is this that orders ecclesial life towards mission, and this mission of evangelization provides the motivation needed for the members and communities of the Ordinariate for transition from the responsive posture of the first decade of existence into the missional activity of evangelization. This essential transition is not a new idea to be tried. An evangelizing mission has marked the beginnings of many Ordinariate groups; and over these early years, steps have been taken to foster a deeply missional self-understanding among the clergy and faithful. As an example, the mission to evangelize can be glimpsed in the introduction to *Architects of Communion: Guide for Parish Development*, which was promulgated on 31 May 2016 by Most Reverend Steven J. Lopes, bishop of the Personal Ordinariate of the Chair of Saint Peter. Asserting that there is more to establishing parishes than administration, the third paragraph of the document declares, 'The establishment and structuring of parishes is therefore ordered to the salvation of souls.' It further states, 'It is ordered to communion with God and the broader Church.'[1] This foundational ordering describes the very identity of the Ordinariate. It gives the diocesan-like structure its personal character.

From this ordering to the salvation of souls, the Ordinariate is given an evangelizing zeal. All of its structures, from its establishment of localized parochial communities to its juridical oversight and all of the various organizational elements of which it consists are to be governed by the central principle so necessary for ecclesial identity and fidelity, 'the salvation of souls, which must always be the supreme law in the Church'.[2] At the same time, this zeal for souls carries with it the deep aspiration for communion. It is much more the personal concern for particular individuals. Rather, it is the longing for that wholeness that unites each soul with God and others in 'one communion and fellowship'[3] within the larger Church.

This expansive way of speaking of the evangelizing mission of the Ordinariate is only beginning to come into the corporate consciousness of the clergy and faithful. The more responsive disposition of the earliest days was identified at the outset of this text. It should be noted that this disposition was in part influenced by the founding documents. Accompanying the publication of *Anglicanorum coetibus* were Complementary Norms that established particular law for the Ordinariate. Of the two paragraphs concerning the faithful of the Ordinariate, the first is regarding the eligibility for membership.

§ 1. The lay faithful originally of the Anglican tradition who wish to belong to the Ordinariate, after having made their Profession of Faith and received the Sacraments of Initiation, with due regard for Canon 845, are to be entered in the apposite register of the Ordinariate. Those baptized previously as Catholics outside the Ordinariate are not ordinarily eligible for membership, unless they are members of a family belonging to the Ordinariate.[4]

The wording of this paragraph appears to be quite restrictive, implying that the only persons eligible for canonical membership in the Ordinariate are former Anglicans who became Catholic and their family members. This implication raised the question as to what persons might be the proper recipients of the evangelizing efforts of various Ordinariate groups or members.

It would be difficult to measure exactly what limitations this lack of clarity placed upon the mission of evangelization within the Ordinariate, but it was a much-discussed matter. This discussion was not limited to the musings of the clergy and faithful belonging to the Ordinariate. The question of membership eligibility was also frequently a topic of conversation between Ordinariate and diocesan officials. This was especially so in cases where new communities were beginning to form or when former Anglican priests make application to the Ordinariate seeking admission to holy orders. Reliance on the founding documents as originally published was often insufficient for resolving diverse interpretations and the conclusions drawn therefrom. At times, this resulted in undue tension between parties with vested interests in communities or persons related to the Ordinariate. Such lack of clarity cannot be conducive to the confidence that is inherent in evangelizing zeal.

On 9 April 2019, the Congregation for the Doctrine of the Faith (CDF) promulgated a revised version of the Complementary Norms for the Apostolic Constitution *Anglicanorum coetibus*. Writing to the clergy of the Ordinariate of the Chair of Saint Peter on that date, Bishop Steven Lopes explained that the revisions were made at the request of all three Ordinariates, the Ordinariate of the Chair of Saint Peter, the Ordinariate of Our Lady of Walsingham and the Ordinariate of the Southern Cross. He further noted the necessity that such revision be made based on the experience and recognized needs of those who participate in the life of the Ordinariate. The original document had been written prior to the erection of the first Ordinariate for the UK, the Ordinariate of Our

Lady of Walsingham, in 2011. This being the case, certain features were theoretical projections of what an unrealized structure might become. The revisions to the Norms take into account the need for greater clarification for the sake of mission.

Of particular interest in this regard are changes to Article 5, which address the issue of membership in the Ordinariate. The first paragraph, quoted above, had been amended in 2013 in a way that does not exclude membership of those who were baptized Catholic but may not have continued in the practice of the faith. Instead, the sentence was edited to read, 'Those who have received all of the Sacraments of Initiation outside the Ordinariate are not ordinarily eligible for membership.' This clearly recognizes the not uncommon situation in which a person is baptized but not fully formed in the faith and whose sacramental life has been neglected over the passage of time. With this revision, not only those who belong to a family that includes members of the Ordinariate but also Catholics who are drawn more fully into the life of the Church through the evangelizing effort of the Ordinariate may be eligible for membership.

This change was further explained by the inclusion of an additional paragraph that followed:

> § 2. A person who has been baptized in the Catholic Church but who has not completed the Sacraments of Initiation, and subsequently returns to the faith and practice of the church as a result of the evangelizing mission of the Ordinariate, may be admitted to membership in the Ordinariate and receive the Sacrament of Confirmation or the Sacrament of the Eucharist or both.[5]

The footnote to this text indicated that his decision has been made by the CDF and approved by Pope Francis in May 2013.

Communications of this decision, at the time it was made, to the clergy and faithful of the Ordinariate have proved helpful in efforts to encourage a change from passive responsiveness to evangelistic action among members and communities. This wording acknowledges that, like all other dioceses and institutions of the Catholic Church, the Ordinariate shares in 'the evangelizing mission' to bring all people to saving faith in Jesus Christ in the full communion of the Catholic Church.

The reality of this mission is further affirmed by an additional paragraph, added to Article 5 in the most recent revision:

> § 3. A person, who has been validly baptized in another Ecclesial Community outside of the Catholic Church, and subsequently desires to enter into full communion with the Catholic Church through the evangelizing mission of the Ordinariate, may be admitted to membership in the Ordinariate upon reception into full communion and conferral of the Sacraments of Confirmation and Eucharist. Also, this applies to the case of those not being validly baptized that have come to the faith through the evangelizing mission of the Ordinariate and therefore receive in it all of the sacraments of initiation.[6]

Twice in these few lines of text, 'the evangelizing mission of the Ordinariate' is affirmed. With this emphasis, it is clear that as the second decade of Ordinariate life begins, it is time to advance beyond a merely responsive posture. It is not enough for members and communities to passively wait for persons outside of the Ordinariate to express curiosity. The Holy See has affirmed that the Ordinariate shares in the mission mandate Our Lord gave to his Church. The mission to make disciples, baptize and teach the fullness of truth revealed in Christ is the mission of the Ordinariate, just as it is the mission of the whole Church. As Bishop Lopes explained in his correspondence with his clergy:

> In explaining the new Norms to our people, we would do well, then, to underscore the missional character of this law and of the Ordinariate itself. The journey into full communion at the origin of our particular Church is but the first movement that gives shape to the Ordinariate, and we cannot get stuck there! The second movement is to go out again – armed with the confidence of Catholic doctrine, the beauty of our English patrimony, and the joy of communion – to draw others into the adventure of faithful discipleship.[7]

Confident in the truth the Church proclaims, worshiping in striking sacral language 'in the beauty of holiness', and rejoicing in the communion that nurtures the fullness of faith, the Ordinariate is uniquely positioned to fulfil the mission of evangelization.

The idea of fulfilling the evangelizing mission immediately raises the questions as to how this is to be accomplished. Too readily, leaders may think in terms of finding a particular programme or identifying resources being used in other dioceses or organizations within the Church. This may be a fruitful step that needs to be taken. However, for the sake of consistency of witness to the particular identity of the Ordinariate, consideration of characteristic identifying features should be given due consideration.

In the Apostolic Constitution, then Pope Benedict XVI wrote of what has often been discussed under the heading 'Anglican patrimony'. Traditions from within Anglicanism that had nurtured faith and motivated desire for the communion of the Catholic Church are described in section III of the Constitution as 'a treasure to be shared'. This treasure, these traditions, are subject to approval by the Holy See and are identified as 'liturgical, spiritual and pastoral'. Each of these elements should rightly influence the manner in which the Ordinariate mission is conducted.

Undoubtedly, the most recognizable characteristic of the Ordinariate is the particular liturgy of *Divine Worship*. Without going into details about the distinctiveness of this form of the Roman Rite, it is sufficient to note that the use of what is often called 'prayer book' language for the texts rings with familiarity in the English-speaking cultures in which the Church exercises the ministry of evangelization. The words of prayer simply sound like prayer, because they have been encountered frequently through much of the most influential literature published in the English language. Additionally, because it is clear, comprehensible language that remains distinct from the informal, common speech used in daily life, the language of the liturgy expresses not merely formality but the reverence that is due the sacred offering. In a world overwhelmed with mundanity, language that exalts, lifting up the mind and heart, expresses value, the worth that underlies the very notion of worship.

The evangelizing efforts of the Ordinariate must always be inspired by and lead to this unique expression of worship. Of course, as the 'source and summit' of the Christian life, the Eucharist must be central in the lives of those participating in evangelization. Regular public celebration of Mass is foundational for the stability and growth of the parochial communities that make up the Ordinariate. At the same time, non-Eucharistic liturgies can provide the settings in which to make and teach disciples. Scheduling and promoting occasions of prayer in the distinctive liturgical language of the Ordinariate to which inquirers and others are invited in the name of the Church might provide the best environment to share the great treasure of our faith with others.

The liturgical tradition that is practiced in the Ordinariate deeply impacts the spiritual life of the clergy and faithful. The Anglican tradition out of which they came is rightly identified with the formative use of *The Book of Common Prayer*. The prayers and devotions contained therein are rightly understood as corporate in nature. They are prayer in common. But many of the individual prayers from within the various rites and the occasional and supplemental prayers supplied therein can be used effectively and devotionally by individuals in private. Likewise, the psalter and the lectionary have guided generations in praying with the scripture. In the Ordinariate, work has been ongoing to provide these same beneficial elements for the use of the people. In addition to the proper liturgical books of *Divine Worship*, the Ordinariate of the Chair of Saint Peter has overseen the publication of the *St. Gregory's Prayer Book*, a collection that includes a simplified Daily Office, the Order of Mass and numerous other prayers and devotions for personal use.

The spiritual life that is fostered by these particular characteristics that flow from the Anglican liturgical tradition is a regularly structured one. It consists of the pattern of a three-fold rule of prayer: Mass, Office and personal devotion. In the fast-paced, over-scheduled modern world, exposure to such a simple, prayerful rhythm provides direction for those seeking to pass beyond the surface of human living. Keeping this pattern, the Ordinariate is able to provide opportunities to share the experience of this structured approach to the spiritual life with all who are feeling directionless in the experience of their daily lives and thus introduce them to the saving faith of the Church.

Another aspect of the patrimony identified in the Constitution is the pastoral dimension. The relational quality of parishes and parochial communities within the Ordinariate has frequently been described as 'domestic' in tone. The typically smaller size of these communities allows for the members to be well known to one another. This is true of the faithful, but it also includes the relationship with the priest and, if he is married, his family. The priest is known and supported as the father of the community, for which and to which he is responsible for providing sacramental care and regular pastoral support. This marked familial sense of the community is sometimes expressed even in terms of one's 'Church family'. This quite naturally includes a strong sense of belonging that can either help or hinder evangelization. When this belonging is perceived as in any way exclusive, it becomes a challenge to welcome newcomers or visitors, and the need to reach beyond the familiar circle of relationships may not even come to mind. But when confidence in one's own belonging and identification with the shared mission of evangelization are combined, they become a motivating force. The various gifts of the clergy work in conjunction with those of all the members and can be employed in establishing the efforts to reach others with the saving Gospel of Christ.

Called into existence a decade ago by the publication of *Anglicanorum coetibus*, the Ordinariate has become more fully established. Some of its parishes have achieved and are maintaining a comfortable stability, while new communities are forming in locales where an Ordinariate presence has not previously existed. At the same time, the majority of the parochial communities remain small and their long-term viability questionable. The necessity of growth in membership is a present reality. Such growth will not be accomplished through a passive responsiveness to those who come to the Ordinariate based on their own personal interest or curiosity. Rather, especially with the publication of the revised Complementary Norms, the time has come for the Ordinariate to embrace its evangelizing mission. Strengthened by the confidence of belonging within the full communion of the Church and inspired by the zeal for souls that desires all to come to saving relationship with Christ within this communion, the rich heritage, liturgical, spiritual and pastoral, that is a great gift to be shared can supply the Ordinariate with the tools and opportunities necessary to discover the means by which it can make disciples, teach the faith and celebrate the sacramental life.

Notes

1 Architects of Communion, 'Guide of Parish Development, Personal Ordinariate of the Chair of Saint Peter' (2016), available at https://ordinariate.net/guide-to-parish-development (accessed: 17 April 2019), p. 3.

2   Code of Cannon Law, Liberia Editrice Vaticana (1983), available at https://www.vatican.va/archive/ENG1104/_INDEX.HTM (accessed: 17 April 2019).
3   *Divine Worship: The Missal* (London: The Catholic Truth Society, 2015), p. 869.
4   Complementary Norms for *Anglicanorum coetibus*, Congregation for the Doctrine of the Faith (2019).
5   Ibid.
6   Ibid.
7   Steven J. Lopes, 'Letter to the Priests and Deacons of the Ordinariate of the Chair of Saint Peter', 9 April 2019.

5

The virtue of religion: The irreducible essence of the Anglican patrimony

Rev. James Bradley

What is the Anglican patrimony? This question has perhaps more than any other vexed, challenged and amused interested parties in equal measure in the decade since the promulgation of *Anglicanorum coetibus*. Yet it is a question of fundamental importance that relates in an essential way to the structure and purpose of the Personal Ordinariates which are the fruit of Pope Benedict XVI's Apostolic Constitution. Commentators on this subject, not few in number, have gravitated towards an almost unanimous position in which the Anglican patrimony is seen principally in its liturgical texts. Certainly there is merit in this point of view, as Augustine Di Noia has said in relation to the Personal Ordinariates, '[The] manner in which an ecclesial community worships uniquely expresses its inner life'.[1] So the liturgical texts and ceremonial and liturgical aesthetics found in the communities of the Personal Ordinariates are important: they relate very strongly to their purpose and mission. The music, hymnody, vesture, language, orientation, ritual and overall style of liturgical celebrations in the parishes and communities of the Personal Ordinariates certainly do speak of, indeed, enunciate, the Anglican patrimony. Nevertheless, one might argue that this is not so much the essence of the patrimony itself, but rather a vehicle for it.

In this paper it will therefore be argued that in seeking to understand what is meant by the Anglican patrimony we have perhaps been asking the wrong question, or at least asking the right question in the wrong way. This is not to contest the view that the Anglican patrimony is identifiable in liturgical texts – it very clearly is – but rather that it is identifiable in these texts because of something more fundamental, some irreducible essence the awareness of which affords the Personal Ordinariates an important opportunity to strengthen their distinctive identity and make a contribution to the wider Church. This irreducible essence is, arguably, the virtue of religion.

Religion as virtue

Saint Thomas Aquinas identifies religion as a subset of the cardinal virtue of justice. A cardinal virtue, a human virtue, is one 'which renders a human act and man himself good'.[2] Justice achieves this in general because it 'regulates human operations' and ensures the right ordering of man's relationship with one another. As Saint Augustine puts it, 'Justice is that virtue which gives every one his due.'[3] Justice achieves this particularly in relation to God when it brings about the right ordering of man's place in relation to the creator; when it allows man to see man as man, and God as God.[4] As Saint Thomas says, 'It is evident that to render anyone his due has the aspect of good, since by rendering a person his due, one becomes suitably proportioned to him, through being ordered to him in a becoming manner.'[5] In true religion, on this account, man 'becomes suitably proportioned' to God. The object of religious obedience, the object of moral living and the object of worship are the same: God. Man renders to God that which is his due as God, and man acknowledges his own place in the order of creation by being 'ordered to [God] in a becoming manner'. In religious obedience, in man's submission of his self to God and before God, man acknowledges God as the creator and source of all life: *God of God, light of light, very God of very God, begotten, not made, being of one substance with the Father, by whom all things were made*, as the Nicene Creed puts it.

In this act of obedience, man also recognizes God as the source of all moral truth and so is obliged by this knowledge to accept and abide by the laws, precepts and commandments of God, not only as a necessary means for moral living but also in order to pursue deeper union with him. Finally, in worship man professes this belief in who God is in the externalized performance of the cult. It is this participation of man in cultic worship that most clearly recognizes God as God, because it is through worship that man ultimately acknowledges God as the source of religion and moral living; not simply the source of its presentation. Jesus Christ is not simply a prophet; God is not simply one being among many. Religion, and particularly the externalization of religion in authentic worship, that is 'in spirit and in truth', makes this clear (Jn 4.24). We can see this in the connection that exists between religious obedience, moral living and worship, and who Christ claims to be in the Gospels: *the way, the truth, and the life* (Jn 14.6).

The acting out of religion can therefore be said to find its zenith in the act of offering worship. But religion is not exhausted by worship, it is crowned by it. As we have already said, the moral life, the subjection of the self to the laws and precepts of God and, thus, the entire culture and ethic of the Christian life are intimately woven together in this act of offering to God that which is his due. John Saward rightly claims, '[There] can be no culture without cult, without worship, the first act of the virtue of religion.'[6] At the same time, it follows that all of human culture has a potential orientation towards the exercise of religion; towards the offering of worship by the created to the creator. When culture seeks truly to reflect the beauty of the created order, and thus the creator from whom all good things come, it becomes clad in the virtue of justice and, thereby, acts as a vehicle for offering to God that which is his due. As we have said of the obligation to moral living that is born of religion, it binds man both as a means of living in a moral way and as a way of acknowledging the divine nature of God as the author of truth. The same can be said of worship: it binds man as a moral action (the reason why the Church prescribes certain worship by means of obligation) and as a way of deepening our union with the Lord God (which is ultimately an action determined by love, itself the fruit of true justice towards the creator).

A further point to be made here is about the choice of the word 'cult' to describe this worship. Conscious that this term carries with it some unhelpful connotations, at least in contemporary general English usage, it is necessary to distinguish between worship that is cultic in nature and that which is not. The offering of worship that is 'given', that is objectively ordered to a particular objectively good end and is received and offered by a community (in this case, the Church), is of a different order from that worship which is formulated by an individual person or community. The Christian cult itself expresses the truth about the nature of God and what God has done for man in Jesus Christ. This means that true worship, cultic worship, is most clearly and authentically found in those expressions received and given by the community of the Church. As recalled above, the way in which a community worships reveals its inner life. This is of fundamental importance in the life of the Church, which is not simply a human institution but the mystical body of Christ. Therefore, the worship undertaken and performed by the Church must express in an authentic and unambiguous way the reality of who Christ is and what he does, even now, in the worship of heaven.

Robin Ward puts it this way: 'The Christian cult conforms to the sacramental economy by being attentive to the outward and visible signs of its celebration, because it is the archetypal exercise of the virtue of religion by the fundamental sacramental sign which is Christ's mystical body.'[7] Thus in order for worship to be faithful to this principle it must be regulated by this same body, Christ's mystical body, the Church. The 'given-ness' of authorized liturgical worship helps to ensure that the worshipper remains faithful to authentic worship, and, thus, ultimately man remains faithful to God by worshipping in a manner that seeks to guarantee he remains 'suitably proportioned'.

Religion in the Anglican tradition

It may be argued that such an understanding of religion runs as a kind of golden thread through the liturgical, spiritual and pastoral traditions of a major strand of classical Anglicanism. This is not to make the claim that the idea of the virtue of religion is a uniquely Anglican attribute, nor that it originated in Anglicanism.[8] Rather it is to contend that a conscious and subliminal understanding of religion as a virtue has acquired a certain virility in the Anglican mind and, thus, in Anglican-influenced expressions of ecclesial life. To quote Richard Hooker (1554–1600), 'So natural is the union of religion with justice, that we may boldly deny there is either, where both are not.'[9]

It is this 'union of religion with justice' that is at the heart of many of those hard-to-explain qualities which commentators have often attributed to the Anglican patrimony, and gone on to identify in externals, particularly in liturgical texts. It is a *way of being*, a *way of doing*, even *a way of speaking*, that can certainly be found in writings, hymnody, liturgical texts and so on, but which at the same time should not be limited to these tangible sources.

It would seem that this classical Anglican tradition, and those communities formed and nurtured in that tradition, has preserved this understanding through certain attitudes, practices and approaches, which offer – in parallel to mainstream Catholic practice in Europe and in remarkable contrast to its Protestant contemporaries – a distinctive way of living the Christian life. Furthermore, within the full communion of the Catholic Church the preservation and promotion of these various attributes not only offers the opportunity 'to maintain the liturgical, spiritual, and pastoral traditions of the Anglican Communion within the Catholic Church, as a precious gift nourishing the faith of the members of the ordinariate[s]' in a manner envisaged by the Apostolic Constitution *Anglicanorum coetibus*, but also, moreover, are 'a treasure to be shared' for the benefit of the wider Church (*Anglicanorum coetibus* III).

Religion in the Anglican tradition of worship

This section will now present a brief outline of how the principles of the virtue of religion can be identified in Anglican liturgical practice as a further means of demonstrating how Anglican liturgical texts communicate these principles, and also how these principles can be understood to have a broader and more fundamental importance in understanding the nature of the Anglican patrimony.[10]

According to the Second Vatican Council, amongst the communities of Christians separated from the full communion of the Catholic Church during the sixteenth century Anglicanism 'occupies a special place'.[11] *Unitatis Redintegratio* notes that '[the] brethren divided from us ... use many liturgical actions of the Christian religion. These most certainly can truly engender a life of grace in ways that vary according to the condition of each Church or Community'.[12] Further still, in relation to the separated communities of the West, 'their form of worship sometimes displays notable features of the liturgy which they shared with us of old'.[13]

This is particularly the case with Anglicanism. Writing in 1962, the convert clergyman and later Bishop of Leeds, Gordon Wheeler, remarked that 'the average Anglican is brought up in a high appreciation of the beauty and dignity of worship'.[14] This appreciation is not generally a mere and simple attachment to liturgical externals, although it may through circumstance lack a complete and integral liturgical ecclesiology, but is rather a product of an understanding inherent in large swathes of the classical Anglican tradition that formal, liturgical worship is important because it offers to God that which is his due. This is surely an identifying mark of the virtue of religion.

Hooker's *Ecclesiastical Polity* is once more a useful source for us on this point. For Hooker public worship may be described as 'the splendor and outward dignity of our religion, forcible witnesses of ancient truth, provocations to the exercise of all piety, shadows of our endless felicity in heaven, on earth everlasting records and memorials, wherein they which cannot be drawn to hearken unto that we teach, may only by looking upon that we do, in a manner read whatsoever we believe'.[15] Indeed, Hooker makes the case for public liturgical prayer, for church buildings set aside as formal places of worship and for the worthy appointment of these churches. He writes warmly of the need to ensure that churches are decorous and decent, saying, 'We every where exhort all men to worship God, even so for performance of this service by the people of God assembled, we think not any place so good as the church, neither any exhortation so fit as that of David, "O worship the Lord in the beauty of holiness."'[16]

The seventeenth-century metaphysical poet and Anglican clergyman George Herbert also pursues a similar point in his own remarks on the obligations of the parson with respect to the cleanliness and ordering of his church building, drawing a clear connection between the proper external ordering of worship and those things set apart for divine service and the intention that undergirds such offering of prayer and praise.

> [All] this he doth, not as out of necessity, or as putting a holiness in the things, but as desiring to keep the middle way between superstition, and slovenlinesse, and as following the Apostles two great and admirable Rules in things of this nature: The first

whereof is, *Let all things be done decently, and in order:* The second, *Let all things be done to edification*, I Cor. 14. For these two rules comprize and include the double object of our duty, God, and our neighbor; the first being for the honour of God; the second for the benefit of our neighbor. So that they excellently score out the way, and fully, and exactly contain, even in external and indifferent things, what course is to be taken; and put them to great shame, who deny the Scripture to be perfect.[17]

This is surely Anglicanism's own rendering of the maxim *lex orandi, lex credendi*. What Hooker and Herbert demonstrate is an understanding of the importance of liturgical worship for several ends, not least the externalization of man's offering of what is due to God through the exercise of the virtue of religion (i.e. justice) within the classical Anglican mindset. At the same time they see that worship is not primarily an act of obligation to the law, but the result of love for God, of man giving God as God that which is his due.

A final note is necessary here on what Hooker calls the 'endless felicity of heaven'. This is a point which deserves greater study, but in brief we can say that worship understood in this way (as the rendering of justice to God through religion) is ultimately worship that is oriented towards heaven, towards beatitude. This focus on worship for the sake of justice towards God, and, thus, on the goal of worship in beatitude, continually directs the worshipper to God and to his eternal presence in the glories of heaven. It avoids viewing authentic worship as merely transactional, as if worship is carried out by man out of pure fear of God, and it instead proposes that God is at least equally worshipped (if not more so) out of the love man has for God, drawn from what God has done for him in Jesus Christ. It is not without reason that Anglican liturgical texts, hymnody and sacred music are laden with references to the life of the world to come, an orientation to worship that is also apparent in the traditional words of the *Act of Contrition* (my emphasis): 'O my God, I am heartily sorry for having offended thee, and I detest all my sins, because I dread the loss of heaven and the pains of hell, but *most of all* because they offend thee, my God, who art all good and deserving of all my love.' John Henry Newman discusses this in one of his *Plain and Parochial Sermons*, linking moral living and religious observance to the desire to be with God in the eternal kingdom of heaven. Newman writes:

To be holy is, in our Church's words, to have 'the true circumcision of the Spirit'; that is, to be separate from sin, to hate the works of the world, the flesh, and the devil; to take pleasure in keeping God's commandments; to do things as He would have us do them; to live habitually as in the sight of the world to come, as if we had broken the ties of this life, and were dead already.[18]

Newman first of all sees the obedience of God's commandments as something in which man should 'take pleasure', and in doing so adopts an orientation towards beatitude: 'to live habitually as in the sight of the world to come'. This desire for heaven, Newman goes on to say, is fundamentally tied to authentic worship:

Heaven then is not like this world; I will say what it is much more like, – *a church*. For in a place of public worship no language of this world is heard; there are no schemes brought forward for temporal objects, great or small; no information how to strengthen our worldly interests, extend our influence, or establish our credit. These things indeed may be right in their way, so that we do not set our hearts upon them; still (I repeat), it is certain that we hear nothing of them in a church. Here we hear solely and entirely of *God*. We praise Him, worship Him, sing to Him, thank Him, confess to Him, give ourselves up to Him, and ask His blessing. And *therefore*, a church is like heaven; viz. because both in the one and the other, there is one single sovereign subject – religion – brought before us.[19]

Some concluding remarks

In the first decade of the project of implementing the Apostolic Constitution *Anglicanorum coetibus*, great importance has been placed on the definition and promulgation of the liturgical books of *Divine Worship*, which 'gives expression to and preserves for Catholic worship the worthy Anglican liturgical patrimony'.[20] This is meet and right. The liturgical expression of the Anglican patrimony is, by its nature, the clearest and most obvious expression of the identity of the communities of former Anglican clergy and faithful who have now found a place in the Catholic Church. Finding an expression of the Anglican patrimony that is at once familiar to the members of the Personal Ordinariates and expressive of the identity of the Anglican patrimony to those outside these communities has been, and remains, of utmost importance.

At the same time the liturgical expression of the Anglican patrimony must be a fundamental expression of a lived reality, of a culture and ethos that runs through the entire life of the communities of the Personal Ordinariates. It is through a greater awareness and cultivation of the virtue of religion that this can take place, and which by God's grace will ensure a happy future for Pope Benedict's youngest children.

Notes

1 Augustine Di Noia, '*Divine Worship* and the Liturgical Vitality of the Church', *Antiphon* 19, no. 2 (2015), pp. 109–15 at 110.
2 Thomas Aquinas, *Summa Theologiae*, II-II, Q. 58, A. 3.
3 Augustine of Hippo, *De civitate Dei*, XIX, 21.
4 Cf. *Catechism of the Catholic Church*, Second Edition (Vatican City: Libreria Editrice Vaticana, 2000) n. 1807.
5 Aquinas, *Summa Theologiae*, II-II, Q. 81, A. 2.
6 John Saward, *The Beauty of Holiness and the Holiness of Beauty. Art, Sanctity, and the Truth of Catholicism* (San Francisco: Ignatius Press, 1997), p. 76.
7 Robin Ward, *On Christian Priesthood* (London: Continuum, 2011), p. 97.
8 On this point see especially the writings of the seventeenth century French School, notably Charles de Condren, Jean-Jacques Olier, Pierre de Bérulle and Saint Jean Eudes. It is of particular interest that this school of spirituality, which produced many of the great seminaries in France, had a following amongst Tractarians and Oxford Movement leaders in the Church of England, including Henry Parry Liddon, vice principal of Cuddesdon College. This influence in turn saw the development of residential theological colleges for the training of clergy in the Church of England from the nineteenth century onwards.
9 A. S. McGrade (ed.), *Richard Hooker: Of the Laws of Ecclesiastical Polity. A Critical Edition with Modern Spelling* (Oxford: Oxford University Press, 2013), V, p. 1.
10 For a discussion of the role of the Anglican tradition of moral theology in relation to this point, see Robin Ward, 'The Anglican Tradition of Moral Theology', *Messenger of the Catholic League* 292 (2010), pp. 144–54. The author is particularly grateful to

Dr Ward, who, as Principal of Saint Stephen's House, Oxford, presented the virtue of religion to us, his students, in a consistent and convincing way.

11 *Unitatis redintegratio*, 13.
12 Ibid., 3.
13 Ibid., 23.
14 Gordon Wheeler 'English Catholicism and the Anglican Tradition', in J. C. Heenan (ed.), *Christian Unity: A Catholic View* (London: Sheed & Ward, 1962), pp. 82–113 at 104.
15 McGrade *Richard Hooker*, p. 71.
16 Ibid., p. 16.
17 George Herbert, in R. Blythe (ed.), *A Priest to the Temple or the Country Parson* (Norwich: Canterbury Press, 2003), p. 33.
18 John Henry Newman, *Plain and Parochial Sermons* (San Francisco: Ignatius Press, 1997), I, p. 1.
19 Ibid.
20 Complementary Norms 2019, Art. 15 §1.

6

Seedtime: St John Henry Newman, personal influence and the evangelizing mission of the Ordinariates

Clinton Brand

'Verily, verily, I say unto you,
except a corn of wheat fall into the ground and die,
it abideth alone:
but if it die, it bringeth forth much fruit.'

JN 12.24 (AV)

That the tenth anniversary of Pope Benedict XVI's Apostolic Constitution *Anglicanorum coetibus* (4 November 2019) so nearly coincided with the canonization of John Henry Newman (13 October 2019) prompts reflection on the providential dynamic linking the two events. Newman is the forerunner, the pioneer, the model and patron of converts, particularly for those coming into the fullness of the Church from the Anglican tradition and for those who would contribute to the richness of the Church from the resources of that tradition. The Ordinariates established by *Anglicanorum coetibus* are the legacy of Newman's conversion and the fruit of his distinctive contributions to both the fullness and the richness of the Church's evangelizing life and work, together with his special awareness of that mission's challenges in the modern world. It should be obvious that the Ordinariates owe much to Newman's example and have much to learn from his writings as the witness of his mind and heart. But, equally, the Church herself owes much and can learn much from that same witness, for the better formation of converts, for the stewarding of their gifts and for more closely aligning and integrating the ethic of conversion and the ethic of evangelization. That Newman's canonization should have preceded by just a few weeks the tenth anniversary of *Anglicanorum coetibus* invites, then, exploration of the saint's lessons for discerning what it might mean to live out 'Anglican patrimony' in the ecology of Catholic communion and for understanding how the Church can receive, shape and fit that patrimony for her evangelizing identity and mission.

In these pages we will look back to a few dimensions of St John Henry Newman's thought, and more broadly at the English spiritual tradition that formed him, in order to identify some resources for the Church's husbandry of this tradition, all for the sake of looking forward to the harvest which awaits. More specifically, this essay aims to discuss Newman's keen and abiding appreciation of 'personal influence' for propagating the truth of the Gospel and making converts. As a golden thread running through his writings, Newman's personalism indicates the evangelizing potential of heart speaking to heart (*cor ad cor loquitur*) for navigating the challenges of change in continuity and of unity in diversity over the course of the soul's (and the Church's) development from shadows and through images to the fuller light of truth (*ex umbris et imaginibus in veritatem*). I should like to argue that Newman's analysis of personal influence in the right habitus of communion provides a compelling context for situating the distinctiveness of the Ordinariates' liturgical life in the bonds of unity. This context, in turn, suggests some corollaries of Newman's personalism, which can be associated with complementary strands of Anglican patrimony, ones given new impetus with the Oxford Movement and which may help characterize how Ordinariate Catholics can enrich the wider Church and contribute to the work of evangelization. These patrimonial strands include a certain charism for rekindling the religious imagination, together with a characteristically English ethic of reserve in approaching sacred mysteries, and a disposition of 'courtesy' and 'homeliness' in pastoral practice and in living out parochial and ecclesial culture on a human scale.

In the nearly two centuries since Newman's conversion to the Catholic Church and, more pointedly, in the decade since his beatification and since the founding charter of the Ordinariates, the soil has been readied and, by God's grace, seeds sown, but many of these seeds have yet to germinate, others to take root and still others to bear fruit. In discussing such things, it must be remembered that the providential dynamic implied by the allusion to Jn 12.24 defies any merely human calculus and points towards something hidden, indeed a mysterious participation in the baptismal and paschal mystery. The seed, the grain of wheat that falls into the ground, must die and, dying, must wait on God's purposes and dilatory time before bringing forth the expected fruit. Newman's life, his successive conversions and the personal influence of his ideas, both among Anglicans and among Catholics, offer a salient illustration of this process, this mystery, and an example with special relevance for fathoming the timing of *Anglicanorum coetibus* and assessing the life and growth of the Ordinariates.

Most saints are commemorated on the calendar dates of their earthly deaths. That St John Henry Newman's feast will be celebrated on the date of his conversion to the Catholic Church (9 October) is apt, for his reception into the Church, by Blessed Dominic Barberi on that rainy day at Littlemore in 1845, had the character of a death. It was not only an experience of devastating loss, albeit one of incalculable gain, but it also signalled the seeming demise of his influence on the course and direction of the Oxford Movement and its summons of Anglicans back to the sources of Catholic truth. And Newman's immense gain in becoming Catholic did not redound to a commensurate influence in the One True Fold. On the contrary, Newman's career in the Catholic Church was fraught with plenty of disappointment, frustration and the failure of many of his dearest projects. His thought as a Catholic, almost entirely forged from ideas developed during his Anglican years,[1] often met with suspicion and misapprehension among his fellow Catholics, a distrust only partially offset with the publication of his great *Apologia Pro Vita Sua* in 1864. In 1866 Newman's fellow convert, Henry Cardinal Manning could still warn against his baleful example: 'I see much danger of an English Catholicism of which Newman is the highest type. It is the old Anglican, patristic, literary, Oxford tone transplanted into the Church.'[2] It was not until Pope Leo XIII made him a cardinal in 1879 that Newman's personal influence really began to be felt, and only in the twentieth century, in the years leading up to the Second Vatican Council, did the compelling power of that influence catalyse with countless other influences to contribute to the energies of Catholic *ressourcement* and renewal.

The Second Vatican Council has been called 'Newman's Council', but, as Avery Dulles and Ian Ker have shown, that facile and sometimes misleading generalization, however well intended, does a disservice both to Newman and to the Second Vatican Council, insofar as the claim often devolves into special pleading for this or that interpretation of the council or of Newman.[3] Nonetheless, there is truth in Pope St John Paul II's observation that Newman's witness as 'a leading figure of the Oxford Movement, and later as a promoter of authentic renewal in the Catholic Church' helped imbue the Second Vatican Council with 'a special ecumenical vocation', one with promise 'not only for his own country but also for the whole Church':

> By insisting 'the Church must be prepared for converts, as well as converts prepared for the Church' he already in a certain measure anticipated in his broad theological vision one of the main aims and orientations of the Second Vatican Council and the Church in the post-conciliar period.[4]

John Paul II's quotation from Newman – 'the Church must be prepared for converts, as well as converts prepared for the Church' – calls for closer examination in context, especially as that context offers particular insights for understanding the ecumenical project of the Ordinariates and, more broadly, for appreciating the reciprocal, mutually reinforcing relationship between evangelization *ad extra* and evangelization *ad intra*. From the time of his own conversion Newman was assiduous in counselling and encouraging Anglican converts to the Catholic faith, but in his private journal for 21 January 1863 he admitted distress at insinuations from Cardinal Wiseman and the offices of Propaganda Fide that he had been 'doing nothing' and had failed to rack up sufficient numbers of high-profile converts:

> The only thing of course, which is worth producing, is *fruit* – but with the Cardinal immediate *show* is fruit, and conversions the *sole* fruit. At Propaganda, conversions, and nothing else, are the proof of doing *any* thing. Every where with Catholics, to make converts is doing something; and not to make them, is 'doing nothing' ... but I am altogether different. ... To me conversions were not the first thing, but the edification of Catholics. ... I am afraid to make hasty converts of educated men, lest they should not have counted the cost, & should have difficulties after they have entered the Church. ... [T]he Church must be prepared for converts, as well as converts prepared for the Church.[5]

As his thousands of letters to prospective and recent converts testify, Newman knew that conversion is ineluctably the work of the Holy Spirit, that it takes time, that it proceeds from antecedent experiences of grace, that it continues after reception into the Church and that it is inevitably beset with internal 'costs' and outward 'difficulties'.[6] Newman worried about those who suffered to come into the Church only then to find themselves abandoned, suffering now for the lack of ongoing formation in the faith, among masses of weakly formed Catholics:

> There are those who only wish to convert, and then leave the poor converts to shift for themselves, as far as knowledge of their religion goes. The other end is so important, is what I call levelling up. If we are to convert souls savingly they must have the due preparation of heart.[7]

Newman understood that the integral preparation of converts necessarily entails the corresponding formation of those already converted – hence his phrase 'levelling up' and his stated priority for the 'edification of Catholics', almost as a precondition for drawing converts.

To attract 'savingly', the Church must be attractive 'savingly', heart to heart, for both those approaching and those already within her gates, and the Church must likewise evince the right staying power to hold and nourish all of her members in the ongoing pursuit of holiness. Evangelization *ad intra* thus supports evangelization *ad extra*, and vice versa, only in a culture of continuous, ever-deepening conversion all round.

For Newman, the dynamic of 'levelling up', particularly in the 'special ecumenical vocation' he pioneered, can be bidirectional and mutually enriching: well-prepared converts entering the Church may raise the bar for better-formed Catholics as much as those Catholics can assist, extend and complete the experience of conversion for those in process and newly arrived. Although he was too modest to say so himself, Newman's own example is a case in point.

His influence, that of many other Anglican converts, as well as the wider aspirations of the Oxford Movement he helped direct, all contributed to the 'Second Spring' of resurgent English Catholicism he celebrated in his famous 1852 sermon. But in the sermon Newman refrained from triumphalism; he knew that any temporal renewal is provisional and that this 'spring-time of the Church' could turn out to be a typically *English* spring 'of bright promise and budding hopes, yet withal, of keen blasts, and cold showers, and sudden storms'.[8] There is a sense, too, that his work was not finished and that the full promise issuing from the Oxford Movement remained unfulfilled, notwithstanding his own refuge in the One True Church. His two sets of lectures, delivered to different audiences in 1850 and 1851, on the *Present Position of Catholics in England* (with its famous advocacy for a better educated Catholic laity) and on *Difficulties of Anglicans* (with its clarion call to conversion), reveal Newman taking stock of both populations, each with an eye to the other, and assessing the challenges of bringing them together for the sanctification of souls and for a fuller realization of the Church's oneness and catholicity. In *Difficulties of Anglicans*, Newman was emphatic that the 'legitimate issue', the 'providential course' and 'destiny of truth' stemming from the Movement of 1833 (as he called the Oxford Movement) point only in the direction of 'communion with the Roman See'. The retrieval of 'Catholic principles', worked and stimulated by the Tractarians, Newman insisted, cannot take root and flourish in a 'national church' nor a 'branch church', and not in a 'party' or a 'sect', as the Anglo-Catholic position had already become within the fissiparous Church of England.[9]

Nonetheless, Newman sympathized with the 'difficulties' of Anglicans still on the far side of the Tiber – they had been his own for many years – and he understood the deep attachment of Anglicans to their native tradition and religious culture, which though fundamentally incoherent had yet managed to preserve, and more recently to revive, much Catholic truth. And he recognized, too, the manifest disorders, abuses and scandals that too often make the human face of the Catholic Church look unattractive and make it difficult even for those well-disposed to take the plunge of conversion and submission. In 1876 he expressed a cautious openness to the scheme of Ambrose Phillipps de Lisle to propose something like an Anglican 'uniate' church or an Anglican 'rite' in communion with Rome.[10] At first, Newman welcomed the prospect for easing erstwhile Anglicans into the Roman fold and as a 'means of drawing to us so many good people, who are now shivering at our gates',[11] but the proposal, he realized, was patently impracticable and premature. Often in the history of the Church, the author of *The Development of Christian Doctrine* reminded de Lisle, we see that 'a thing is in itself good, but the time has not come for it'.[12] The circumstances not yet propitious, too few Anglicans were prepared and too few Catholics were willing to embrace such a development. Nor had the post-Reformation Catholic Church herself, one might observe, yet fully developed the requisite theology of evangelization, or the right ecumenical orientation, to render the idea compelling and articulate. Neither the soil nor the seeds were ready for a sowing, which had to wait for another season, more than a century later, with Pope Benedict XVI's discernment of the climate and conditions that made *Anglicanorum coetibus* possible.

In his own time, Newman himself discerned that the Oxford Movement, while pointing inescapably to the imperative of Catholic conversion, had taken on a life of its own, short of its proper telos, and had yet to run its course in campaigning for a Catholic revival outside of the Church of Rome. After the furore stirred up by his infamous *Tract 90* (which desperately, rather tortuously argued that the Thirty-Nine Articles could be reconciled with the teachings of the Council of Trent) and after his subsequent 'defection' to Rome, Newman believed that the Tractarian movement was expiring in Oxford itself. But he knew that the energies he had unleashed were morphing and making progress in the rest of the country and even having an impact in Anglican quarters throughout the English-speaking world.[13] The post-Tractarian development of the Oxford Movement, a wild chiaroscuro of light and darkness, must have been vexing to Newman. On one hand, even as a Catholic, he saw 'the wonderful revival of religion in the Established Church' as a work coming 'from God'. But, on the other hand, he could see this revival as a negative influence inhibiting conversions, as much as encouraging them, by keeping its followers in an ecclesial allegiance that he came to view less as the instrument than 'the enemy of truth'.[14] Though he never shrank from encouraging conversion, he did acknowledge that some Anglo-Catholics may have been providentially 'kept where they are, with no more light than they have, being Anglicans in good faith in order gradually to prepare their hearers and readers in greater numbers than otherwise would be possible for the true and perfect faith'.[15] In other words, Newman perceived from his own experience and that of countless others that the Anglican tradition, under the right influences, could serve as a valuable *praeparatio evangelica* and even, for a time, as a 'breakwater' against a rising tide of unbelief.[16] But he also had a sense that, despite manifest evidence of sincerity and sanctity in its ranks, Anglicanism, considered as a 'system' of compromise and equivocation (one lacking a visible centre of unity and a living magisterium), would over time reveal its fundamentally liberalizing character as a fatal solvent to truth, though perhaps thereby sharpening for some of its adherents the imperative summons to a deeper, truer conversion.

Again, we see Newman's extraordinary prescience and prudence in both waiting on and anticipating the developments that would come to shape the evangelizing promise of *Anglicanorum coetibus*. And again, we see his patience before the mystery of germination and his acute sense that the human apprehension of truth is the daughter of time and the issue of the catalytic interplay of influence, conscience and providence. 'Great acts', he said, 'take time'.[17] Although his own influence among both Anglicans and Catholics alike was, in his lifetime, intermittent and mixed, not always reaching its intended audience and objects exactly as he might have wished, the example of the clarity of his conscience points to something profoundly providential. If Newman did not always appreciate this fact about himself, there were others who did.

After Newman's 'defection' to Rome, the mantle of leadership in the Oxford Movement fell on the shoulders of Edward Bouverie Pusey such that followers of the movement became known as 'Puseyites'. Within a fortnight of Newman's reception into the Catholic Church, Pusey penned an astonishingly magnanimous letter in which he wrote of his former comrade's conversion: 'It is perhaps the greatest event which has happened since the communion of the Churches has been interrupted, that such a one, so formed in our Church, and the work of God's Spirit as dwelling within him, should be transplanted to theirs'. Rather than expressing any bitterness or mourning the loss to the Church of England of the man 'marked out as a great instrument of God ... to carry out some great design for the restoration of the [Anglican] Church', Pusey instead commends the courage of Newman's conscience and the strength of his holiness:

> He has gone as a simple act of duty with no view for himself, placing himself entirely in God's hands. And such are they whom God employs. He seems then to me not so much gone from us, as transplanted into another part of the Vineyard, where the full energies of his powerful mind can be employed, which here they were not.

The letter goes on to speculate about 'the mysterious purposes of God's good providence' in calling Newman to the Catholic Church for the softening of Catholic prejudices against Anglicans while rebuking Anglicans for the abiding 'heresy existing more or less within us', all in order that 'what now hinders the union of the Western Church will fall off'.[18]

Newman was not to be the apostle of the wholesale corporate reunion that some imagined and Pusey might have dreamed. Yet Pusey's insight does prefigure John Paul II's characterization of Newman's 'special ecumenical vocation' in ways not only retrospective of his accomplishment but also prospective of how his witness might be renewed and continued in the Ordinariates established by *Anglicanorum coetibus*. If Newman understood that the consciences of many Anglicans still needed time to ripen towards conversion, he also may have intuited, as Pusey seems to have, that the Catholic Church too needed time to absorb the positive influence of converts like Newman himself and to forge thereby a more ecumenical perspective beyond the polemics of the Reformation era. Newman's abandoned theory that the Anglican Church could persuasively model a via media between Catholicism and Protestantism did succeed in building a bridge, the notion of a 'bridge church' – and bridges, of course, are made for crossing. Newman not only crossed over but, in doing so, he laid the planks that would, in the fullness of time, make the passage easier for others and make their reception on the other side more hospitable. To the degree that the 'full energies of his powerful mind', formed and exercised among Anglicans, found more fruitful employment on the Roman side, Newman really did stimulate the Catholic Church's belated appreciation of 'elements of sanctification and truth' outside her visible boundaries 'as forces impelling to Catholic unity'.[19] In calling Anglicans back to the sources of their professed faith in the Bible and in the Church Fathers and then subjecting this heritage to a rigorous historical and psychological study for the sake of energizing salvific truth, he honed the insights that would combine with other similar influences and point the way forward to fruition at the Second Vatican Council and later in the pontificates of John Paul II and Benedict XVI.

The Ordinariates that Benedict XVI established, building on John Paul II's Pastoral Provision for Anglican converts,[20] have been described as the achievement of a kind of *'realized* ecumenism', as distinct from the ecumenism of interminable, often futile dialogue having only vaguely eschatological horizons – and that is surely true. However, 'ecumenism' was not a word in Newman's vocabulary, and the modern sense of the term was foreign to him. He knew nothing of institutional 'dialogue' aimed at shared understanding or consensus of belief in order to creep towards institutional realignment or eventually engineer the reconciliation of ecclesial structures.[21] Rather for Newman, what we have come to know as the ecumenical 'project' was coterminous with, and indistinguishable from, the orientation and ends of conversion and evangelization as the growth of individual souls and the community of the faithful in ever-greater apprehension of truth and closer conformity to the very person of Christ. As Newman would have understood, the realization of ecclesial union here and now – living out and living into the unity *of* the Church, *in* the Church and *for* the Church – is an ongoing, continuous challenge, with an interior dimension (like conversion and evangelization), and allows no complacency, admits no slackening. Anglican converts to the Catholic faith would do well to adopt, for their own sense of mission, Newman's lifelong watchwords, as learned from the evangelical Thomas Scott when he was still a boy: '*Holiness rather than peace*, and *Growth the only evidence of life*'.[22] For all of Newman's patience, prescience and prudence, we cannot overlook his sense of insistence and even urgency in propagating the saving truths of the Gospel.

This essay has spoken much of Newman's influence and how that influence was spun from and out of his particular personality. The time has come to reflect a bit on Newman's teaching about 'personal influence', in general, as the indispensable instrument of evangelization and, then, on how the special influence of his example and of the tradition that formed him might shape the evangelizing work of the Ordinariates in the fullness of Catholic communion.

What Newman did, both as an Anglican and as a Catholic, and what the Ordinariates are called anew to continue, was to take the 'dogmatical principle', as he called it, faith in a 'definite creed', and make it personally compelling, imaginatively thrilling, intellectually exacting and vibrantly credible in an age already confronted by the rising tide of secularism and unbelief. He tackled the toughest questions of religious epistemology in the modern world, not only with theological acuity and precision but also in a way that would vindicate the humblest habits of belief, the natural instincts of worship and the simple piety of ordinary Christians.[23] Similarly, Newman had an uncanny gift for holding together, in unity and creative tension, two persistent dispositions that are always in peril of flying apart or being set at odds (perhaps no more acutely than in the Church of our own time), that is, the priority of human persons, as such, and the priority of divine truth, as such. For Newman, the dangers of watery subjectivity, on one hand, and of ossified abstraction, on the other, are offset and avoided in the conviction that heart-to-heart communication is the necessary mode of perceptive life leading through shadows and images to the personal utterance, the vital truth, of the divine Word himself.[24] Heart speaks to heart for the sake of communion with the Sacred Heart of Jesus. Newman, of course, used the word 'heart' constantly, but we miss the sense of the term if we associate it with the seat of the emotions or confuse it with Victorian sentimentality. Rather, Newman's usage derives from the Bible and the Fathers in a meaning perfectly captured by Joseph Ratzinger: 'In biblical language, the "heart" [Hebrew *leb*] indicates the centre of human life, the point where reason, will, temperament and sensitivity converge, where the person finds his unity and his interior orientation.'[25] It was precisely this sense of personal unity and interior orientation that Newman sought to unpack in his writings on 'personal influence'.

Newman dated the beginning of the Oxford Movement to 14 July 1833, when John Keble preached the Assize Sermon from the university pulpit under the title 'National Apostasy' and protested the parliamentary suppression of ten Anglican bishoprics in Ireland.[26] Keble's rebuke of state control of the Church of England, though delivered during the university's vacation and attracting little attention at the time, did help launch the publication of the *Tracts for the Times*. But the real impetus for what would become the Oxford Movement came from the sermons that Newman himself had been preaching at the university church of St Mary the Virgin over the previous few years. Charles Stephen Dessain and others have argued that the fire was, in fact, sparked eighteen months earlier than the Assize Sermon, in January 1832 when Newman preached on 'Personal Influence, the Means of Propagating Truth':[27]

> [Truth] has been upheld in the world not as a system, not by books, not by argument, nor by temporal power, but by the personal influence of such men ... who are at once the teachers and the patterns of it.[28]

The truth Newman had in mind is saving truth, that which proceeds from and summons back to the very author of truth: 'it is not a mere set of opinions ... which may lodge on the surface of the mind', but rather that truth which changes 'the heart' and models its recipient after 'the One above himself, who is the beginning of a new creation'.[29] Divine truth, argues Newman, makes its way through the world by an 'economy' of incremental disclosure, by interactions in time and then by the combined witness of those called to holiness and shaped therein, the witness of those whose 'personal influence' becomes both attractive and diffusive of the good in them concentrated and then expanded:

> Men persuade themselves with little difficulty to scoff at principles, to ridicule books, to make sport of the names of good men; but they cannot bear their presence: it is holiness embodied in personal form, which ... they cannot steadily confront and bear down.[30]

This insight about personal influence as a 'catching force'[31] of sanctity serves as the foundation for Newman's distinctive and lifelong apologetic for Christian truth, one with roots deep in biblical revelation and patristic antiquity but which spoke to the crisis of belief in Victorian Britain and which can yet speak to our own modern or post-modern predicament. It is an apologetic based more on the personal attraction of holiness than on the intellectual appeal of reasonableness, yet which by no means shuns the intellect but rather engages reason and all the human faculties as they converge in persons and touch and move the human heart. Newman's personalism found its theological orientation even earlier when he preached on 'The Influence of Natural and Revealed Religion Respectively' in 1830: 'The philosopher aspires towards a divine *principle*; the Christian towards a Divine *Agent*'. That the Triune God is considered the *personification* of 'the Word, the Light, the Life, the Truth, Wisdom', is no bit of anthropomorphic projection, suggests Newman, no trick of rhetoric or poetic fancy, but rather the very substance and mode of God's self-disclosure: truth is personal because revealed truth proceeds from the relational communion of Father, Son and Holy Spirit. Therein alone, as mediated through the relational communion of the Church and the personal nourishment of the sacraments, can we find our bearings and our happiness and come to share that happiness with others. This 'method of personation (so to call it)', continues Newman, 'is carried throughout the revealed system',[32] and the same 'method', I would say, is carried throughout Newman's writings to serve as a quarry for personal analogies of faith and for shaping his habitual idiom of thought in deeply, pervasively personalist terms.[33] For Newman, evangelization works not by sophisticated plans or programs, nor on an industrial scale for mass results, but heart to heart, obscurely, humbly, personally, radiating outward from the small kindled fire of personal influence, lighting the way for 'the keen, vivid, constraining glance of Christ's countenance'. As Ian Ker puts it, quoting Newman:

> It is not a philosophical or theological abstraction but the 'piercing, soul-subduing look of the Son of Man' who fulfils the otherwise unfulfillable human longing for an 'object of life.' The new evangelization, Newman would insist, must preach not Christianity but Christ.[34]

Such is the radical and fundamental character of evangelization, in itself. But as it was for Newman, so for Ordinariate Catholics following in his path, the relevant collocation of personal influences is rather distinctive and gathers up patrimonial elements of that 'old Anglican, patristic, literary, Oxford tone', once decried by Manning, but now newly transplanted into the Church and given a fresh lease on life. These elements, though filtered through experiences more diverse than Newman's, might find their place in an assimilative mode of Catholic communion, which, like his example, proceeds by inclusion without reduction, correction without elimination and distinction without denial.[35] For Newman, the way to truth passed through Oxford and the network of influences lovingly recounted in the pages of the *Apologia* – Hawkins, Whately, Keble,

Froude, Pusey and many others. Then, almost as intimately and even more decisively for making him Catholic, he communed with the early Church Fathers, regarding them not as ancient avatars or theological data sets but 'as contemporaries, as participants in the theological conversations and controversies of his own day'.[36] Along the way, Newman absorbed, concentrated and channelled in his leadership of the Oxford Movement, as well as his witness thereafter, nearly all the features of Anglican patrimony that the Catholic Church has judged worthy of 'repatriating' for her own evangelizing mission.

Though we must be careful not to render Newman as more *representatively* 'Anglican' than he really was – in many respects, he was *sui generis* and, like all great saints, idiosyncratic – still I would like to suggest that his legacy indicates some dimensions of Anglican patrimony, as corollary modes of personal influence, which can help fructify a new, more vibrant and counter-cultural style of evangelization for our own age. These patrimonial strands might also assist the work of preparing the Church for converts, in preparing converts for the Church and help achieve something of the effect of 'levelling up' that Newman prescribed and hoped for.

Newman offers a model and a rationale for rekindling the Catholic *imagination* from traditionally Anglican sources and habits as instruments calling the faithful to a richer contemplation of divine mysteries and the beauties of Catholic dogma. As John Coulson has argued and widely explored in his studies of Newman, the chief accomplishment and most enduring contribution of the Oxford Movement was its re-enchantment of the religious imagination.[37] For Newman, reflecting back on the motives of the movement yet writing as a Catholic in his *Grammar of Assent*, what he called 'real assent' to the truths of the faith, as opposed to merely 'notional' agreement, is virtually identical with 'imaginative' apprehension as a fully personal means of grasping concrete and vital images, symbols and icons of otherwise invisible and elusive realities. Contrary to more escapist notions of the imaginative faculty, Newman understood the imagination as the conduit of knowledge carried to the heart and invested with persuasive and motivating power for living into the splendor of truth:

> The heart is commonly reached, not through the reason, but through the imagination, by means of direct impressions ... Persons influence us, voices melt us, looks subdue us, deeds

inflame us. Many a man will live and die upon a dogma; no man will be a martyr for a conclusion.[38]

This account has relevance for the Ordinariates' stewardship of their distinctive liturgical, musical and artistic tradition in the conduct of public worship. Though Newman did not write widely on liturgy per se, he did have a deeply liturgical sensibility and appreciated ritual as a veil of 'marvelous disclosures' and as the privileged 'means, both moral and mystical, of approaching God, and gradually learning to bear the sight of Him'.[39] Newman held that 'habits of personal religion', formed through prayer and liturgical participation, shape 'a religious imagination' for 'a living hold on truths which are really to be found in the world, though they are not upon the surface', and for 'a more and more consistent and luminous vision of God'.[40]

His great preaching, like that of the other Oxford fathers, unfolded according to the festivals of the liturgical year with its round of mysteries and sought to form not just minds but hearts with a grasp of reality that is pervasively, personally Trinitarian, incarnational, sacramental and ecclesial, firmly rooted in 'the faith once delivered to the saints'. Listen to Newman descanting on the imaginative power of the Athanasian Creed, that great affirmation of Trinitarian orthodoxy, once so prominent and regular a feature in Anglican worship and now lovingly reclaimed by Ordinariate Catholics:

> It is not a mere collection of notions, however momentous. It is a psalm or hymn of praise, of confession, and of profound, self-prostrating homage, parallel to the canticles of the elect in the Apocalypse. It appeals to the imagination quite as much as to the intellect. It is the war-song of faith, with which we warn, first ourselves, then each other, and then all those who are within its hearing, and the hearing of the Truth, who our God is, and how we must worship Him, and how vast our responsibility will be, if we know what to believe, and yet believe not.[41]

How many contemporary Catholics have even heard of the Athanasian Creed, much less been nourished by its cadences to feel its august, thrilling, monitory force? Today, at a time when the religious imagination in much of the Western world has all but atrophied (even among Catholics) and often dwindled into something coarse, banal and thin, one can see how the more robust liturgical life of the Ordinariates could serve a special need and have a particular appeal in reawakening imaginative resources for living out the truths of the faith in all the confidence and authority of Catholic teaching. In their own little way, the Ordinariates could use select aspects of Anglican patrimony to help fertilize the Church's good soil, to grow the seeds of grace and thereby assist, in the language of Charles Taylor, the 'buffered' selves of our secular age in becoming once again more 'porous' and open to the signals of transcendence.[42]

For the Ordinariates, a particular stewardship of the religious imagination might go hand in hand with the important Tractarian principle of 'holy reserve', a modest, reverent reticence in approaching divine mysteries, as exemplified by Newman, for the sake of safeguarding and nurturing the 'life hidden with Christ in God'.[43] And this sense of reserve, in turn, could join with a quintessentially English ethic of what Julian of Norwich called 'courtesy' and 'homeliness' in the conduct of pastoral ministry and parochial fellowship – an enactment of communion whereby God's 'courteous' and 'homely' embrace of his faithful models the 'courteous' and 'full homely divinity' of the faithful with one another in the household of Christ.[44] All these elements together – imagination, reserve, courtesy and homeliness – under the aegis, influence and patronage of St John Henry Newman could promote fruitfulness in the Ordinariates' apostolate of evangelization. All these together, in the right mixture, under the right conditions, could also serve to check and correct certain pathologies of religious life which Newman astutely identified in his own time and which still afflict the health of the Church today. While affirming the personal expression of faith, he advocated a habit of reserve to counter any tendency towards emotivist enthusiasm, even as he called upon the imagination and a 'poetical' piety to arouse, without exciting, feelings of wonder in order to preserve awe before mystery and to counter the dangers of desiccated rationalism. Similarly, Newman counselled and illustrated a style of religious communication that was brave and forthright, uncompromising in calling out what he labelled the 'religion of the day' with its 'unreal words' of vapid, conformist respectability (the Victorian version of today's 'moralistic therapeutic deism'). At the same time, he criticized the vice that he named 'viewiness' (the besetting sin of the contemporary 'blogosphere' in which every religious topic or event becomes an opportunity for spouting all manner of cocksure, half-baked opinions).⁴⁵ Likewise, in a more satiric vein, he warned Anglicans against the dangers of misplaced nostalgia and the temptations of any self-indulgent aestheticism detached from real belief and the demands of personal holiness.⁴⁶ Synthesizing in himself the best of the English tradition that formed him, Newman points the way to an ethos at once deeply traditional yet forward-looking, humble yet bold, genteel yet unaffected, tough yet hospitable, sinewy yet attractive, one that might serve as a magnet and a beacon for converts and all who find their home in God's holy Church.

In the ten years since the promulgation of *Anglicanorum coetibus*, some seeds have sprouted and others are beginning to break through the soil, with promise of further growth in due season. As St John Henry Newman's life and writings testify, the most authentic flowers of Anglican patrimony can find their true and lasting home in the garden of the Catholic Church, albeit transplanted, only if they can grow and bloom afresh in the right ecology of communion for evangelistic fruitfulness. The Apostolic Constitution and its revised Complementary Norms refer to this ecology in exacting terms, even as the process of sowing, germination and growth yet continues amid patient, prayerful waiting on propitious weather and rainfall. *Anglicanorum coetibus* mentions the 'precious gift' and 'treasure' found in the Anglican tradition, particularly its liturgical expression, while describing these riches, not as alien growths, but 'as gifts properly belonging to the Church of Christ'. Such 'elements of sanctification and truth' may have had an extra-territorial life for a time (scattered among rocks and thorns) but are now brought home, 'transplanted' back to the Catholic Church's own good ground.⁴⁷ The Complementary Norms, speaking of the approved liturgical texts of the Ordinariates, further characterize this patrimony 'as that which has nourished the Catholic faith throughout the history of the Anglican tradition and prompted aspirations towards ecclesial unity'.⁴⁸ Just so. But we might miss the energizing motives and personal sense of mission in the phrase 'aspirations towards ecclesial unity' if we construe the language only in abstract or institutional terms and forget the personal itineraries of pilgrims and converts like Newman. Rather, in a personalist idiom he would have appreciated, the theological preface of the Apostolic Constitution specifies that the relevant analogy of faith for grasping the matrix and rationale for ecclesial unity is nothing other than the dynamic, interpersonal life of the Trinity and the Church's own life as the extension in time and space of the 'the mystery of the Incarnate Word'. This extension, 'one complex reality formed from a two-fold element, human and divine', works through the complexities of change and continuity and unity in diversity with a corresponding intention towards reconciliation, to draw all men into the communion of Christ, into his very personhood and the hypostatic union therein of his two natures, human and divine. Accordingly, some elements of Anglican patrimony are worthy of repatriation insofar as they are genuinely personal influences impelling towards unity in Christ and insofar as they might come to inhere and subsist in Christ's Church, per the Chalcedonian definition of Jesus' two natures, *'without confusion, without division'*. Archbishop Joseph Augustine Di Noia, one of the architects of *Anglicanorum coetibus* and the president of *Anglicanae traditiones* (the commission that prepared the Ordinariates' liturgical texts), put it more simply:

> Anglican patrimony is not really worth preserving *in itself*. Rather, its value and virtue is measured to the degree that it positively contributes to making better Catholics and more Catholics by fanning the flames of faith, hope, and charity.[49]

Without confusion, without division: This formula, defining the unity in diversity of Christ's two natures, seems to me an apt characterization for understanding the relationship between the particularity of Anglican patrimony in Catholic communion and the universality of the Church's wider reach and mission. Patrimony brought home subsists distinctively (*without confusion*) yet inheres integrally (*without division*) in the oneness of the Church's salvific life and work. Another metaphor might help make the point. Anglicans and Catholics alike have long delighted in singing a well-known setting of St Patrick's Lorica, 'I bind unto myself today'. Memorably, this beloved hymn couples two different tunes from old Irish melodies, one sung after the other. The first is called *St. Patrick* (as adapted by Sir Charles Villiers Stanford), and the second is named *Deirdre* (as harmonized by Ralph Vaughn Williams). Per the headnotes often found in Anglican hymnals with instructions for singing, the first tune should be sung '*In unison, with energy*', while the second tune is sung '*In harmony, with breadth*'.[50] These directions together suggestively capture the challenge of Anglican patrimony in service of the universal mission of Catholic evangelization. On one hand, the Ordinariates are an expression of Catholic unity and must sing *in unison, with energy* and with the whole Church. On the other hand, though, the Ordinariates have a particular character and a distinctive work, one harmonized with the Church's unity yet enriching that oneness with a special breadth. This one hymn, the Church's song, with its two different tunes and different verses, also integrates dogmatic declaration with personal consecration, binding its singers in the 'strong Name of the Trinity' and then invoking 'Christ in hearts of all'. This musical analogy is, I think, one that Newman would have understood and might have relished, Newman the musician and the singular symphonist of truth, dogmatic and personal, Newman the pioneer and model for the Ordinariates.

His restless heart always sought a personal faith in communion with a personal God, a quick and quickening faith for propagation and fellowship. Reflecting on his aspirations for the Oxford Movement, he wrote:

> I wanted to bring out in a substantive form a living Church of England, in a position proper to herself, and founded on distinct principles; as far as paper could do it, as far as earnestly preaching it and influencing others towards it, could tend to make it a fact; – a living Church, made of flesh and blood, with voice, complexion, and motion and action, and a will of its own.

Paper and preaching, alone, could not do it, nor could the Anglican Church answer to his longing. In the Catholic Church, he found a differently complex reality: 'I looked at her; – at her rites, her ceremonial, and her precepts; and I said, "This *is* a religion."'[51] He found the already given, living 'fact' of the *corpus permixtum*, mingling wheat and tares with flesh and blood, both the 'substantive form' of our messy, gritty, fallen humanity and also the supersubstantial form of that Flesh and Blood of the speaking Word who is our souls' life and the deepest personal influence of all. Participating in Christ's own husbandry, St John Henry Newman's influence has helped sow seeds far and wide. But in one of the Church's smallest, yet most far-flung, patches of soil, in God's good time, he has for the Ordinariates specially lent his hand and heart to plant a few choice flowers and scatter some corns of wheat, perhaps with a couple of mustard seeds.

Notes

1. See Geoffrey Rowell, 'Newman, the Church of England and the Catholic Church', *New Blackfriars* 92, no. 1038 (2011), pp. 130–43.
2. Henry Edward Manning to George Chetwynd Talbot, 25 February 1866, quoted in Ian Ker, *John Henry Newman: A Biography* (Oxford: Oxford University Press, 1988), p. 609; and Edmund S. Purcell, *Life of Cardinal Manning, Archbishop of Westminster* (London: Macmillan, 1896), p. 323.
3. Ian Ker, *Newman on Vatican II* (Oxford: Oxford University Press, 2014); and Avery Dulles, SJ, *Newman* (London: Continuum, 2002), pp. 150–64.
4. John Paul II, 'Letter on the Centenary of the Cardinalate of John Henry Newman', in *Acta Apostolicae Sedis* 71 (7 April 1979); also in *L'Osservatore Romano*, English edition (21 May 1979), p. 582, available at http://w2.vatican.va/content/john-paul-ii/en/letters/1979/documents/hf_jp-ii_let_19790514_100-newman.html.
5. *John Henry Newman: Autobiographical Writings*, ed. Henry Tristram (New York: Sheed & Ward, 1957), pp. 257–8.
6. See Stanley Jaki's rich study of Newman's many letters to prospective and recent converts, *Newman to Converts: An Existential Ecclesiology* (Pinckney, MI: True View Books, 2001).
7. *The Letters and Diaries of John Henry Newman*, ed. Charles Stephen Dessain et al. (31 vols): I–X (Oxford: Clarendon Press, 1978–84); XI–XXII (London: Thomas Nelson & Sons, 1961–72); XXIII–XXXI (Oxford: Clarendon Press, 1973–77), here XXV, p. 3.
8. John Henry Newman, 'Second Spring: A Sermon Delivered to the First Provincial Council of Westminster, 1852', *Sermons Preached on Various Occasions* (London: Longmans, Green, 1908), p. 180.
9. *Certain Difficulties Felt by Anglicans in Catholic Teaching*, Vol. I (London: Longmans, Green, 1901), pp. xiii, 124.
10. See Ker, *John Henry Newman: A Biography*, pp. 695–6; and Louis Allen, 'Ambrose Phillipps de Lisle, 1809–1878', *Catholic Historical Review* 40, no. 1 (1954), pp. 1–26.
11. *Letters and Diaries* XXVIII, p. 20.
12. Ibid., XXVIII, p. 66.
13. On Newman's influence and the spread of the Oxford Movement in the United States in the nineteenth century, see George E. DeMille, *The Catholic Movement in the American Episcopal Church* (Philadelphia: Church Historical Society, 1950); and Clinton A.

Brand, 'That Nothing Be Lost: America, Texas, and the making of *Anglicanorum coetibus*', *Catholic Southwest: A Journal of History and Culture* 22 (2011), pp. 48–67.

14 For a study that remains an astute analysis of the immense promise and then the eventual failure of the Oxford Movement, after Newman's conversion to Rome, see Christopher Dawson, *The Spirit of the Oxford Movement* (London: Sheed & Ward, 1945).

15 *Letters and Diaries* XXV, pp. 129, 260; XXVIII, pp. 167–8; XXX, p. 120.

16 See Dulles, *Newman*, pp. 121–4.

17 John Henry Newman, *Apologia Pro Vita Sua*, ed. David J. DeLaura (New York: W. W. Norton, 1968), pp. 136.

18 Quoted in H. P. Liddon, *The Life of Edward Bouverie Pusey* (London: Longmans, Green, 1893), Vol. 2, pp. 460–1.

19 Benedict XVI, Apostolic Constitution *Anglicanorum coetibus*, quoting the Second Vatican Council, Dogmatic Constitution *Lumen gentium*, 8: http://w2.vatican.va/content/benedict-xvi/en/apost_constitutions/documents/hf_ben-xvi_apc_20091104_anglicanorum-coetibus.html.

20 On John Paul II's 1980 Pastoral Provision for Anglican converts in the United States, from a perspective predating *Anglicanorum coetibus*, see Clinton A. Brand, 'Restoring All Things in Christ: Some Reflections on the Pastoral Provision for the Anglican Use of the Roman Rite', *Mapping the Catholic Cultural Landscape*, ed. Paula Jean Miller, FSE, and Richard Fossey (Lanham, MD: Rowman & Littlefield, 2004), pp. 259–74.

21 See Dulles, *Newman*, 127; see also Avery Dulles, 'Newman, conversion, and ecumenism', *Church and Society: The Laurence J. McGinley Lectures, 1988–2007* (New York: Fordham University Press, 2008), pp. 51–67.

22 *Apologia*, p. 17.

23 Newman always criticized 'the common mistake of supposing that there is a contrariety and antagonism between a dogmatic creed and vital religion ... The formula, which embodies a dogma for the theologian, readily suggests an object for the worshipper.' *An Essay in Aid of the Grammar of Assent* (Notre Dame, IN: University of Notre Dame Press, 1979), pp. 108–9. The whole passage, between the ellipses, is worth reading for the points at hand.

24 For an elegant distillation of this and other insights about Newman's personalism, see George W. Rutler, 'Newman and the Power of Personality', *Essays in Honor of the Centenary of John Henry*

Cardinal Newman (1801–1890) (Front Royal, VA: Christendom Press, 1989), pp. 111–31.

25 Joseph Ratzinger, 'Theological Commentary on the Third Secret of Fatima', *L'Osservatore Romano* (8 June 2000), Special Insert.

26 *Apologia*, p. 41.

27 See C. S. Dessain, *The Spirituality of John Henry Newman* (Minneapolis: Winston Press, 1977), p. 31.

28 John Henry Newman, 'Personal Influence, the Means of Propagating Truth', *Newman's University Sermons: Fifteen Sermons Preached before the University of Oxford 1826–43* (London: SPCK, 1970), pp. 91–2.

29 Ibid., pp. 86–7.

30 Ibid., p. 92.

31 John Henry Newman, *Prayers, Verses, and Devotions* (San Francisco: Ignatius Press, 2000), p. 390.

32 John Henry Newman, 'The Influence of Natural and Revealed Religion Respectively', *Newman's University Sermons*, pp. 28–30.

33 On Newman's use of *analogia fidei*, as especially derived from the Alexandrian Fathers, and suffusing his thought, see Thomas J. Norris, *Newman and His Theological Method* (Leiden: E. J. Brill, 1977). Among the many studies of Newman's personalism, see John F. Crosby, *The Personalism of John Henry Newman* (Washington, DC: Catholic University of America Press, 2014); *Personality and Belief: Interdisciplinary Essays on John Henry Newman*, ed. Gerard Magill (Lanham: University Press of America, 1994); and Ian Ker, *Healing the Wound of Humanity: The Spirituality of John Henry Newman* (London: Darton, Longman & Todd, 1993).

34 Ker, *Newman on Vatican II*, p.154, quoting from Newman's *Sermons Bearing on Subjects of the Day* (pp. 312–13) and *Sermons Preached on Various Occasions* (pp. 52–3).

35 Inspired by Newman's example and by his own conversion from Lutheranism, Louis Bouyer (still one of the best writers on Newman) argued, similarly, that the most compelling insights of Protestant experience need not be rejected but can be gathered up, rightly contextualized, indeed authenticated in Catholic communion. See *The Spirit and Forms of Protestantism*, trans. A. V. Littledale (Westminster, MD: Newman Press, 1961).

36 Uwe Michael Lang, 'Newman and the Fathers of the Church', *New Blackfriars* 92, no. 1038 (2011), p. 144.

37 See John Coulson, 'Faith and Imagination', *The Furrow* 34, no. 9 (1983), pp. 535–2; as well as *Newman and the Common Tradition: A*

Study of the Language of Church and Society (Oxford: Clarendon Press, 1970) and *Religion and Imagination* (Oxford: Clarendon Press, 1981). See also Gerard Magill, *Religious Morality in John Henry Newman: Hermeneutics of the Imagination* (New York: Springer, 2015); together with Ian Ker, 'Newman on Imagination and Religious Belief', *Logos: A Journal of Catholic Thought and Culture* 1, no. 1 (1997), pp. 96–110.

38 John Henry Newman, 'The Tamworth Reading Room', *Discussions and Arguments* (London: Longmans, Green, 1907), p. 293.

39 John Henry Newman, 'Worship, a Preparation for Christ's Coming', *Parochial and Plain Sermons* (London: Longmans, Green, 1907), vol. 7, pp. 10–11. See also Joseph Alencherry, 'Newman, the Liturgist: An Introduction to the Liturgical Theology of John Henry Newman', *Newman Studies Journal* 13 (2016), pp. 6–21.

40 *Grammar of Assent*, p. 106.

41 Ibid., p. 117.

42 See Charles Taylor, *A Secular Age* (Cambridge, MA: Harvard University Press, 2007), pp. 37–41 *et passim*; and James K. A. Smith, *How (Not) to Be Secular: Reading Charles Taylor* (Grand Rapids, MI: Eerdmans, 2014).

43 See Robin C. Selby, *The Principle of Reserve in the Writings of John Henry Newman* (Oxford: Oxford University Press, 1975); together with the extensive selections, including many by Newman, on the Tractarian 'Doctrine of Reserve' in *Firmly I Believe: An Oxford Movement Reader*, ed. Raymond Chapman (Norwich: Canterbury Press, 2006), pp. 131–149.

44 See Anna Maria Reynolds, CP, '"Courtesy" and "Homeliness" in the *Revelations* of Julian of Norwich', *Fourteenth-Century English Mystics Newsletter* 2 (1979), pp. 12–20.

45 See John Henry Newman, 'The Religion of the Day', *Parochial and Plain Sermons*, I, pp. 309–24; and 'Unreal Words', V, pp. 29–45.

46 See the delicious satire scattered throughout Newman's novel, *Loss and Gain: The Story of a Convert*, ed. Alan G. Hill (Oxford: Oxford University Press, 1989), pp. 16–17, 61–2, 191–6.

47 *Anglicanorum coetibus*, III.

48 Congregation for the Doctrine of the Faith, *Complementary Norms of the Apostolic Constitution 'Anglicanorum coetibus'* (19 March 2019), Art. 15.1, available at http://www.vatican.va/roman_curia/congregations/cfaith/documents/rc_con_cfaith_doc_20190319_norme-anglicanorum-coetibus_en.html.

49 J. Augustine DiNoia, 'Divine Worship and the Liturgical Vitality of the Church', *Antiphon* 19, no. 2 (2015), p. 112.

50 *The Hymnal 1940* (New York: The Church Hymnal Corporation, 1940), Standard Harmony Edition, No. 268; cf. *The Hymnal 1982* (New York: The Church Hymnal Corporation, 1982), No. 370.

51 *Apologia*, pp. 67, 254.

7

The spirit of *Anglicanorum coetibus*: Beauty in the development of Anglican patrimony

Robert M. Andrews

Introduction

> [Oxford] was the sacred city of Anglicanism, into which nothing common or unclean could enter, and where neither Popery nor Dissent could obtain a foothold. ... Elsewhere the old order seemed to represent nothing but the vested interests of pluralists and place hunters: in Oxford it still stood for an ideal. No doubt it was an anomaly in the age of utilitarianism and industrial development. It was inefficient, cumbersome, out of date. But it was beautiful; more beautiful perhaps than any other place in England which was still rich in beauty: and consequently it could still inspire loyalty and affection.[1]

So wrote the twentieth-century Catholic meta-historian and convert from Anglicanism, Christopher Dawson (1889–1970), in *The Spirit of the Oxford Movement* (1933), written to commemorate the first centenary of the Oxford Movement. Why did Dawson write a history of a religious event that was mostly concerned with a nineteenth-century Anglican phenomenon and theological questions related to Anglican identity? John Henry Newman's spiritual journey that led to Rome in 1845 was clearly a focus. More than this, however, Dawson saw in Newman and the leaders of the Oxford Movement the genuine and authentic spirit of Christianity, of the need to see the English Church as a living presence rather than just an embodiment of contemporary political, cultural or societal norms.[2] For Dawson 'the religious movement of 1833'[3] said something important about the vivifying effect that post-Reformation Anglicanism, despite its defects, had had upon the West. Aesthetically, Dawson still felt a noticeable pull towards the post-Reformation English spiritual tradition – as he put it, 'The spirit of Hooker and Andrewes, and Laud and Sandcroft and Henry Vaughan and Thomas Ken … The perfume that still clings to the chapel of Little Gidding.'[4] The Oxford Movement's embodiment of ecclesial and spiritual vitality during the period of the 1830s was, for Dawson, of major influence to the development of nineteenth- and twentieth-century religious history – Catholic and Protestant.

Literary descriptions of an Anglican aesthetic by other writers and intellectuals (usually, but not always, English) give off a similar air to that of Dawson. There are, indeed, many examples one could cite, such as George Orwell's reference to 'old maids biking to Holy Communion through the mists of the autumn mornings'.[5] More recently, the late Sir Roger Scruton spoke with fondness of the 'scents of damp stone and plaster, of altar flowers and dusty kneelers' that, for him, one only seems to find in old Anglican churches.[6]

Undoubtedly idealistic, such descriptions are nonetheless at the heart of the 'spirit' that Dawson and others sought to articulate and that the Apostolic Constitution, *Anglicanorum coetibus*, has made a reality within the Roman communion when, on 4 November 2009, this historic document was promulgated by Pope Benedict XVI.[7] More specifically, beauty, or rather the Anglican patrimonial expressions of it, go to the heart of the vision of *Anglicanorum coetibus*. 'Inefficient, cumbersome, [and] out of date', *Anglicanorum coetibus* and the patrimony that it embodies is also beautiful and, therefore, embodies the spirit of a creed that can save the world.

In a sense this essay poses the question that numerous commentators put forward when *Anglicanorum coetibus* was promulgated in 2009: what is Anglican patrimony? No description of Anglican patrimony is without its problems, even within the Personal Ordinariates where modest liturgical differences may be found.[8] Indeed, seen as a concept that encompasses the whole Anglican experience since the Reformation, including the phenomenon of Anglicanism as a worldwide communion that now uses a variety of languages and liturgical expressions, there is no definition of Anglican patrimony that would ever satisfy anyone – Anglican or Catholic. In brief, however, and at the risk of oversimplification, Anglican patrimony may be defined as representing a religious vision that is in its origins both medieval and modern, thoroughly Anglican and English in nature and that is at its heart aesthetic – that is, concerned with beauty. This is not to suggest that beauty is the only defining quality of Anglican patrimony, but it is nonetheless central to the spirit of *Anglicanorum coetibus* and cannot be excluded without doing fundamental damage to the concept. Crucially, beauty – notably its liturgical and aesthetic expressions by the Christian tradition over the centuries – is also at the heart of the theology of the retired pontiff who made the concept of *Anglicanorum coetibus* a reality.[9] In a society that so often seems intent on neglecting beauty, or at least putting forward poor substitutes, beauty continues to stand, as Roger Scruton put it, 'as an independent witness to the meaning of the universe'[10] and, therefore, along with truth and goodness, of paramount importance to the Christian witness.

The Long English Reformation and the foundations of patrimony: The Cranmerian legacy, 1534–1829

The phrase 'Long English Reformation' refers to the drawn-out nature of the legacy of the sixteenth-century English break from Rome and the subsequent development of Anglicanism – 1534 being reference to Henry VIII's declaration of the royal supremacy and 1829, on the other hand, being a reference to Catholic Emancipation, whereby Anglicanism was effectively dethroned from its place of legal supremacy.[11] Making note of this period in relation to the development of Anglican patrimony, the dominating achievement of the Archbishop of Canterbury Thomas Cranmer (1489–1556), the chief composer of the prayer book tradition, looms large. Indeed, it is rare for exponents of dignified, sombre, poetic and consoling liturgical English not to mention Cranmer's legacy.

Cranmer was a masterful linguist, both in his translations of medieval liturgical texts and in his composition of entirely new prayers. There is, for example, what is arguably Cranmer's most famous composition: 'The Prayer of Humble Access', said by the congregation before the reception of Holy Communion:

> We do not presume to come to this thy Table, O merciful Lord, trusting in our own righteousness, but in thy manifold and great mercies. We are not worthy so much as to gather up the crumbs under thy Table. But thou art the same Lord, whose property is always to have mercy: Grant us therefore, gracious Lord, so to eat the flesh of thy dear Son Jesus Christ, and to drink his blood, that our sinful bodies may be made clean by his body, and our souls washed through his most precious blood, and that we may evermore dwell in him, and he in us. *Amen*.[12]

At Evening Prayer (Evensong), the Anglican service that combines Vespers and Compline, can be found the 'Collect for Aid Against All Perils', a prayer taken from early Western liturgical sources. This collect's imaginative contrasting symbolism of light and divinity, juxtaposed with nocturnal darkness and diabolic malevolence, is powerful:

> Lighten our darkness, we beseech thee, O Lord; and by thy great mercy defend us from all perils and dangers of this night; for the love of thy only Son, our Saviour, Jesus Christ.[13]

It is prayers and sentences such as this, read week by week by the village parson (whether he wanted to or not), that provides one of the explanations as to why, during the sixteenth and seventeenth centuries, much of England adopted Anglicanism as a popular faith – in so doing, abandoning, by degrees, their native Catholicism for the ambiguous Protestantism of the Thirty-Nine Articles. In the *Stripping of the Altars*, Eamon Duffy writes of how 'Cranmer's sombrely magnificent prose, read week by week, entered and possessed their minds, and became the fabric of their prayer, the utterance of their most solemn and their most vulnerable moments'.[14]

Vulnerability, indeed, requires consolation. It does not need to be stressed that the Reformation was a period of violence and suffering, not just for England but for Europe – Protestant and Catholic. Religion was not only the cause of violence but also a consolation from it. Recently, in a short piece written as part of a volume to celebrate the 350th anniversary of the 1662 Prayer Book, Terry Waite, who was famously held hostage in Lebanon during the 1980s, described how the words of the Book of Common Prayer – memorized during his youth in a Church of England school – comforted him while he was kept in solitary confinement, chained to a wall in a room with no natural light. As he put it, '"Lighten our darkness, we beseech thee, O Lord; and by thy great mercy defend us from all perils and dangers of this night" ... takes on a deep significance when one is afraid and sitting in darkness.'[15] One can imagine the 'soothing' effect that such a prayer may have had upon a troubled soul trying to navigate their conscience during the sixteenth and seventeenth centuries.[16] Such navigation was a part of life for many English men and women. Catholic memory of the English Reformation within anglophone memory can often become dualistic in its conception of the choices available to souls during those centuries. There are thus the heroes (the devout Recusants) and the villains (the devout Protestants). But there were also the middle, the lukewarm – who, whether out of weakness or for reasons unknown, preferred to live in peace or simply chose not to take a stand, especially when religious choices were also seen as political choices. There were, for example, those known derisively by both Catholics and Protestants as 'Church papists', the name given to Catholics who partially conformed for a variety of social, political or religious reasons.[17] They were, in a sense, Catholics who worshipped as Anglicans. Cranmer's 'Collect for Aid Against All Perils' would have taken on a very different theological meaning when prayed by, say, the head of a Catholic family who – on behalf of his family – was forced to attend parish worship so as to avoid a fine, or perhaps for the layman or laywoman who simply lacked the courage to make a public protest. Another individual, far more common than Catholic memory instinctively perceives, is the English Catholic who chose to be loyal to the reigning Tudor or Stuart monarch and to whom Pope Pius V's *Regnans in Excelsis* (1570) was an undesired – or simply unrealistic – call to rebellion.[18] In sixteenth-century England, a prayer for a luminous deliverance from diabolical darkness would have varied greatly among those of all social classes and occupations. Cranmer's prose may, on the one hand, have been a prayer for the deliverance from popery, but it also could just as easily have been a simple cry for assistance to get through life's daily tasks.

Stella Brook, in a 1965 study of the prayer book's literary achievement, contended that outstanding liturgical writing had to have both aural and textual qualities:

> Liturgical writing calls for simultaneous and balanced use of the physical and intellectual aspects of language ... Since the whole purpose of liturgical composition is to be uttered and to be heard, many of its relationships are with spoken rather than with written style. It has to meet, simultaneously, the workaday but important requirements of articulation and the need to create aural effects of sonority and dignity and rhythmic balance. But beautiful sounds are not enough. Liturgical writing has also to give clear expression to profound and subtle thought, ordered into formal shape and pattern. Although its primary impact on the mind is made through the ear, it has also to be capable of bearing the more testing and critical scrutiny of the eye of a reader.[19]

Cranmer undoubtedly achieved this and his project understandably has earnt a foundational place in the history and development of liturgical English, not to mention the English literary tradition. Able to be memorized and recited by a child, it can also be placed in the same literary category as Shakespeare – a remarkable feat and one that speaks to the fact that not only did Cranmer create a liturgy to be heard, spoken and remembered, but he also created a text to be read and contemplated. Even the unchurched, long after the adaptation by the English-speaking parts of the Anglican Communion, of contemporary English services that have rare aural power or literary merit, still know parts of the traditional prayer book, even if they may not recognize the precise source. One notable example in this category is the preamble to the marriage service (quoted here from the original 1662 text), which begins with that most familiar of Anglican clerical greetings, 'Dearly beloved', and continues:

> we are gathered together here in the sight of God, and in the face of this congregation, to joyn together this Man and this Woman

in holy Matrimony; which is an honourable estate, instituted of God in the time of mans innocency, signifying unto us the mystical union that is betwixt Christ and his Church; which holy estate Christ adorned and beautified with his presence, and first miracle that he wrought, in Cana of Galilee, and is commended of Saint Paul to be honourable among all men; and therefore is not by any to be enterprized, nor taken in hand unadvisedly, lightly, or wantonly, to satisfie mens carnal lusts and appetites, like brute beasts that have no understanding; but reverently, discreetly, advisedly, soberly, and in the fear of God, duly considering the causes for which matrimony was ordained.[20]

It is worth observing that in the official Personal Ordinariate service book containing the marriage service, *Divine Worship: Occasional Services*, the text of the above has been amended – notably with the phrase 'to satisfy mens [sic] carnal lusts and appetites, like brute beasts that have no understanding' having been removed.[21]

For both the literate and the illiterate, the prayer book has been remembered by generations since as a composition of beauty – an invitation, as Cranmer put it in the service of Morning Prayer, 'unto the throne of the heavenly grace'.[22] Yet notwithstanding this acclaim, it needs to be remembered that Cranmer would likely have been appalled by 'Papists' using his prayers for the 'superstitious abomination of the Mass', as he and the Reformers thought of it as. The surprise would also have been shared by many on the Catholic side, for that matter – shock at the thought of a Protestant heretic's writings being absorbed into the Western liturgical patrimony. Nonetheless, though Cranmer's work may have had as its initial justification the conversion of England from the supposed corruptions of 'popery', it is difficult to deny the effect such prayers had on the English people as a whole, Protestant and Catholic. Combined with the Authorized Version of the Bible, the plays of Shakespeare and the music of William Byrd, it can be argued that post-Reformation England had, by the seventeenth century, given the Christian West more than enough for a place within the history of Christian civilization, though not the complete preservation of Catholic culture.[23] In the *Grammar of Assent* (1870), Newman discussed this type of national religious heritage within the epistemological category of 'notional assent'.[24] Writing as a Catholic, Newman regarded Anglicanism's formularies as a kind of national or creedal umbrella over an ecclesial body separated by church parties and styles of churchmanship. This was, for Newman, essentially the means for the presentation of what he described as, '"Bible Religion" ... the recognized title and the best description of English religion'. Newman went on: '[Bible Religion] consists, not in rites or creeds, but mainly in having the Bible read in Church, in the family, and in private.'[25] Arguably a description that included the Book of Common Prayer (though Newman did not explicitly delineate it), this 'Bible Religion' had been the dominant religious inheritance of Newman's upbringing prior to his evangelical conversion. If such a minimalistic description of Anglicanism reads as though Newman was disparaging out of hand the Anglican patrimony as something merely cultural, like a body of art held in common by a nation, his subsequent elucidation shows that he was by no means referring to such a portrayal:

> I am far indeed from undervaluing that mere knowledge of Scripture which is imparted to the population thus promiscuously. At least in England, it has to a certain point made up for great and grievous losses in its Christianity. The reiteration again and again, in fixed course in the public service, of the words of inspired teachers under both Covenants, and that in grave majestic English, has in matter of fact been to our people a vast benefit. It has attuned their minds to religious thoughts; it has given them a high moral standard; it has served them in associating religion with compositions which, even humanly considered, are among the most sublime and beautiful ever written; especially, it has impressed upon them the series of Divine Providences in behalf of man from his creation to his end, and, above all, the words, deeds, and sacred sufferings of Him in whom all the Providences of God centre.[26]

The creative spirit and the pursuit of the sublime – in literature, art, music and architecture – was, consequently, present in force and power, even if it was not a 'real' notional assent that was unified or held in common, as Newman contended Catholicism had been in medieval Europe or in nineteenth-century Spain.[27] As Augustus Welby Pugin (1812–1852) vividly outlined in his exaggerated polemic, *Contrasts* ([1836] 1841), much was gone from post-Reformation England that would never return.[28] For devout Recusants, inflamed and encouraged – sometimes with violent intent – by the papal excommunication of Elizabeth I in 1570, persecution and limited toleration was their lot. Yet, with Anglicanism's episcopal structure intact, the cathedrals with their choral traditions present, a prayer book that had a large scattering of traditional elements, the seeds of future 'catholicizing' developments within the Church of England – a body 'haunted by its Catholic past'[29] – were entirely possible. However, it would not be until the nineteenth century that the radical and romantic notion of a Catholic Anglicanism could properly bloom, let alone the concept of an Anglican 'Uniate' body in Roman communion.

'Adorned and Beautified': Tractarianism, Anglo-Catholicism and the expansion of patrimony

Tracing the rise and development of Anglican patrimony out of a history that includes centuries of anti-Roman sentiment and non-Roman ecclesiastical jurisdiction is complex. The end of the 'Long Reformation', mentioned earlier, clearly played a role. Specifically, in the 'constitutional revolution' that took place from 1828 to 1833 (a period that included the repeal of the Test and Corporations Acts, Catholic emancipation, the Great Reform Act and the Irish Church Temporalities Bill), Anglicanism was essentially dethroned from its place of political privilege to denominational equality (though it retained many of its social privileges).[30] As an initial response to these political events,[31] the patristic and medieval idealism of the early Tractarians eventually led, for some, to a desire to clothe the theology of the Oxford Movement in either pre-Reformation or Tridentine spirituality and ceremonial – what became the Anglo-Catholic Revival.[32] In this sense, both Tractarianism and Anglo-Catholicism have been rightly associated with the Romantic Movement – both in the idealism of heroic individuals and in the advocacy of a hermeneutic that creatively sought to return Anglicanism to sources of Catholic identity.[33] Consequently, the nineteenth and twentieth centuries witnessed major changes to the visual and spacial elements of the Anglican patrimony – those aspects of patrimonial beauty that are beheld by the senses (art, vestments, liturgy, architecture, etc.) and that complement the more textual and aural elements of Anglican patrimony inherited from Cranmer and the English Reformation.

The visual and spacial contributions of Anglo-Catholicism to the emerging Anglican Communion were, by the early twentieth century, extensive and visible. No longer were chasubled priests offering the sacrifice of the Mass (possibly with incense and a radically altered liturgy and sanctuary) to be found only in English Catholic chapels, but instead could be found within England's established parishes – much to the horror of evangelicals and nonconformists.

Though Anglo-Catholicism had its eccentric elements, its achievements were nonetheless substantial. Undergirded by belief in the apostolic succession (despite *Apostolicae Curae*'s 1896 declaration of Anglican orders as 'absolutely null and utterly void'),[34] Anglo-Catholics nevertheless, with sincerity, regarded themselves as a branch of the universal Catholic Church. They built an ecclesiastical world that, by the early twentieth century, included cathedrals, foreign missions, seminaries, convents and monasteries. While in England Anglo-Catholicism had frequently to do battle with Protestant Anglicans who saw them as traitors to the Reformation, within the freedom of the colonies Anglo-Catholic missions came to dominate various areas of the imperial periphery, such as Africa and the South Pacific. By the turn of the early twentieth century, even in England, there were signs of growth and confidence. When, in 1933, the movement celebrated the centenary of the Oxford Movement, around seventy thousand people were said to have enrolled in the Anglo-Catholic Congress for that year. The various books of authors such as Peter F. Anson (1889–1975), himself a convert to Rome, with his own hand-drawn illustrations of churches, monasteries and convents, depict a world that, though now largely depleted, was once confident, thriving and, most importantly, exhibited numerous expressions of spiritual, theological, liturgical, artistic and architectural beauty.[35] Indeed, Anson's art itself may be taken as both a depiction of Anglican patrimony, as well as a reproduction of its beauty.

What emerged from Anglo-Catholicism was an assimilation of post-Reformation Anglican spirituality with revived and creative pre-Reformation expressions. Though the historical accuracy of these constructions frequently verged on the mythical,[36] they 'adorned and beautified' the Protestantism of Anglicanism sufficiently enough for a genuine revival of an English aesthetic that made reference to either the Gothic or Tridentine past, yet with a simultaneous reference to its Anglican present. With the remnants of a Protestant – Cranmerian – liturgy (either the prayer book itself

The Anglican Benedictine Abbey of Caldey, South Wales. Drawing by Peter F. Anson. Anson was a monk of Caldey. Source: Peter F. Anson, A Roving Recluse: More Memoirs (Cork: Mercier Press, 1946), p. 49.

St Cyprian, Dorset Square, London. Designed by Sir Ninian Comper (1903). Drawing by Peter F. Anson (1945). Source: Peter F. Anson, Churches: Their Plan and Furnishing (Milwaukee: Bruce Publishing Company, 1948), p. 58.

or *The English Missal* of 1912, a translation of the Roman Missal into prayer book English), one can imagine how a setting such as St Cyprian, Dorset Square, London (designed by Sir Ninian Comper in 1903), brought a genuine feeling of living reality to the Anglo-Catholic movement.

Its sincerity and boldness of vision notwithstanding, problems of ecclesial identity, derived mostly from the meaning and interpretation of the English Reformation, became a problem for Anglo-Catholicism. Some Anglo-Catholics, for example, sought to 'Catholicize' the prayer book without changing it or its doctrines drastically. Others, in various ways, sought to reinterpret the Reformation, usually by minimizing – unconvincingly – the prayer book's Protestant elements (sometimes to the point of dismissing them altogether).[37] Those who minimized or denied the value of the Reformation sought to either revive pre-Reformation English usages and styles, or to dismiss the Reformation altogether – sometimes, in extreme cases, even the English language itself through the adoption of the Roman Missal in Latin. Nonetheless, despite the position of a minority who dismissed their own native traditions, most Anglo-Catholics sought to retain elements of the prayer book tradition, seeking to reconcile (as best they could) post-Reformation Anglican beliefs and practices with both pre-Reformation Catholicism and contemporary Roman Catholic practice.

An Uncertain Courtship: Anglo- and Roman-Catholicism

Anglican proposals for corporate reunion began well before the nineteenth century. The concept can, in fact, be traced back to the Stuarts and their various (unsuccessful) attempts to steer the Church of England back to Roman communion. Understandably, numerous proposals appeared from the mid-nineteenth century onwards, such as the Association for the Promotion of the Unity of Christendom (founded in 1857) and, in the 1920s and 1930s, at the height of Anglo-Papist influence, various Anglo-Catholic initiatives for corporate reunion. These included the 'Malines Conversations' (between Cardinal Mercier, Archbishop of Malines, Belgium, and Lord Halifax, the second Viscount), which took place between 1921 and 1925, and a proposal made by the Committee for Promoting the Church Unity Octave in 1933, which garnered the signatures of around seven hundred clergy.[38]

It is difficult to judge how sincere these calls for corporate reunion were owing to the obvious fact that, in the end, they never resulted in any substantial corporate reconciliation. Not only did

Low Church Evangelicals within the Church of England publicly oppose such moves, but for those Anglo-Catholics, however, who were sincere, their proposals were often met by conservative Catholic opposition. W. S. F. Pickering has described Anglo-Catholic declarations for reunion during the early twentieth century to an unrequited romance, and there is much truth to this assessment.[39] Nineteenth-century ultramontanism, with its many zealous English-convert adherents, combined with *Apostolicae Curae*'s repudiation of Anglican orders, helped foster a Roman attitude that was largely dismissive of the concept of corporate reunion. The entry on the Oxford Movement in the 1911 edition of the *Catholic Encyclopedia* stated that *Apostolicae Curae* 'shuts out the hope entertained by some of what was termed "corporate reunion"'.[40] During the 1920s and 1930s, when Anglo-Catholicism was at its height – as were calls for corporate reunion – it is interesting to ask whether a more irenic and creative ecclesiology on Rome's part could have led to a much larger 'Anglican Uniate' body. The counterfactuals are stimulating, giving rise to the notion that an Apostolic Constitution like *Anglicanorum coetibus*, present at an earlier date, could have had a much more substantial impact, not to mention size. The Anglo-Catholic embodiment of English sacral beauty, elucidated in this essay, with its imaginative *via media* of pre- and post-Reformation theology and praxis could have enriched the general atmosphere of Catholic *ressourcement* present in the early twentieth century. A corporate union with Rome during this period would have led, in a much more expansive way, to the type of vision that Aidan Nichols described in *The Panther and the Hind* in 1993. His description of an Anglican style 'uniate' Church in communion with Rome – of a body that preserves 'the best in Anglicanism' without doctrine moving like 'a weathercock for ev'ry wind' – is now well known. Referring to his pessimism regarding the ecumenical efforts of the Anglican–Roman Catholic International Commission (ARCIC), certainly in regards to its ability to practically bring about any sort of corporate reunion, Nichols asked 'What is to be done?' answering that an 'Anglican church united with Rome but not absorbed, an Anglican Uniate church, is perfectly feasible', a Church that, absorbing

> numerous elements of the Anglican theological tradition – 'classics', both as texts and persons – could find re-patriation in the Western patriarchate, in peace and communion with that see with which the origins of English Christianity are for ever

connected. ... Such an Anglican Uniate community might be relatively small in numbers, yet, provided with its own canonical structure, liturgical books, parishes, and means of priestley formation, it would enrich Roman Catholicism with its own theological patrimony, and – in the atmosphere of ecumenical détente which holds good in the West, though not, alas, the East – fulfil the rôle of 'bridge-Church' between Canterbury and Rome.[41]

Nichols had written *The Panther and the Hind* during the Church of England's debate over the ordination of women in the early 1990s. The frustration of Catholics and Anglicans supportive of a corporate home for Anglican patrimony during the 1990s had, however, in an ironic turnaround on Rome's part, been largely prevented by an attitude – influential during the decades following the Second Vatican Council (1962–5) – that sought to not upset ecumenical dialogue with the Anglican Communion.[42] Though individual conversion was encouraged, any sort of corporate option was considered a step too far by most Catholic bishops and curial officials within the Anglosphere – with the notable exception of a minority of individuals, notably Joseph Ratzinger, prefect of the Congregation for the Doctrine of the Faith from 1981 to 2005.[43]

The (other) Benedict option[44]

Ratzinger obviously becomes central to the events that led to *Anglicanorum coetibus*, not simply because of his papacy but his own ecclesiology.[45] Exasperated with the timidity of the English Catholic hierarchy during the 1990s,[46] Ratzinger understood – then, as he later did as pope – that genuine ecumenism has to be conducted in accordance with the ecclesiological position of *Lumen gentium*, that the Church Christ founded 'subsists in the Catholic Church'.[47] At the same time, however, this belief could also include support for notions of corporate reunion (and, of course, continuing dialogue), thus similtaenously affirming *Lumen gentium*'s related affirmation that not only are 'many elements of sanctification and of truth ... found outside of its visible structure', but also these elements are 'gifts belonging to the Church of Christ, [and] are forces impelling toward catholic unity'[48] – a sentence from *Lumen gentium* repeated in *Anglicanorum coetibus*.[49] The two principles were not contradictory for Ratzinger – indeed, they are central to the ecumenical enterprise.[50]

Moreover, as Pope Benedict XVI, all the evidence suggests that Ratzinger has long regarded the 'elements of sanctification and of truth' found within Anglo-Catholicism to be expressions of beauty, and, as has been highlighted, beauty has been central to his theological vision. Noting the centrality of the theology of beauty advanced by St Augustine of Hippo to Ratzinger's thought, Tracey Rowland writes of how 'Ratzinger's Augustinian pedigree has also been manifest in the attention he gives to beauty and his understanding of the catechetical importance of language and symbols and the relationship between matters of form and substance'.[51] Elsewhere, Ratzinger has endorsed Dostoevsky's statement in *The Idiot* that 'beauty will save the world',[52] and has linked this with the ability of Christians down through the centuries to creatively produce tangible – sacramental – links with 'the great artist' himself, the *Logos*. This is why, for Ratzinger, needless inattentiveness to sacred beauty falls so far below the standard all Christians are called to invoke, emulate and treasure. Even if it is not the within the psychological nature of all Christians to orient themselves to making aesthetic beauty a priority, the Church's commitment to truth and goodness should not exclude beauty – at least not without necessity. This is because, as Ratzinger put it, created beauty is inseparably linked to 'the *Logos* himself ... the great artist, in whom all works of art – the beauty of the universe – have their origin'. Consequently, 'all true human art is an assimilation to the artist, to Christ, to the mind of the Creator'.[53]

The Anglican tradition, for all its faults, has produced individuals who have been able to achieve this. It is seen in the liturgical legacy of Thomas Cranmer, the art of Peter Anson, the designs of Ninian Comper or in that archetypal Anglican depiction of Christ, 'The Light of the World' (1851-3) by William Holman Hunt. In communion with Rome, the Anglican patrimony – in its various service books – has been absorbed, adapted and creatively added to. Creations of beauty, whether they be literary, liturgical, artistic or architectural, produced by individuals living the spirit of *Anglicanorum coetibus* can in this regard contribute, however small, to the salvation of the world. Such creations are not ends in and of themselves: they are lanterns illuminating the only beauty that matters, 'the Beauty of Christ Himself'.[54] As Ratzinger said in August 2002, to the Communion and Liberation Meeting at Rimini,

Northern Italy, 'Nothing can bring us into close contact with the beauty of Christ himself other than the world of beauty created by faith and light that shines out from the faces of the saints, through whom his own light becomes visible.'[55] Human expressions of beauty are, consequently, signposts pointing towards Christ. This Christological foundation is the reason *Anglicanorum Coetibus* and the Personal Ordinariates of the United Kingdom, North America and Australia ultimately exist.

Indeed, while Pope Francis's criticism of those within the Church who display 'an ostentatious preoccupation for the liturgy'[56] needs to be kept in mind as a caution, the desire to promote aesthetic beauty is not contradictory to the Christian witness – a distractive addition to the simplicity of the Gospel. Beauty is a timeless and eternal reality and its various human manifestations – which invoke Catholicism's incarnational and sacramental nature – cannot needlessly be dismissed as irrelevant to Catholicism's witness in the world. The various elements of Anglican patrimony that the Personal Ordinariates possess are their unique contributions to a Church called to witness the 'beauty of Christ'. This is the spirit of *Anglicanorum coetibus*. 'Inefficient, cumbersome, [and] out of date', the manifestations of Anglican patrimony that exist within the Personal Ordinariates are also expressions of beauty. The maintenance of 'the liturgical, spiritual and pastoral traditions of the Anglican Communion within the Catholic Church' is not only 'a precious gift nourishing the faith of the members of the Ordinariate', but it is also 'a treasure to be shared'.[57]

Notes

1 Christopher Dawson, *The Spirit of the Oxford Movement* (London: Sheed & Ward, 1945), p. 77.

2 Dawson, however, overstated the pervasiveness of ecclesiastical corruption – 'the vested interests of pluralists and place hunters'. On the whole, recent scholarship has largely positive things to say about the individuals who held order in the Church of England at the turn of the nineteenth century. See W. M. Jacob, *The Clerical Profession in the Long Eighteenth Century, 1680–1840* (Oxford: Oxford University Press, 2007); Jeremy Gregory, 'Introduction', in Jeremy Gregory (ed.), *The Oxford History of Anglicanism Volume II: Establishment and Empire, 1662–1829* (Oxford: Oxford University Press, 2017),

pp. 1–21 at 17–18; J. C. D. Clark, *English Society 1660–1832*, 2nd edn (Cambridge: Cambridge University Press, 2000).

3 John Henry Newman, *Apologia Pro Vita Sua & Six Sermons*, ed. Frank M. Turner (New Haven, CT: Yale University Press, 2008), p. 162.

4 Dawson, *The Spirit of the Oxford Movement*, p. 13.

5 George Orwell, *Inside the Whale and Other Essays* (London: Penguin, 1972), p. 64.

6 Roger Scruton, *Our Church: A Personal History of the Church of England* (London: Atlantic Books, 2012), p. 41, see also, 89.

7 See Benedict XVI, *Anglicanorum Coetibus*, 4 November 2009, http://w2.vatican.va/content/benedict-xvi/en/apost_constitutions/documents/hf_ben-xvi_apc_20091104_anglicanorum-coetibus.html.

8 Many clergy within the Personal Ordinariate of Our Lady of Walsingham in the UK, for example, use the Novus Ordo, rather than the approved liturgical use found in the *Divine Worship* Missal. The UK Ordinariate has also produced its own office book. See Andrew Burnham and Aidan Nichols (eds), *Customary of Our Lady of Walsingham: Daily Prayer for the Ordinariate* (London: Canterbury Press, 2012). An official, Roman-approved, office book, making use of the prayer book tradition is currently in preparation.

9 Tracey Rowland, *Ratzinger's Faith: The Theology of Pope Benedict XVI* (Oxford: Oxford University Press), pp. 8–9.

10 The author is unable to find a written source for this quote, but it is used in the online video: 'Roger Scruton: Reclaiming Beauty', https://www.youtube.com/watch?v=5zHg7vxrAJo&t=82s (accessed: 19 December 2017). See also Roger Scruton, *Beauty: A Very Short Introduction* (Oxford: Oxford University Press, 2011).

11 See, for example, Nicholas Tyacke (ed.), *England's Long Reformation: 1500–1800* (London: UCL Press, 1998).

12 Brian Cummings (ed.), *The Book of Common Prayer: The Texts of 1549, 1559, and 1662* (Oxford: Oxford World's Classics, 2011), p. 402.

13 Ibid., 256.

14 Eamon Duffy, *The Stripping of the Altars*, 2nd edn (New Haven, CT: Yale University Press, 2005), p. 593.

15 Terry Waite, 'A Very Present Help in Trouble', in Prudence Dailey (ed.), *The Book of Common Prayer: Past Present & Future* (London: Continuum, 2011), pp. 193–8 at 195.

16 This was the exact word John Keble used to describe the prayer book. See [John Keble], *The Christian Year* (Oxford: J. Parker, 1827), pp. vi–vii.

17 For an irenic study of the phenomenon of 'Church papists', and of the complexities of religious identity during this period, see Alexandra Walsham, *Church Papists: Catholicism, Conformity and Confessional Polemic in Early Modern England* (Woodbridge: Boydell Press, 1999).

18 See Arnold Pritchard, *Catholic Loyalism in Elizabethan England* (London: Scholar Press, 1979); Peter Holmes, *Resistance and Compromise: The Political Thought of the Elizabethan Catholics* (Cambridge: Cambridge University Press, 1982).

19 Stella Brook, *The Language of the Book of Common Prayer* (London: Andre Deutsch, 1965), p. 122.

20 Quoted here from the original 1662 text. Cummings, *The Book of Common Prayer*, pp. 434–5.

21 Overall, the text for the Ordinariates has been simplified, though its full literary power have been maintained: 'Dearly beloved, we are gathered here in the sight of God and in the presence of this congregation, to witness the joining together of this man and this woman in Holy Matrimony; which is an honourable estate, instituted of God himself, signifying unto us the mystical union that is betwixt Christ and his Church; which holy estate Christ adorned and beautified with his presence, and first miracle that he wrought, in Cana of Galilee, and is commended in Holy Writ to be honourable among all men; and therefore is not by any to be enterprised, nor taken in hand, unadvisedly, lightly, or wantonly; but reverently, discreetly, soberly, and in the fear of God, duly considering the causes for which Matrimony was ordained.' See *Divine Worship: Occasional Services* (London: Catholic Truth Society, 2014), p. 61.

22 Cummings, *The Book of Common Prayer*, p. 240.

23 Kenneth Clark, *Civilisation* (London: BBC & John Murray, 1969), p. 163.

24 John Henry Newman, *Grammar of Assent* (Notre Dame, IN: University of Notre Dame Press, 1979), pp. 52–76.

25 Ibid., p. 63.

26 Ibid.

27 These are the examples Newman gives. He refers to Tsarist Russia as 'quasi-Catholic'. 'To them', Newman writes, 'the Supreme Being, our Lord, the Blessed Virgin, Angels and Saints, heaven and hell, are as present as if they were objects of sight' (Newman, *Grammar*, p. 62).

28 See Augustus Welby Pugin, *Contrasts: Or, A Parallel Between the Noble Edifices of the Middle Ages, and Corresponding Buildings of*

the Present Day; Shewing the Present Decay of Taste; Accompanied by Appropriate Text, 2nd edn (London: Charles Dolman, 1841).

29 Diarmaid MacCulloch, *The Later Reformation in England: 1547–1603* (New York: St Martin's Press, 1990), p. 6.

30 See Geoffrey Best, 'The Constitutional Revolution, 1828–1832 and its Consequence for the Established Church', *Theology* 62, no. 468 (1959), pp. 226–34; David Hempton, *Religion and Political Culture in Britain and Ireland: From the Glorious Revolution to the Decline of Empire* (Cambridge: Cambridge University Press, 1996), pp. 1, 22–3, 33.

31 See John Keble, *National Apostasy Considered in a Sermon Preached in St. Mary's, Oxford, before His Majesty's Judges of Assize, on Sunday, July 14, 1833* (Oxford: J. H. Parker, 1833); [John Henry Newman], 'No.1. thoughts on the ministerial commission', in [Anon.], *Tracts for the Times* 1 (London: Rivington, 1834), pp. 1–4.

32 Most historians link the Oxford Movement and Anglo-Catholicism, seeing the latter as being grounded in the former. This is, in my view a justifiable connection, though both movements were not monolithic, there were inevitable differences and variations. See Jeremy Morris, *The High Church Revival in the Church of England: Arguments and Identities* (Leiden: Brill, 2016), pp. 46–9.

33 George Herring, *What Was the Oxford Movement?* (London: Continuum, 2002), pp. 33–4.

34 *ordinationes ritu anglicano actas, irritas prorsus fuisse et esse, omninoque nullas* (Leo XIII, *Apostolicae Curae*, 13 September 1896, https://w2.vatican.va/content/leo-xiii/la/apost_letters/documents/litterae-apostolicae-apostolicae-curae-13-septembris-1896.html).

35 The author acknowledges the continuing presence of the Anglo-Catholic tradition in its various liberal and conservative traditions. They would understandably assert that Anglo-Catholicism, in developed forms, remains within the Anglican Communion, not to mention the many 'Continuing' Anglican churches that have a distinctive Anglo-Catholic identity. Nonetheless, the perspective of W. S. F. Pickering, that Anglo-Catholicism 'is but a shadow of its former self', remains difficult to deny, even if one were to qualify the assertion. See W. S. F. Pickering, *Anglo-Catholicism: A Study in Religious Ambiguity*, revised edn (Cambridge: James Clark, 2008), pp. 247, 283. See also Jeremy Morris's thoughtful and balanced discussion on the fortunes of Anglo-Catholicism since the 1930s (Morris, *The High Church Revival*, pp. 251–4).

36 See Diarmaid MacCulloch, The Myth of the English Reformation, *History Today*, July 1991, pp. 28–35.

37 See for example, John Mason Neale's (1818–1866) confident declaration that 'the Church of England never was, is not now, and I trust in God never will be, Protestant'. See John Mason Neale, *The Bible, and the Bible Only, the Religion of Protestants* (London: Joseph Masters, 1852), p. 3.

38 Aidan Nichols, *Catholics of the Anglican Patrimony: The Personal Ordinariate of Our Lady of Walsingham* (Leominster: Gracewing, 2013), pp. 12–18; Richard Waddell, 'Canonical and theological aspects of the Personal Ordinariates established pursuant to the Apostolic Constitution Anglicanorum coetibus' (JCL thesis, Pontifical Gregorian University, 2016), pp. 3, 6–7; Bernard Barlow, *'A Brother Knocking at the Door': The Malines Conversations 1921–1925* (Norwich: Canterbury Press, 1996).

39 Pickering, *Anglo-Catholicism*, p. 180.

40 William Barry, 'Oxford Movement', in Charles G Herbermann et al. (eds), *The Catholic Encyclopedia* xi (New York: Universal Knowledge Foundation, 1911), pp. 370–7 at 377.

41 Aiden Nichols, *The Panther and the Hind: A Theological History of Anglicanism* (Edinburgh: T&T Clark, 1993), pp. 178–9.

42 See William Oddie, *The Roman Option: Crisis and Realignment of English-Speaking Christianity* (London: HarperCollins, 1997).

43 Nichols, *Catholics of the Anglican Patrimony*, pp. 27–32.

44 See Rod Dreher's recent thesis invoking the sixth-century monastic pioneer: *The Benedict Option: A Strategy for Christian in a Post-Christian Nation* (New York: Sentinel, 2017). Dreher has referred to the pope emeritus as the 'second Benedict of *The Benedict Option*'. See Rod Dreher, 'Benedict XVI & *The Benedict Option*', https://www.theamericanconservative.com/dreher/benedict-xvi-ganswein-benedict-option (accessed: 15 September 2018).

45 William Tighe, 'The Genesis of Anglicanorum Coetibus', The Anglican Use Conference, Church of St Mary the Virgin, Arlington, Texas, July 2011, https://ordinariateportal.wordpress.com/2011/07/19/william-tighe-the-genesis-of-anglicanorum-coetibus/; Rowland, *Ratzinger's Faith*, pp. 98–9.

46 Joseph Ratzinger, 'What Are the English Bishops Afraid Of?', Eastertide, 1993, in Oddie, *The Roman Option*, 1. See *Lumen gentium* 8§2, 21 November 1964, http://www.vatican.va/archive/hist_councils/ii_vatican_council/documents/vat-ii_const_19641121_lumen-gentium_en.html.

47 Ibid.

48 See *Lumen gentium* 8§2.

49 *Anglicanorum Coetibus* [preamble].
50 Rowland, *Ratzinger's Faith*, pp. 98–9.
51 Ibid., p. 8.
52 Joseph Ratzinger, '"The Feeling of Things, the Contemplation of Beauty", Message to the Communion and Liberation Meeting at Rimini (24–30 August 2002)', in John F. Thornton and Susan B. Varenne (eds), *The Essential Pope Benedict XVI: His Central Writings & Speeches* (New York: HarperCollins, 2007), p. 52.
53 Joseph Ratzinger, *The Spirit of the Liturgy* (San Francisco: Ignatius Press, 2000), pp. 153–4.
54 Ratzinger, 'The Feeling of Things, the Contemplation of Beauty', p. 52.
55 Ibid.
56 Pope Francis, *Evangelii gaudium*, 24 November 2013, http://w2.vatican.va/content/francesco/en/apost_exhortations/documents/papa-francesco_esortazione-ap_20131124_evangelii-gaudium.html#II.%E2%80%82Temptations_faced_by_pastoral_workers.
57 Dawson, *The Spirit of the Oxford Movement*, p. 77.

8

A rich heritage of sanctity: The cultural impact of pre-Reformation English and Welsh saints

Petroc Willey

This chapter is concerned with the impact of the English and Welsh pre-Reformation saints on both their local and European culture. The area is one of considerable interest and there are a number of well-developed studies identifying some of the highlights in these contributions.[1] The period under consideration is a lengthy one, of almost fifteen hundred years, and would usually be divided into two main phases, that of Romano-British Christianity, dominant until the sixth and seventh centuries, giving way to the second Roman Christian phase, during which the various barbarian waves of Angles, Saxons, Jutes, Danes and Vikings[2] were drawn into a single Christian culture.

Out of the heady ethnic mix from which a Christian England and Wales gradually emerged, we find a shaping of culture by faith into something distinct, expressed in and through the geographical as well as historical character of this island: a relatively small area of land, ringed by a sea that both protects and provides avenues for mission and outreach,[3] with a temperate climate, a sense of proportion between the person and nature, an environment that requires hard work and yet rewards it, and the sense of a Providence whose hand can be felt in the small dells and rivulets as well as the wide sweep of hills.

Each person will capture this distinctiveness in a different way, identifying what he or she sees as its mature expressions, in places, people or work. I would like to choose two points of reference for this discussion, reading this period 'with the perpetual interpretation of Christendom', as Newman requests, seeking 'the mind of the Church acting upon facts'.[4] Both of them speak to the irreducibly *personal* way in which the heritage of sanctity is received and passed on; both witness to the importance of *geography and place*; both witness to the way in which a commitment to *transcendence* inspires the embodiment of holiness in works of art and institutional forms.

Two reference points

My first reference point is the collection of poems by George Herbert. If I begin outside of our pre-Reformation historical reference area (Herbert died in 1633), and outside of the Catholic confession (he was an Anglican priest), it is to make the point that the legacy of sanctity from this period has endured in many forms and shapes beyond it.

At its best the culture of Christian sanctity from the pre-Reformation period, reflected in Herbert's work, is one of natural and religious sensitivity. The spirituality we find quintessentially in Herbert, and in the saints of Herbert's Christian heritage is – as he described prayer to be – 'heaven in ordinary'.[5] The heritage is that of transcendence embodied.

Gathered together in the volume *The Temple*, Herbert's poems draw links between the physical parish church and the 'temple' of the human person, each feature mirroring aspects of a Christian anthropology.[6] Both his understanding of the person and the parish building in which he ministered date back to before the Reformation. His understanding of the person draws upon the medieval view of man as a microcosm of the universe, at once embracing the spiritual and the material:

> Nothing hath got so far
> But man hath caught and kept it as his prey;

His eyes dismount the highest star;
He is in little all the sphere.[7]

The simple parish church of St Andrews at Bemerton in Wiltshire, in which he served, dates from the Norman period. There is evidence of a medieval arch and lists of priests dating back to 1344. Reflecting on its architecture he aligns building and person in poems such as *The Church Porch*, *The Altar*, *The Sacrifice*, *The Church-floore* and *Church Musick*. The one who is the microcosm of the created world finds a pale reflection of himself, and of the world, in this small church. His poem *The Windows* speaks to the challenges of the incarnation of sanctity:

Lord, how can man preach thy eternal word?
He is a brittle crazy glass;
Yet in thy temple thou dost him afford
This glorious and transcendent place,
To be a window, through thy grace.

But when thou dost anneal in glass thy story,
Making thy life to shine within
The holy preachers, then the light and glory
More reverend grows, and more doth win;
Which else shows waterish, bleak, and thin.

Doctrine and life, colors and light, in one
When they combine and mingle, bring
A strong regard and awe; but speech alone
Doth vanish like a flaring thing,
And in the ear, not conscience, ring.[8]

The South East Nave window in Herbert's church is from the so-called 'Decorated Period' (c.1250–1350) and the poet uses this feature to propose that the human person has a 'transcendent place' in nature, but that place must necessarily be lit up by the colours of grace in order to 'win' others. Hearing must be accompanied by seeing – form must become visible in the person for the conscience of another to 'ring'. This is the work of grace bringing about the sanctification of the person: just as a maker of the window anneals in the glass the vibrant colours, so God's grace 'anneals' the soul, writing the divine story in the person so that the divine light can shine through.

The image is both transcendent and homely. The many challenges to holiness are reflected throughout the volume of poems. At times it seems as though his 'little cosmos' must break under the strain:

> Although there were some fourtie heav'ns or more,
> Sometimes I peere above them all;
> Sometimes I hardly reach a score,
> Sometimes to hell I fall.
>
> O rack me not to such a vast extent;
> Those differences belong to thee;
> The world's too little for thy tent,
> A grave too big for me.

Herbert movingly recognizes that the complexities in the spiritual-material composition of the human person place enormous challenges before the person who is truly seeking holiness of life. Nonetheless, the poem moves towards resolution: the tension holds, and Herbert finds a way forward in a spirit of humility and trust. The promise is held out for a spiritual life incarnated in the person – and also in the soft contours and arches of the small parish church, probably only ever built to seat around thirty people.

> Yet take thy way; for sure thy way is best;
> Stretch or contract me thy poor debter:
> This is but tuning of my breast,
> To make the musick better.
>
> Whether I flie with angels, fall with dust,
> Thy hands made both, and I am there.
> Thy power and love, my love and trust,
> Make one place everywhere.[9]

Herbert helps us to see how the cultural achievements associated with English and Welsh spirituality to which he in indebted hold together the magnificent ranges of the life of grace with a proportionality measured by the fragile human frame and against the gentle undulating natural environment.

My second reference point is taken from within our period, from a particularly intense time of the gathering of a spiritual heritage that could mark and characterize the new Anglo-Saxon kingdom.

Alfred (849–899) is at the centre of this work. With the assistance of Latin scholars, he worked personally on the translation of various Christian classics, in order to assist in the formation of a Catholic mind and culture in his new kingdom. The preface he wrote for his very free translation of Augustine's *Soliloquies* is striking in the abundant use it makes of imagery of wood-gathering and homebuilding in order to reflect upon the necessary but fragile tasks involved in the making of a Christian culture and upon the debts this kingdom would owe to Christian saints as they took their 'place' in this kingdom:

> I then gathered for myself staves, and stud-shafts, and crossbeams, and helves for each of the tools that I could work with; and bow-timbers and bolt-timbers for every work that I could perform – as many as I could carry of the comeliest trees. Nor came I home with a burden, for it pleased me not to bring all the wood home, even if I could bear it. In each tree I saw something that I needed at home; therefore I exhort every one who is able, and has many wains, to direct his steps to the self-same wood where I cut the stud-shafts. Let him there obtain more for himself, and load his wains with fair twigs, so that he may wind many a neat wall, and erect many a rare house, and build a fair enclosure, and therein dwell in joy and comfort both winter and summer, in such manner as I have not yet done. But He who taught me, and to whom the wood was pleasing, hath power to make me dwell more comfortably both in this transitory cottage by the road while I am on this world-pilgrimage, and also in the everlasting home which He hath promised us through Saint Augustine and Saint Gregory and Saint Jerome, and through many other holy Fathers; as I believe also for the merits of all those He will both make this way more convenient than it hitherto was, and especially will enlighten the eyes of my mind so that I may search out the right way to the eternal home, and to everlasting glory, and to eternal rest, which is promised us through those holy Fathers. So may it be.[10]

Alfred wants to erect 'many a rare house' and put up a 'a fair enclosure' and he is conscious of the role of the saints in his endeavor: they point the way to eternity and they also 'make this way more convenient'. Within this long analogy comparing the task of Christian culture-construction to that of wood-making,

Alfred appeals directly to the saints to whom he is indebted. The homestead he is seeking to build depends upon *their* guidance and assistance. They help us carve out a place of habitation, and also remind us of its temporary nature, that it is placed 'by the road'. The imagery is of his beloved Wessex and of the Southern downs that lead down to the sea. All of *this place* can become truly habitable if it is made holy.

Alfred mentions saints Augustine (of Hippo), Gregory the Great and Jerome in this introduction. Some of the guidance, the timbers and wood shafts for making his tools, he took from these giants of the Christian tradition. But, as we shall see, he was also able to draw from closer to home for staves and props, from the local schools of England, such as those founded by saints Adrian and Theodore of Canterbury.

Transcendence embodied: The character of culture impacted by sanctity

We have seen the themes of history and geography coming together in order to inform the way in which a peculiarly English and Welsh spirituality was formed, one which aligns the person not only to perennial spiritual themes in the pursuit of holiness but also to the particularities of time and place. The tension within which we must always place the saint and his or her impact on culture is that of referencing the transcendent while incarnating this in a particular form of life. The two points are inseparable. The veracity of the witness of sanctity lies both in the capacity of the saint to point to the transcendent and also to enshrine the form of holiness in a convincing way.

Let us consider the point about transcendence first. In a discussion on the merits or otherwise of utilitarianism, Bernard Williams makes the point that only if there are some people in a society who hold to certain moral standards is the slide towards a generalized understanding of happiness being conceived in more and more comfortable terms halted. There have to be enough people who decide that there are 'a range of things that they cannot consider doing, or bring themselves to do, or put up with being done, whatever other people do or may do'.[11] The virtuous person, prizing personal integrity, holds to the absolute norm and in doing so holds more than just him or herself to that norm. Ground is gained for others as well. Virtue is social. A secure reference point is hammered into the mountainside on which more than a single climber can be held safely. A group of climbers may be roped to that same point, held by that same key. The significant reformers in any nation or group's history are such because of their conviction that an unswerving personal commitment is necessarily inseparable from the institutional and cultural forms in which that commitment is enshrined.

When we treat of the impact of sanctity on culture we are moving into a further, but related, world. Expressing Williams's point in religious terms, we might say simply that there is no substitute for personal holiness. The saint is the personal meeting point of the worlds of nature and of grace, of the work of grace clothing that of nature. Here untiring moral effort is united to the even greater persistence of grace so that new forms of life, cultural and institutional, can be born 'from above' (cf. Jn 3.24) – precarious models because never dependent on the human lives that inhabit and express them, but recognizably lit, nonetheless, by a more than human light.[12] The religious form of life embraces the paradox that the mountain key by which the social body is held is placed there by One who comes down to provide safe ways for the ascent.

The most profound impact of the saints on a culture in any period is that of bearing witness to the reality of the supernatural and of its inevitable shaping of cultural forms. For the saint, it is not the development or the restoration of culture that is the end point or focus. The saint transforms the culture around him or herself precisely by looking *beyond* culture and, in doing so, lifts it to that further horizon point.[13] Thus an outward-facing culture is developed, not just towards other persons but towards the Other, the transcendent. G. K. Chesterton characterized the Christian saint as having eyes opened wide.[14] The gaze of the saint embraces, but does not finally rest on, the proximate forms of natural life – ethnic group, local loyalties, family allegiances and immediate communities. The form of life is stable but its security derives not from the incarnate form, but from its divine governing point. We might describe this point using the familiar landscape of the English countryside. Dotted throughout the small towns and villages we see the spires and towers of the churches. Normally understood as a sign of our reaching up to heaven, we could perhaps more accurately see these spires as the secure reference point for the local community – fixed and rooted in heaven rather as the huge crucifix in the apse of San Clemente is held from heaven. The spires are the visible reminder to everyone in the surrounding area of Christ who descended from heaven in order to bring the secure point of grace by which the ascent to God may be made.

The saints are rooted in heaven. At the same time, they impact society so powerfully because they not only point towards the transcendent but also because their lives provide an *apologia* for the Incarnation by demonstrating that the Form of the Eternal, made uniquely present in time in Christ, can not only inspire but can also make present cultural patterns of holiness in stable ways of life, capable of being shared by others. Stuart Sutherland offers an extended discussion of this general theme in his *Atheism and the Rejection of God* where he considers Dostoevsky's response to the problem of evil raised by Ivan in *The Brothers Karamazov*.[15] He proposes that Dostoevsky's chosen rejoinder to Ivan takes the form, not of an intellectual argument but rather of demonstrating that a theistic way of life is possible, even in the face of great evil and misery. To do this, Dostoevsky provides us with the figure of the monk Zossima to stand as a living answer to Ivan's rejection of the world as a place 'not possible' for him to live in, a creation where he must 'return the ticket'. There is a possible 'form of life' in which holiness may be pursued, which through its very existence provides an answer to the challenging 'problem' of evil.[16]

Every culture which we can call 'Christian' has this character of holiness marking it in some way, expressing transcendence and its embodiment. We can identify a number of ways in which this is expressed in our period.

In the first place, we can see the way in which, rather than detach one from earthly concerns, the hope for heaven provides a deep strength and power for renewal and rebuilding. What might appear to be simply encouraging a detachment from the present in the light of expected eschatological happiness in fact allows for a thoroughly practical, patient concentration upon the present. It is the unique vantage point of the saint, gained through grace, that provides the unquestionable vitality that characterizes the dynamism of cultural shaping we find throughout this extended period of English and Welsh history. We might capture it in the vivid image of Alcuin's (735–804) determination to rebuild Christian culture in and through the Carolingian Renaissance, even in the face of the burning of his magnificent library by the Vikings in the ninth century.

Newman wrote elegantly of this salient characteristic as that which made possible the patient restoration of local culture by the Benedictines – in England and elsewhere – of their embracing of cultural dislocation and trauma for the sake of a higher loyalty, one that did not dismiss or seek to subvert the troubling earthly realities but sought to re-establish the 'school for the Lord's service', *dominici schola servitii*[17] even in its act of breaking:

> [St Benedict] found the world, physical and social, in ruins, and his mission was to restore it in the way, not of science, but of nature ... not professing to do it by any set time or by any rare specific or by any series of strokes, but so quietly, patiently, gradually ... Silent men were observed about the country, or discovered in the forest, digging, clearing, and building; and other silent men, not seen, were sitting in the cold cloister, tiring their eyes, and keeping their attention on the stretch, while they painfully deciphered and copied and re-copied the manuscripts which they had saved. There was no one that 'contended, or cried out', or drew attention to what was going on; but by degrees the woody swamp became a hermitage, a religious house, a farm, an abbey, a village, a seminary, a school of learning, and a city ...
>
> And then, when they had in the course of many years gained their peaceful victories, perhaps some new invader came, and with fire and sword undid their slow and persevering toil in an hour ... and nothing was left to them but to begin all over again; but this they did without grudging, so promptly, cheerfully, and tranquilly, as if it were by some law of nature that the restoration came, and they were like the flowers and shrubs and fruit trees which they reared, and which, when ill-treated, do not take vengeance, or remember evil, but give forth fresh branches, leaves, or blossoms, perhaps in greater profusion, and with richer quality, for the very reason that the old were rudely broken off.[18]

What Newman identifies as a Benedictine virtue is characteristic of the need to rebuild and reform throughout our period, a process of renewal reaching a high point in the covering of Catholic England by Cistercian monasteries. One of the founders of this reformed order was of course from England, St Stephen Harding, who suffered his own losses as a member of the Anglo-Saxon nobility after the Norman conquest, yet went on to author the *Carta Caritatis*, the Charter of Charity[19] while the English Cistercian saint *par excellence*, St Aelred of Rievaulx, the 'second St Bernard', authored his *Mirror of Charity* in the midst of English and Scottish war and upheaval.

Three other expressions of sanctity, of embodied transcendence, which we find in our period alongside the monastic form are those of martyrdom, virginity and mission. Each in its own way points beyond a purely earthly culture. The place of the *martyr* saints is particularly significant for this point since they bear witness in the clearest way to the insufficiency of the merely human, providing the greatest impetus to this turning of the gaze towards heaven. 'Martyrdom, accepted as an affirmation of the inviolability of the moral order, bears splendid witness both to the holiness of God's law and to the inviolability of the personal dignity of man, created in God's image and likeness.'[20] The impact of the saints on culture most strongly emerged, on the British and English landscape, out of the period of greatest cultural trauma. As Lewis Mumford characterized the period of the fifth and sixth centuries in general, 'One by one, the old classic lamps went out; one by one, the new tapers of the Church were lighted.'[21] The English proto-martyr is, of course, Alban. The *Old English Martyrology*, probably compiled in the ninth century, is now a significant source for understanding the cult of saints in our period.[22]

The witness of the martyr saint to the primacy of the transcendent meaning of the person was captured in the shrine to that saint, which often became a place of physical as well as spiritual healing. The shrine of Thomas Becket in Canterbury is well known in this regard, with examples of healings granted through his prayers narrated in the stained glass windows of the cathedral so that pilgrims on their way to the shrine could be inspired by these miracles. The shrine is always the place of the world's end, not so much a conclusion as a connecting point and entrance into the place from which the Most High speaks and reaches down to lift the pilgrim to what is higher, to provide the hope of resurrection out of death. It is perhaps no coincidence that the name 'St Peter' was given to so many churches in early England – the one who was both the focal point of ecclesiastical authority and stability and the 'door-keeper of heaven'.[23]

Closely related to this theme of martyrdom (and of course to monasticism) we must mention chosen *virginity*. In England and

Wales, as elsewhere, the deliberate relinquishing of family life and bonds for the sake of a closer belonging to the wider family of God, both spoke to the higher claims of the transcendent and protected the sanctity of sexuality and marriage. The shrines often embraced this theme also, as at St Winefride's Well. Dating from the seventh century, St Winefride was a Welsh virgin martyr who was beheaded by the young prince, Caradoc, after rejecting his advances. A miraculous spring of water appeared where her head fell and the shrine at the well became associated with miraculous healings and was immensely popular as a place of pilgrimage and prayer up to the time of the Reformation.

Finally, under this theme of attentiveness to the transcendent we need to include the 'form' of *mission* – that constant going out of oneself for the sake of others, leaving behind established form and context and placing oneself at the service of the proclamation of the heavenly Word. This extended Christian period, both in its British and Anglo-Saxon phases, is characterized by its mission orientation.[24] Missions took place despite the many dangers and hardships, and typically out of a genuine zeal for serving others with the truth of the Gospel. The missions of the saints took place not only during their lifetime, but also – and often more extensively – after their death, in the form of relics. As we have seen, the power of the intercession of the saints was evidenced by miracles of healing that took place associated with the relics. These enduring marks of holiness were sought after, reverenced and, of course, featured extensively in the liturgy, being housed in the altars of the churches. The earlier 'British' relics continued to be revered alongside those of the Anglo-Saxon saints; so, for instance, St Winefride's relics were transferred in 1138 to Shrewsbury, while St Petroc's relics were stolen in 1177 and given to the Abbey of St Meen in Brittany and took the intervention of King Henry II to restore them.[25]

Gathering the tools: A sense of place

We have noted the broad ethnic and cultural streams that flowed into England and Wales from which the British and Anglo-Saxon forms of sanctity were gathered. It is also clear that the stability provided by monastic forms of life, above all, in both the British and Anglo-Saxon traditions, enabled distinctive forms of Christian culture to be established and disseminated.[26] England and Wales were rarely the originating points of these cultural achievements, but through the advantages of an island geography they often provided a place of hospitable incubation, enabling a maturing of the 'form' for the sake of its energetic spread.[27] There remain many mysteries surrounding details of the rich interaction between the cultures of mainland Europe, Britain and Ireland. What we can see, nevertheless, is a beautiful tapestry of mutual enrichment and organic development, with the ocean encircling the island placing a pause on the concourses, allowing time for what has been received to exhibit its own distinctive character.

Alcuin's own contribution is a good example of this. Called 'blessed' in some traditions,[28] and described as the 'greatest cultural transmitter' of his time and 'the most learned man of the age',[29] he is a product of the Northumbrian Renaissance[30] that was characterized not only by a striking missionary zeal inherited from an original Irish monastic outreach but also by an unusually fine grasp of classical languages, perhaps gifted from that same source. That Irish mission from which he had received had in turn taken much of its founding impetus from the endeavours of St Patrick and his disciples who, most claim, originally came from Wales, and benefitted from a later education in Gaul. Alcuin's work reached a stage of settled maturity in the north of England, where he directed the Christian school at York for fifteen years and grew his famous library. It was at this point that he was invited by Charlemagne to direct the Palace School at Aachen. Once transferred to the court of Charlemagne, Alcuin oversaw the gathering, translation and dissemination of key texts, rescued from the Western ruins of the old Roman Empire. These included manuscripts such as the works of St Gregory the Great. It is some of these that were to find their way back into Alfred's English kingdom in the ninth century where the king oversaw the translation of selected texts, such as Boethius's *Consolation of Philosophy* and Gregory's *Pastoral Care*, into the vernacular for distribution to all of the bishops.[31]

The story of mutual dependence and the enrichment of Western culture, guided by Providence, is a moving one in which the pre-Reformation English and Welsh Churches clearly played a central role. As our example indicates, that impact found a particular focus in the development of monastic and cathedral schools under the Carolingians. The educational vision emanating from Aachan is famously represented by Alcuin in one of his letters:

It may be that a new Athens will arise in France, and an Athens fairer than of old, for our Athens, ennobled by the teaching of Christ, will surpass the wisdom of the Academy. The old Athens had only the teachings of Plato to instruct it, yet even so it flourished by the seven liberal arts. But our Athens will be enriched by the sevenfold gift of the Holy Spirit and will, therefore, surpass all the dignity of earthly wisdom.[32]

The relaunching of an education more widely accessible under the Carolingians was powerful. Nonetheless, the monastic schools remained closely associated with this development and were not left behind in the new emphasis on cathedral schools: Alcuin himself, during his final years, was Abbot of St Martin's at Tours, where he set to work building up a monastic school. Jean Leclercq's famous study of monastic culture, *The Love of Learning and the Desire for God*, sums up an important principle from this period, that the cultural impact of Christianity was inseparable from the liturgy: that it was truly cult that gave birth to culture.[33] In these schools, formed by the liturgy, there was an opportunity to study the traditional liberal arts, but ordered to the glory of God. To the Gregorian chant originating in the monasteries was joined the development of polyphony from the cathedral schools. As we have also noted, it was not only in France that the English contribution was being made. Monastic and cathedral schools were home-grown in England also. For example, St Theodore (602–690) and St Adrian (635–710) founded the great monastic School of Canterbury, which became a revered centre of learning during their age.[34] From royal Winchester and the cathedral school there, we also have the earliest European evidence of polyphony.[35]

The climax to these developments in the field of education was the birth of the universities. These, too, exhibited their clear debt to the monastic and cathedral schools and to the liturgy. The chapels were central to their life and their quadrangles modelled on the monastic cloister. It is no accident, also, that the foundations and development of these centers of learning in England and in continental Europe were so closely associated with the mendicant orders, focused on uniting education to *mission*. Prompted and energized especially by the twelfth-century Christian Renaissance – the flowering that appeared after centuries of steady growth – they ensured that the learning previously available only to small numbers of lay people could now be much more widely enjoyed.

Conclusion

We began with a consideration of how Herbert expressed the unity of Christian culture in a distinctively Christian understanding of the human person, conceived as a temple, as a place of worship, and how this understanding was, in turn, echoed in the architecture of the small Wiltshire church in which he served. Both his understanding of the person and the Church itself derive from before the Reformation, in the way the liturgy and educational initiatives growing out of both the Romano-British and Anglo-Saxon communities were shaped and molded in decidedly local ways. The saints are the 'high points' of these developments, the respected and revered points at which grace is recognized in its working to transform nature.

We also began our considerations with Alfred, a king about whom there are a remarkable number of stories of humility and self-deprecation. (Indeed, Alfred's humility in the passage cited is evident in his brief interpolation, 'as I have not yet done!') In the striking pastoral tone and clear spiritual focus of his concerns, we see the emerging model of Christian monarchy, a lay king serving, with his subjects, spiritual ends. In the estimation of Eamon Duffy, one of the achievements of the Catholic period prior to the Reformation was a religious culture in which there is 'no substantial gulf ... between the religion of the clergy and the educated elite on the one hand and that of the people at large on the other'.[36] The growth of the universities and the movement towards an egalitarianism is a natural outflow from the concerns that had led to the prizing of sanctity above wealth and earthly lordship. In the best of the period under our consideration, transcendence and embodiment are not opposed, not wasted in a strained dualism, but flow together, uniting 'the life of Christ and the high mysteries of the faith' with the 'homely realities of common life'. Those words are Dawson's[37] and his comments here refer to one of *his* selected reference points for understanding the achievements of pre-Reformation Christian culture in England and Wales, William Langland's *Piers Plowman*. Langland's vision of how a truly Christianized culture is accessible to all in its essentials, drawing all into one society, we might take as a reminder of the centrality of our theme: the conviction that social cohesion is ultimately a divine work brought about, above all, by those who turn their lives towards the transcendent, towards the work of grace:

For we are all Christ's creatures, and by his coffer are we wealthy,
And brothers of one blood, beggars and nobles.
Christ's blood on Calvary is the spring of Christendom,
And we became blood brethren there, recovered by one body,
As *quasi modo geniti* – and gentle without exception,
None base or a beggar, but when sin cause it.[38]

Notes

1 Some of the more important treatments would be Samuel Crawford's *Anglo-Saxon Influence on Western Christendom, 600–800* (London: Oxford University Press, 1933); Wilhelm Levison's post-war work, *England and the Continent in the Eighth Century* (Oxford: Clarendon Press, 1946), which traces not only the European contribution of the great English missionary saints and scholars such as Willibrord, Boniface and Alcuin but also treats more generally of the place of shrines, relics and pilgrimages; Christopher Dawson's wide-ranging Gifford Lectures, *Religion and the Rise of Western Culture* (New York: Sheed and Ward, 1950), given in 1948–9, and Donald Bullough's volume on Alcuin, that most remarkable monk of the ninth century, D. A. Bullough, *Alcuin: Achievement and Reputation: Being Part of the Ford Lectures Delivered in Oxford in Hilary Term 1980* (Leiden: Brill, 2004). We should also mention Eleanor Duckett's eminently readable biographical studies of Aldhelm, Wilfred, Bede and Boniface, gathered in her *Anglo-Saxon Saints and Scholars* (London: Macmillan, 1947) and volumes I and II of Newman's classic *Historical Sketches* (Westminster: Christian Classics, 1970; originally London: B. M. Pickering, 1876) which for elegance and saintly insight are matchless.

2 The complexity of relations between the 'two churches' (see Hugh Williams, *Christianity in Early Britain* (Oxford: The Clarendon Press, 1912)), the British and the Anglo-Saxon, has often been treated. Both were Roman in origin, even though the British church developed in unusual ways due to the pressures upon it at the end of the classical Roman era. The key ancient accounts upon which we depend and which we must interpret are, of course, those of Gildas and of Bede. To Aelfric we owe around fifty stories of saints in Old English. For a helpful survey of the evidence of the British church, until AD 500, see C. Thomas, *Christianity in Roman Britain to AD 500* (Berkeley: University of California Press, 1981), especially his

conclusions at pp. 345–55. For the British period in general, see the thoughtful work of Malcolm Lambert, *Christians and Pagans: The Conversion of England from Alban to Bede* (New Haven, CT: Yale University Press, 2010); and for a selection of Anglo-Saxon lives capturing the dynamism of mission, see C. Albertson, *Anglo-Saxon Saints and Heroes* (New York: Fordham University Press, 1967).

3 As an example, we see the way in which Alfred developed nautical analogies which he added to the Old English translations of Boethius's *Consolation of Philosophy* and St Augustine's *Soliloquies* (see Carnicelli 1969: 32.5) while his evident knowledge and love of the English downs and woodlands shines out in his Preface to Augustine's work. See also the detailed comments relating to Alfred's translation of the *Soliloquies* in R. Waterhouse, 'Tone in Alfred's Version of Augustine's Soliloquies', in P. E. Szarmach (ed.), *Studies in Earlier Old English Prose* (Albany: State University of New York Press, 1986), pp. 47–86.

4 John Henry Newman, *St. Aelred: Abbot of Rievaulx* (London: James Toovey, 1845), p. 3.

5 George Herbert, *The Works of George Herbert in Verse and Prose* (London: George Routledge, 1854), p. 45.

6 For a full bibliography on Herbert, both literary and historical, and for details of the parish church, see www.GeorgeHerbert.org.uk.

7 Herbert, *The Works of George Herbert*, p. 90.

8 Ibid., p. 63.

9 Ibid., pp. 49–50.

10 H. L. Hargrove, *King Alfred's Old English Version of Augustine's Soliloquies*, Yale Studies in English XXII (New York: Henry Holt, 1904), available at http://www.gutenberg.org/files/40341/40341-h/40341-h.htm. For the original text see T. A. Carnicelli (ed.), *King Alfred's Version of St Augustine's Soliloquies* (Cambridge: Harvard University Press, 1969), pp. 47–8.

11 B. Williams, *Morality: An Introduction to Ethics* (New York: Harper and Row, 1972), p. 105; see also his contributions in J. J. C. Smart and B. Williams, *Utilitarianism For and Against* (Cambridge: Cambridge University Press, 1973).

12 Cf. Thomas Merton, who argued that a monk 'is essentially someone who takes up a critical attitude towards the world and its structures' which he does 'in view of his desire for change', in T. Merton, 'Marxism and Monastic Perspectives', in J. Moffitt (ed.), *A New Charter for Monasticism*, (Notre Dame, IN: University of Notre Dame Press, 1970), pp. 71, 74.

13 In regard to intellectual trends and the development of scholastic philosophy, Newman proposed that the 'sweet language' of St Aelred, with the 'commanding eloquence' of St Bernard, and indeed the whole Cistercian movement 'purified the schools by keeping aloof from them'. He argues, 'The church was not yet ready for the schools; or rather the schools were not ready for the church; men must learn to love the truth before they can safely philosophise upon it.' See: Newman, *St. Aelred*, pp. 144–5.
14 G. K. Chesterton, *Orthodoxy* (San Francisco: Ignatius Press, 1995), pp. 138.
15 S. Sutherland, *Atheism and the Rejection of God: Contemporary Philosophy and The Brothers Karamazov* (Oxford: Blackwell, 1977).
16 While Sutherland is indebted to a Wittgenstinian framing of this response, especially in the latter's concept of 'language-games', stressing the necessary unity of language and 'the actions into which it is woven', that philosophical context is not necessary for the general point we are making here. See Ludwig Wittgenstein, *Philosophical Investigations* (Oxford: Blackwell, 1953), p. 7.
17 T. Fry, OSB (ed.), *The Rule of St. Benedict*, Prologue 45 (Collegeville: The Liturgical Press, 1980).
18 John Henry Newman, *Historical Sketches*, Vols II and III (Westminster: Christian Classics, 1970), pp. 410–11.
19 J. B. Dalgairns, *The Cistercian Saints of England: St Stephen, Abbot* (London: James Toovey, 1845).
20 John Paul II Encyclical Letter, *Veritatis splendor* (London: Catholic Truth Society, 1993), p. 93.
21 Lewis Mumford, *Condition of Man* (New York: Harcourt 1944), p. 81.
22 For ongoing work on this see Christine Rauer's project at St Andrew's University, C. Rauer, *The Old English Martyrology: An Annotated Bibliography* (2019), https://www.st-andrews.ac.uk/~cr30/martyrology/.
23 W. Levison, *England and the Continent in the Eighth Century* (Oxford: Clarendon Press, 1946), p. 35.
24 See also the assessment of Dawson, *Religion and the Rise of Western Culture* , pp. 12–19.
25 More generally, we see the ongoing importance of links between Celtic Christianity in Cornwall, for example, and the new Anglo-Saxon Kingdom of Alfred in the Old English Life of St Neot. See M. Godden, 'The Old English Life of St. Neot and the Legends of King Alfred', *Anglo-Saxon England* 39 (2011), pp. 193–225.

26 Newman is surely right in his judgement that 'In the monastic system lay the remedial system of the Church ... the monks were the real reformers of the Church' (*St. Aelred*, p. 47).

27 Aidan Nichols, OP, referencing Michelle Brown's work, *The Lindisfarne Gospels: Society, Spirituality and the Scribe* (London: British Library Publishing Division, 2003), offers us the Lindisfarne Gospels as a striking example of 'synthetic power' representing the fusion of a number of cultures which were then placed 'at the service of the divine Word'. See Aidan Nichols, *The Realm: An Unfashionable Essay on the Conversion of England* (Oxford: Family Publications, 2008), pp. 35–8.

28 Alcuin's cult has never been formally confirmed, although a number of martyrologies list him as *beatus*. See P. Willey, 'Blessed Alcuin, Deacon', in *New Diaconal Review* (London: International Diaconate Centre, 2012), for an overview of his life; and P. de Cointet, et al. *The Catechism of the Catholic Church and the Craft of Catechesis* (San Francisco: Ignatius Press, 2008), pp. 8–15, for a discussion of his relevance for the new evangelization. For Alcuin's life and for a discussion of sources, especially his collections of letters, see Bullough, *Alcuin*. Note also the caution in Rosamond McKitterick's analysis in R. McKitterick, 'Review of D.A Bullough, *Alcuin: Achievement and Reputation*', *Catholic Historical Review* 91, no. 2 (2005), pp. 350–4.

29 The first description is Paul Johnson's in *A History of Christianity* (Harmondsworth: Penguin Books, 1976), p. 160. The second is the judgement of the royal biographer Einhard, in *Vita Karoli magni*, trans. L. Thorpe, *Two Lives of Charlemagne* (Harmondsworth: Penguin Books, 1969), p. 25.

30 The great Northumbrian centre of culture that was the inspiration of St Wilfrid (AD 634–709) and Benedict Biscop (AD 628–690) and which had a fruitful interaction with the Celtic centre at Lindisfarne.

31 For Alcuin's clear influence on Alfred's translations see W. F. Bolton, 'How Boethian is Alfred's *Boethius*?', in P. E Szarmach (ed.), *Studies in Earlier Old English Prose* (Albany: State University of New York Press, 1986), pp. 153–70.

32 Cited in Dawson, *Religion and the Rise of Western Culture*, p. 71 and see P. Riché, *Écoles et Enseignement dans le Haut Moyen Age*, 3rd edn (Paris: Picard Éditeur Riché, 1999), pp. 115–18.

33 J. Leclercq, *The Love of Learning and the Desire for God: A Study of Monastic Culture*, 3rd edn (New York: Fordham University Press, 1982).

34 King's School in Canterbury has some claim to be the oldest extant school in England, possibly dating back to St Augustine's original foundation in AD 597.
35 The Winchester Troper dates back to the turn of the first millennium. See S. Rankin (ed.), *The Winchester Troper: Facsimile Edition and Introduction* (London: Stainer and Bell, 2007).
36 Eamon Duffy, *The Stripping of the Altars: Traditional Religion in England 1400–1580* (New Haven, CT: Yale University Press, 1992), p. 2.
37 Dawson, *Religion and the Rise of Western Culture*, p. 269.
38 W. Langland, *The Vision of Piers Plowman*, XI, trans. H. W. Wells (New York: Sheed and Ward, 1935), pp. 201–6.

9

Service in perfect freedom: The precious gift of the Caroline Divines

Jacob Phillips

Introduction

The seventeenth century was pivotal for the development of Anglican theology and culture, and can be called 'the greatest age of the English Church'.[1] It was a time of unparalleled importance primarily as 'the first century of the Reformation'.[2] A 'reflective Anglican consciousness' had begun to emerge during the reign of Elizabeth I[3] and this developed in the following decades. Increasingly sophisticated theological rationales for understanding Anglicanism thus took shape in the writings of various English theologians. Much of this centred on situating Anglicanism in relation to the Continental Reformation on the one hand, and a Catholicism generally classed as pertaining to 'Rome' on the other. This reflected the tension between Anglican reformers who sought more faithfulness to the teaching of Luther and (particularly) Calvin, and those who looked to ground the Church of England's enduringly episcopal structure by situating it closely to the pre-Reformation English Church. Richard Hooker's *Lawes of Ecclesiastical Politie* had been published in 1594 and 1597, but this had not settled the 'controversy between those satisfied with the Elizabethan settlement ... and those desiring a more reformed church'.[4] Arguably, this Anglican tension between reform impulses and Catholic heritage proved long standing and intensified in the decades preceding the promulgation of *Anglicanorum coetibus* some four centuries later. For this reason, there is much to be gained by approaching these early explorations of Anglicanism in light of this document. That is, from when the theology of 'a Protestant Church which remained haunted by its Catholic past' was first being established.[5]

It was not only this theological tension that defined the ecclesiastical contours of seventeenth-century England. It was also a high-water mark of the English Renaissance. William Shakespeare died in 1616, Christopher Marlowe in 1593 and Ben Johnson in 1637. Spencer's *The Faerie Queene* had been published in full in 1596. Musically, this was the era of Thomas Tallis, Orlando Gibbon, William Byrd and John Dowland. Theological developments were therefore taking place as a distinctively 'English' cultural identity was coming to fruition. The theologians of this time were educated in universities which, by the time of Charles I, 'had long been steeped in the study of ancient authors', particularly Cicero and Aristotle.[6] It has been said that 'never before' had the Church of England 'contained within its bounds such a wealth of scholarship'.[7] So this was a period which was both ecclesiastically and culturally fertile. Again, one can see an impressive cultural legacy enduring in Anglicanism long after the seventeenth century. This legacy is acknowledged in *Anglicanorum coetibus*, which speaks of 'Anglican patrimony' as a 'precious gift' and 'a treasure to be shared'.[8] There are good grounds, therefore, to study the culturally rooted aspects of this period too, in order to understand more fully what this 'precious gift' might involve for Catholicism today.

The Caroline Divines

The churchmen of the seventeenth century are generally known as the Caroline Divines. Because the period is so significant, they are elevated to high status in Anglican self-understanding. For various reasons, providing an exhaustive list of those to whom the title can pertain is challenging, but the names usually attached to this title would include at least Lancelot Andrewes, Jeremy Taylor,

George Herbert, John Donne, William Laud, John Cosin, Herbert Thorndike and Mark Frank.[9] The term 'Caroline' was first used of those divines active during the reign of Charles I (1625–49), whereas it now tends to be used as a generic term for seventeenth-century theologians and devotional writers from the reigns of James I (1603–25), Charles II (1660–85) and James II (1685–8) as well.[10]

Interestingly, the term is often used in a way which is not merely signifying *when* the divines were active, but as something closer to what we might term – loosely – a particular theological 'school'. The defining marks of this group arise from the way they navigate the tension between Continental 'Reformism' and 'Romanism' in a distinct way. The overarching impulse is to explicate the Elizabethan settlement by drawing on elements of the pre-Reformation Church of England. In other words, 'it describes those theologians who set out to show the Church of England of the 17th Century as both Catholic and Reformed' and who represent an 'extensive attempt ... to reclaim the full theological and spiritual legacy discernible from earlier periods'.[11] The typical foci of this reclamation include firstly, a rediscovery of the early fathers, particularly the Greek fathers (whose early *depositum fidei* had paled in significance with the Reformers' approaches to Scripture). Secondly, there is more confidence in the 'application of reason as a critical and imaginative faculty in the discernment of religious truth' (a faculty which was downplayed in the wake of Luther's writing). Thirdly, these divines embark on 'typological' readings of contemporary events in British history through the lens of Scripture, and fourthly, the facilitation of an emergent Anglican piety – 'applying Christian devotion to daily discipleship'[12] – something the faith-works dichotomy of the Reformation threatened to engulf.

The term 'divines' might seem to require little or no explanation, it being a word which functions broadly as a synonym for 'theologians'. As is often in the case in dealing with Anglicanism, however, apparently slight ambiguities can reveal hidden depths. For this group also includes devotional writers like Herbert and Donne, so 'divine' carries a broader and more suggestive sense than today's formal use of the word 'theologian'. This will prove important in what follows, in connection with the aforementioned culturally rooted aspects of what *Anglicanorum coetibus* calls the 'precious gift' of Anglican patrimony. For the diversity of writing genres pertaining to the Caroline Divines means that we are dealing not only with formal theological argumentation but also with a certain literary, aesthetic sensibility, and it is precisely this element of Anglicanism which today's Catholics are encouraged to participate in by the document which this volume celebrates.

With the theological argumentation itself, however, a challenge arises in giving attention to the Caroline Divines for contemporary Catholic reflection. Put simply, there are crucial elements of Caroline thinking and writing which, for the most part, are very difficult to align with key tenets of Catholic theology. Much of this arises from the generally antithetical attitude to the teachings of the Council of Trent, or other instances of what were considered 'the popish extremes of Counter Reformation Catholicism'.[13] Several examples of genuine variance follow from this. To give just one, divines like Laud and Andrewes would differentiate 'traditions of the present Church' as secondary to the status of the 'indefectible' authority of the 'tradition of the early or "undivided" Church'.[14] As put memorably by Andrewes, this was a faith in 'One canone [sic] reduced to writing by God himself, two testaments, three creeds, four general councils, five centuries, and the series of Fathers in that period – the centuries that is, before Constantine, and two after' which, he said, 'determine the boundary of our faith'.[15]

It is not necessary to belabour why the Catholic understanding of the Magisterium will not permit this gradation of indefectibility commencing at some particular moment in time. Although it could be argued that the Caroline affection for the Fathers constitutes something analogous to the *Ressourcement* movement of the twentieth century, this would be problematic. The *Nouvelle Théologie* critique of neo-scholastic modes of thinking pertained more to questions of theological method and style than the enduring rectitude of dogma or doctrine; it was by no means a denial of authoritative teaching like that of Trent. The Carolines do not point to a need to emphasize ancient styles of theology as more appropriate or fitting for their time, but rather apportion doctrinal errors pertaining to the Church of Rome. That said, Walter Kasper has highlighted the concern with the early Church as something to be applauded in the Caroline Divines. In an address to the Anglican Lambeth Conference in 2008, Kasper responded to a question he had been asked by Rowan Williams: '*What kind of Anglicanism do you want?*' He then mentions the Caroline Divines as an example of a 'critical [moment] in the history of the Church of England and subsequently of the Anglican Communion, [when] you have been able to retrieve the strength of the Church of the Fathers when that tradition was in jeopardy'.[16] But it is important to note that Kasper is suggesting that the Caroline Divines' concern with the early Church is something it would be beneficial for Anglicanism to rediscover, not advocating Caroline theology as a fruitful resource for Catholicism. As it stands, then, it is challenging for Catholics reading theological texts which consider the Church of Rome to have gone severely astray. Taking William Laud as an example, he considered Rome to be 'so erring and corrupt that salvation was only possible in her to those who either were invincibly ignorant or were engaged in efforts to reform her from within'.[17]

Anglicanorum coetibus itself takes a balanced line on things. Of course, it maintains that 'the *Catechism of the Catholic Church* is the authoritative expression of the Catholic faith professed by members of the Ordinariate'.[18] This statement will not permit Andrewes's scheme outlined above. But at the same time the document holds that the time of post-Reformation exile is certainly not without considerable value, because Anglican patrimony constitutes a 'precious gift' and 'treasure to be shared'. A chapter of this length is not the place to engage in a detailed study of where, exactly, irreconcilable doctrinal differences are and are not found. Instead, it will investigate how the ancient Catholic heritage of the Church of England resurfaced and fused with the emerging cultural identity in and around the Caroline Divines. This is one example of what *Unitatis redintegratio* calls the 'special place' held by Anglicanism in relation to the Catholic Church.[19] The points of resonance between Caroline writing and Catholicism today are not so much theological as aesthetic, therefore. They are centred on particular tropes of Caroline spirituality. The task undertaken here seeks to respond to a prophetic challenge made by Aidan Nichols back in 1993. Nichols writes, 'If a Uniate Anglican Church is ever set up one of its chief goals will be the salvaging of ... 17th Century patrimony, corrected and amplified by union with the apostolic church of the West, the see of Rome.'[20] Assuming the theological corrections of *Anglicanorum coetibus*, let us enter into what Nichols calls the 'profound debt' contemporary Catholics sense towards 'the heritage of Anglicanism – as literature and music, thought and scholarship, liturgy and devotion, and works of charity'.[21]

Caroline moderation and discretion

The seventeenth-century fusion of religion and culture is highly pertinent for this volume. The Caroline Divines have been called 'masters of English writing as well as of restrained spirituality'[22] and this statement hints at a key aspect of this fusion, with the word 'restrained'. Terms like 'restraint', 'moderation' and 'discretion' are common in writings by and about the Carolines. These words gain importance after early notions of the via media understanding of Anglicanism began to take root. This via media situates Canterbury as treading a 'middle-path' between 'popish' Rome and the Calvinist Zurich. We see in the Carolines a salient constellation of themes emerging from this, particularly in application to the spoken and written word. This constellation promises to offer just one example of a process whereby culturally rooted values, in fusion with religion, can reach to a more universal provenance. This process is explicated by Joseph Ratzinger, and termed 'interculturality'. For Ratzinger, when religious faith comes into contact with culture, a profound transformation can occur, insofar as elements of 'truth' are shared by each. Once moments of interculturality have occurred, the resulting fusion – as radiating the 'true' – can inform and enlighten situations beyond that in which they originate.[23] In short, the result is the sharing of a 'precious gift'.

It should be borne in mind that 'the first task of the conforming theologians immediately after Elizabeth's reign, was ... to defend ... the *status quo* of the national Church, demonstrating its authenticity and suitability for the English people'.[24] 'English moderation', we read elsewhere, 'combined with a dislike of foreigners, ... produced among many people favourable to the break with Rome a very cautious attitude to the continental Reformation.'[25] This 'dislike' of both Rome and the Reformation, of course, relates to the via media, but the key word here is 'suitability'. The immediate task was to show how this particular outworking of the Christian religion should be considered the most appropriate form of faith for the people on English shores, to 'establish the Church of England in the hearts of its citizens as the *natural* form of religion for the country'.[26] In doing so, an emerging sense of the English as 'moderate', and antithetical to 'extremes', became increasingly important. This gave rise to something spoken of as the 'golden mediocrity' of the English Church by Archbishop Matthew Parker, something to which Hooker's measured approach in the *Lawes* had already given voice. Hooker had presented the Elizabethan settlement as 'the natural and reasonable form of religion for the English people', partly through a 'tone of debate that was reasoned and moderate': a 'measured tranquillity'.[27] The result was what might be termed a 'taste for decorum', which was both theological and related to personal conduct. A locus classicus of this can be found in Herbert's poem, *The Familie*:

> First peace and silence all disputes controll,
>   Then Order plaies the soul,
> And giving all things their set forms and houres,
>   Makes of wild woods sweet walks and bowres.[28]

In William Laud's work, particularly, we see the values of moderation and reticence growing in sophistication. It soon became evident that deliberate reticence over theological aspects of belief and practice could be highly valuable pragmatically. Leaving precise definitions unsaid – that is, moderating the desire for absolute knowledge – enabled the holding together of the ever-strained factions at play in Anglicanism. Laud's followers were 'prepared to make the Church of England's doctrinal boundaries flexible to increasingly outspoken and crypto-popish defences of them, on the grounds that the Church of England's official formularies did not explicitly renounce them'.[29] We see much the same impulse at work in Anglicanism to this day, in the deliberate lack of rubrics in Anglican liturgical books. Because the rubrics are not explicitly stated, the same Anglican rites can be a full smells-and-bells liturgy in one parish and charismatic all-singing-and-dancing service in the parish next door.

Moderation and discretion had more than a merely pragmatic function, however. They were connected to a Caroline affection for 'order', for that which Herbert said 'plaies the soul'. To be controlled and moderate in word – not to lay claim over realms beyond our understanding – should be situated within a broader proclivity for 'unity and order' in the Caroline thought-world. With Laud, for example, these are not to be regarded 'as irksome restrictions imposed from without upon unwilling individuals, but as the necessary conditions of the development of freedom and personality'.[30] In short, Laud was a primary 'upholder of ordered freedom',[31] which meant not being enslaved by ideological adherences and tribal impulses, by the rush to extremes indicated by fixations on precise explications of theological minutiae. Dealing with mystery in theology thereby combines with a disposition of humility and reticence towards the human desire for systematization. This constellation of themes is perhaps best expressed in the words of the 1662 *Book of Common Prayer*, and the Collect for Peace from Evensong: 'O God, who art the author of peace and lover of concord ... whose service is perfect freedom.'

This constellation, at least in Laud, is closely related to that great signifier of a 'Catholic impulse' in the Anglican mind: liturgical uniformity. Laud's prescriptions for uniformity in worship iterate his 'passion for tidiness' or decorum, which was itself 'an expression of the love of order which was far more deep-rooted'.[32] A widely acknowledged defining feature of the Caroline era is an appreciation for the 'beauty of holiness', connected with Ps. 29.2 ('Give unto the Lord the glory of his name/Worship the Lord in the beauty of holiness'). This need for beauty in worship gave rise to a concern for liturgical order. The beauty of holiness 'was expressed not only in godliness of life but in an insistence upon dignity and decorousness in liturgy and furnishings'.[33] The result was a 'suitably restrained, ceremonial liturgy', and the 'rare temper and proportion' of the Anglican rites. Again, *The Book of Common Prayer* is exemplary for this, 'with its dignified and restrained austerity of liturgy and ceremonial' which 'provided a form of worship no less attractive and satisfying to the average Englishman than the more exuberant Roman rite'.[34] This dignified and restrained austerity applied also to 'godliness of life', in the shape in peculiarly English concerns around 'civility and urbanity of language'.[35] Turning to Herbert, again:

> In conversation boldnesses now bears sway.
>   But know, that nothing can so foolish be,
> As empty boldnesse: therefore first assay
> To stuffe thy minde with solid braverie;[36]

To modern readers, this interpenetration of virtues pertaining both to 'godliness of life' and to 'liturgy and furnishings' might appear strange. But it is important to bear in mind that moderation, order and discretion had developed into key theological themes against an intellectual background very different to our own. This is best demonstrated by considering English Renaissance cosmology. This cosmic vision can be detected in Hooker, with his 'idea that the cosmos is constituted by a web or a network of giving and receiving'.[37] This was an enchanted, pre-modern cosmos, where the self-offering or mutual service of the constituent parts is undertaken for the good of the whole, in perfect freedom. It is paramount for Laud, and for his champion, King Charles I, who agreed that order is always closely and inextricably related to beauty. This applies to the cosmic reality of nature, which appears beautiful on account of its 'order and purposiveness'. It applies also to the arts, where beauty emerges from the formation of order within what is otherwise a 'chaotic manifold of sensation and emotion'. Moreover, these come together in liturgy, in which 'uniformity' was meant to quell the threat of human 'profaneness and irreverence'.[38]

This cosmic vision was an English inheritance. Its most well-known exponent is undoubtedly Shakespeare, and its paradigmatic expression is found in Ulysses's speech in *Troilus and Cressida*:

The heavens themselves, the planets and this centre
Observe degree, priority and place,
Insisture, course, proportion, season, form,
Office and custom, in all line of order

Note how human affairs are ordered to the cosmic whole, how 'office and custom' mirror the planetary spheres, so godliness of conduct has cosmic dimensions. This heavenly order is reflected in the hierarchical ordering of human society, and this was not without significance for those adhering to the episcopal structure of the English Church:

Take but degree away, untune that string,
And, hark, what discord follows!
Each thing meets
In mere oppugnancy: the bounded waters.[39]

The Carolines extended this cosmic basis for corporate order into the ecclesiastical realm. They also exemplified another phrase of Shakespeare's, that those who 'have discretion ... know the world'.[40] Leaving things deliberately unsaid does not therefore indicate a lack of knowledge, but quite the opposite. In terms of theological substance, this is best demonstrated in the vexed seventeenth-century discussions of the Eucharist. Here, the intertwining of mystery and reticence functions importantly in the development of

Anglican theology. It follows from the aforementioned via media. On one side, there were Anglican reformers who sought for a fideistic interpretation of the Real Presence, in which Christ is only bodily present for those who believe him to be so: *sola fide*. On the other side, there was the all-encompassing emphasis of Counter-Reformation Catholicism on an objective change which in no way depends on the faithfulness of believers: transubstantiation. The amount of writing on the issue of how best Anglicans should have understood the Real Presence in the seventeenth century is of course voluminous, but for present purposes let us bear in mind Hooker's comment that theologians are wasting time and energy on arguments over the precise mechanics of the Eucharistic change, claiming that to do so is to 'vainly trouble' oneself with 'fierce contentions'.[41] As the debates raged throughout the seventeenth century, the via media was applied to a disposition of reticence about the precise nature of the Eucharistic change. This meant that this process remained '*deliberately* undefined' by many.[42]

This is not only a matter of pragmatic utility, but also reflects the fact that the transformation of the elements is held to be an unutterable mystery. For Herbert Thorndike, moreover, to focus all one's attention 'on the *nature* of the change provided an unnecessary and unwelcome distraction from the true *significance* of the Real Presence, which bore fruit in the lives of those who received it'. The issue centres here on moderating our human tendency to grasp at extensive knowledge in favour of that which is more important: 'the very purpose for which the Eucharist was instituted; the life-giving encounter between the faithful and Christ'. While Thorndike would not pass the *anathema sit* of Trent unscathed, he does maintain what he considers the key point of the Tridentine definition; that a real, objective change occurs which does not depend on the disposition of the communicant. It happens, he says, 'by virtue of the consecration, not of their faith'. Simultaneously, he insists that this encounter with what Trent called 'the body and blood, the soul and divinity' of Christ himself in the Eucharist is to be understood in the broader narrative scheme of salvation history, which he terms, the 'Covenant of Grace'.[43] This is highly salient for this discussion, because the present *Catechism* inserts the article on transubstantiation into an extensive elucidation of the broader narrative framework of the economy of salvation.[44] The *Catechism* thus gives the impression that while the proper definition of transubstantiation is entirely necessary, of course, it is something which grounds the objectivity of the miraculous change conceptually, whereas its significance is in the life-giving encounter between Christ and his people.

Contemporary examples

This chapter works from the conviction that reading the Caroline Divines promises to be highly fruitful for Catholics today, in light of *Anglicanorum coetibus*. The previous section discussed particular aspects of Caroline writing which are culturally rooted, but which provide resources for drawing on this era in Anglican patrimony in a way which can avoid what *Unitatis redintegratio* calls the 'false irenicism'[45] of denying genuine doctrinal difference. In what remains, the task is to enquire into how these culturally rooted tropes, in their fusing with the elements of truth in the English Church which endured after the Reformation, have the potential for wide-ranging provenance for Catholics today. That is, to ask where moderation and reticence resonate in today's Catholic scene, showing something of how Caroline approaches serve as apt examples of a 'precious gift' and 'treasure to be shared' with the Church universal.

A theme of Caroline writing yet to be mentioned, but related to the prior discussion of transubstantiation, is *adiaphora*, or 'things indifferent'. This was obviously taken from the classically Lutheran position that along with the bare essentials of the faith discerned *sola scriptura*, there are a host of other matters of Christian practice which do not necessitate theological correction. For Hooker, the contention that there are ecclesiastical matters about which theologians can be indifferent resonated with his tendency for reticence about unnecessary speech, and he could hold, therefore, that things may 'vary from place to place and time to time' without undermining anything fundamental about the faith. This was extended by Laud to the point that 'everything fundamental is not of a like nearness to the foundation, nor of equal primeness in the faith'.[46] At first glance, this seems close to the problematic apportioning of indefectibility to only the early Church which was typical of the Carolines, and it certainly cannot be fully understood apart from that. But uncoupled from its doctrinal problems, and placed in context with moderation and reticence, it promises to be of value for a key aspect of today's Catholic theology, the New Evangelization.

The New Evangelization involves the transmission and perpetuation of the faith in contexts far removed from classically evangelistic contexts, particularly 'post-Christian' and/or 'secular' societies. This change in context, of course, requires a change in method, for an evangelism St John Paul II described as new in 'its ardour, methods and expression'.[47] The recipients may include those who are already familiar, at least superficially, not only with the basic tenets of the Gospel, but also the more challenging situation pertaining to those raised with a world view in which any transcendent reality is beyond consideration, where the metaphysical is only ever presented as outdated and expired, and where even notions of truth, beauty and goodness are, at best, relative. In this context, evangelizing needs to take shape in forms other than the explicit proclamation which led to the dissemination of the Church across the Roman Empire in the first centuries of our era. It requires wisdom and creativity in choosing when and how to describe and make available aspects of the faith, in a way fitting and suited to the situation in context. More precisely, it calls for a moderate disposition, which might leave unsaid key tenets of the faith which simply cannot gain immediate traction in the twenty-first-century West. What *is* said, needs to be chosen carefully; all things need to be done 'decently and in order'.[48]

This aspect of the New Evangelization is markedly resonant with Caroline moderation and reticence, and for this reason it is important that it is highlighted in a recent Magisterial document. This is Pope Francis's *Evangelii gaudium*. In §36, the Holy Father navigates the duality of *Unitatis redintegratio* through the application of moderation. On the one hand, he does not deny the danger of the 'false irenicism' of denying the fullness of the Catholic faith, saying, 'All revealed truths derive from the same divine source and are to be believed with the same faith.' On the other hand, however, he maintains that some of 'these truths are more important', practically, 'for giving direct expression to the heart of the Gospel'. The least 'indifferent' thing, or rather the thing about which hearers of the Word can least afford to be indifferent, 'is the beauty of the saving love of God made manifest in Jesus Christ who died and rose from the dead'. So, while nothing is strictly indifferent, considered contextually in light of the New Evangelization, 'there exists an order or a "hierarchy" of truths'.

A second example of Caroline moderation and reticence in connection to today's Catholicism comes from the recently published writings of Cardinal Robert Sarah. These writings are proving popular among the faithful, and are strongly endorsed by Benedict XVI. Sarah's *The Power of Silence: Against the Dictatorship of Noise* is focused on the need for a contemporary rediscovery of ascetic discipline, following from the cultivation of silence. The text applies this rediscovery to the internal wrangles within the Church, particularly in reference to the life of clergy, to the personal and corporate piety of believers, to the liturgy and even to such challenging territory of the problem of evil. Of particular interest, here, is Sarah's diagnosis of the contemporary West, which he sees as under 'the dictatorship of noise'. This is seen particularly in the inexorable fixation on digital communication in contemporary life. Sarah is clear that the reason for the inescapable prevalence of noise is secularity. He quotes Thomas Merton, saying, 'The turmoil and confusion and constant noise of modern society are the expression of the ambiance of its greatest sins – its godlessness, its despair.' Our world of 'endless argument, vituperation, criticism, or simply of chatter, is a world without anything to live for'.[49]

Sarah's diagnosis is compelling, but it is his suggested remedy which is of interest here. His writings are not formal theology as such, but he is clear that theology itself has all too frequently fallen under the dictatorship of noise. He speaks of 'garrulous theologians' who 'are pretentious and infatuated with their own arguments'.[50] Contemporary theology must beware of the 'sterile enthusiasm', 'intense passions' and 'disordered excitement' which are today mistaken as indicators of profundity.[51] As was true for the Caroline Divines, the core element here is mystery. Sarah writes that 'words often bring with them the illusion of transparency, as though they allowed us to understand everything, control everything, put everything in order'. But, 'words spoil anything that surpasses them'. Therefore, we are warned, 'if we no longer know how to be quiet, then we will be deprived of mystery'. He reiterates the point, 'Without silence we are deprived of mystery.'[52] For Sarah, 'renewed entrance into the mystery would allow everyone to experience a silent, contemplative approach to doctrine and theology', because 'these disciplines are the result ... of receptiveness in silence to the Word of God'.[53]

Sarah's writing suggests that a renewed engagement with the constellation of themes around moderation and reticence in Caroline theology could be beneficial for today's contemporary Catholic scene. There is something here which promises to be a 'precious gift' and 'treasure to be shared' well beyond the confines of seventeenth-century England. Indeed, given the challenges of contemporary lifestyles, an attentiveness to this 'precious gift' might indeed seem pressing. Sarah tells us that 'today many people are drunk on speaking', so 'if we are to avoid harming or soul and the souls of others ... moderation and reticence are necessary'.[54] Imposing 'silence on the labour of thought' is not oppressive, but liberating: 'silence is the supreme freedom of man'.[55] One might suggest here that silence indeed speaks of the God described by the *Book of Common Prayer*, whose service is 'perfect freedom', of he who is 'the author of peace and lover of concord'. He who is, as such, the ultimate antidote to the incessant wranglings of this era of noise. It has been said of William Laud, that he is 'the upholder of just that ideal of ordered freedom which provides the best pathway of escape for the chaos that an unbridled individualism has brought upon the Western world'. One wonders if the same could be said of Sarah himself, as one who, like Shakespeare, considers silence to be the 'perfect herald of joy', with sights set firmly on the Gospel. Given our circumstances today, then, we would do well to follow *Anglicanorum coetibus* and receive the gift of the Caroline Divines as a 'treasure to be shared' with the faithful today.

Notes

1. E. C. E. Bourne, *The Anglicanism of William Laud* (London: SPCK, 1947), p. 1.
2. Aidan Nichols, *The Panther and the Hind: A Theological History of Anglicanism* (London: T&T Clark, 1993), p. 9.
3. Ibid., p. xix.
4. Ibid., p. 54.
5. Diarmaid MacCulloch, *The Later Reformation in England, 1547–1603* (London: Palgrave, 2001), p. 5.
6. P. G. Stanwood, 'Patristic and Contemporary Borrowing in the Caroline Divines', *Renaissance Quarterly* 23(4) (Winter, 1970), pp. 421–9 at 421.
7. Bourne, *The Anglicanism of William Laud*, p. 1.
8. *Anglicanorum coetibus*, §5/ VI: 5.
9. Cf. Kenneth W. Stevenson, 'Caroline Divines' in Adrian Hastings (ed.), *The Oxford Companion to Christian Thought* (Oxford: Oxford

University Press, 2000), pp. 97–8 and Stanwood, 'Patristic and Contemporary Borrowing in the Caroline Divines', pp. 421–9.

10 Some are more specific in limiting the term 'Caroline' to divines active only under the reigns of Charles I and II, such as Benjamin Guyer in *The Beauty of Holiness: The Caroline Divines and their Writings* (London: Canterbury Press, 2012), p. 1; yet others specify 'Jacobean divines' for those active during the reigns of James I and II, for example Mark Langham, *The Caroline Divines and the Church of Rome: A Contribution to Current Ecumenical Dialogue* (London: Routledge, 2018), p. 2.

11 Stevenson, 'Caroline Divines', pp. 97–8.

12 Ibid., p. 98.

13 Nichols, *The Panther and the Hind*, p. 38.

14 Ibid., p. 61.

15 Lancelot Andrewes, *XCVI. Sermons by the Right Honorable and Reverend Father in God, Lancelot Andrevves, Late Lord Bishop of Winchester. Published by His Majesties Speciall Command* (London: George Miller, 1629), p. 91.

16 Walter Kasper, 'Roman Catholic Reflections on the Anglican Communion' (BBC, 1 August 2008), available at https://www.bbc.co.uk/blogs/ni/2008/08/cardinal_kasper_and_the_anglic.html.

17 Nichols, *The Panther and the Hind*, pp. 61–2.

18 *Anglicanorum coetibus*, §5: II.

19 *Unitatis redintegratio*, §13.

20 Ibid., p. 77.

21 Ibid., p. xix.

22 Stevenson, 'Caroline Divines', p. 98.

23 Joseph Ratzinger, 'Lecture by Cardinal Joseph Ratzinger', *The Patrician* (February 1999).

24 Mark Langham, *The Caroline Divines and the Church of Rome: A Contribution to Current Ecumenical Dialogue* (London: Routledge, 2018), p. 1.

25 Nichols, *The Panther and the Hind*, p. 38.

26 Ibid., p. 38.

27 Langham, *The Caroline Divines and the Church of Rome*, p. 1 n13.

28 George Herbert, *The Poems of George Herbert* (Oxford: Oxford University Press, 1961), p. 127.

29 Nichols, *The Panther and the Hind*, p. 38 n7.

30 Bourne, *The Anglicanism of William Laud*, p. 9.
31 Ibid., p. 24.
32 Ibid., pp. 20–1.
33 Langham, *The Caroline Divines and the Church of Rome*, p. 7.
34 Bourne, *The Anglicanism of William Laud*, p. 1.
35 Langham, *The Caroline Divines and the Church of Rome*, pp. 15, 21.
36 George Herbert, *The Poems of George Herbert*, p. 16.
37 Nichols, *The Panther and the Hind*, p. 46; cf. John F. Danby, *Shakespeare's Doctrine of Nature: A Study of King Lear* (London, Faber & Faber, 1949).
38 Bourne, *The Anglicanism of William Laud*, p. 21.
39 William Shakespeare, *Troilus and Cressida*, Act I, scene III.
40 William Shakespeare, *Merry Wives of Windsor*, Act II, scene II.
41 Quoted by Mark Langham in *The Caroline Divines and the Church of Rome*, p. 31.
42 Ibid.
43 Herbert Thorndike, *The Theological Works of Herbert Thorndike Volume V* (Oxford: Parker, 1854), p. 578.
44 *Catechism*, §1333–44; 'The Eucharist in the Economy of Salvation', article on transubstantiation, §1376.
45 *Unitatis redintegratio*, §11.
46 Langham, *The Caroline Divines and the Church of Rome*, p. 23.
47 St John Paul II, CELAM address, 1983.
48 1 Cor. 14.40.
49 Robert Sarah, *The Power of Silence: Against the Dictatorship of Noise* (San Francisco: Ignatius, 2017), p. 31.
50 Ibid., p. 42.
51 Ibid., pp. 49, 106.
52 Ibid., pp. 125–7.
53 Ibid., pp. 133–4.
54 Ibid., pp. 39–40.
55 Ibid., pp. 81–2.

10

The place of the Monarchy in Anglican culture

James Bogle

For many Anglicans and members of the Ordinariate in countries of the former British Empire and Commonwealth, the institution of the monarchy is a cultural, historical and political treasure. This attachment to the monarchy is not, of course, a matter of fundamental Christian dogma or doctrine. It is not part of the patrimony understood theologically. Nevertheless, many Anglicans and Commonwealth Ordinariate members, sincere and earnest in their faith, are also sincere and earnest in their preference for a monarchical form of constitutional government.

Likewise, American Episcopalians and Ordinariate members, loyal to their own countries' traditions, are proud of their own nation's constitution and system of government, based, as it is, upon the English Common Law. Some even argue that the American political system is, in fact, a form of elective, time-limited monarchy. Indeed, at its inception, there had even been a suggestion by Vice President John Adams that the first president, George Washington, be styled 'his Elective Majesty'[1] although this idea was roundly rejected by Thomas Jefferson, Benjamin Franklin and James Madison.

Even countries of the Commonwealth which have become republics nevertheless continue to recognize the British monarch as the Head of the Commonwealth out of a residual historical respect for British culture and empire – and to a certain degree religion – to which they were once so closely connected.[2]

It is fashionable in our day to mock this residual respect as culturally immature. That judgement, however, is largely rebutted by the fact that even republican members of the Commonwealth still wish to retain the link, to a greater or lesser degree. It is indicative of a deep cultural resonance which remains live and relevant, not merely as some temporary political expedience but rather as an ancient historical, cultural and spiritual heritage.

Moreover, monarchy has certain oft-neglected advantages. No one in the past ever attempted the fundamentalist folly of imposing absolute egalitarianism on society. Our ancestors knew that it would give rise to anarchy and chaos, not equality and justice. Simply put, if all are absolutely equal, then to whom does one apply for redress of grievances against one's neighbour's wrong-doing? If none are above us, we can apply for such redress to no superior (whether parent, employer, judge or other authority), there being none. Redress of grievance can then only be settled by majorities or force of numbers, that is, by the principle that 'might is right', the very harbinger of injustice, war, strife and anarchy. The librettist W. S. Gilbert put it more succinctly: 'When everyone is somebody, then no-one's anybody.'[3]

It was left to our age to square the circle and argue that absolute fundamentalist egalitarianism is beneficial and equates to democracy. Of course, it is neither. Democracy gives a valid and formal voice to the governed subjects of the Crown. It does not flatten all to the same level. Moreover, in the Westminster system at least, the Crown is (or should be) the final protection for democracy and its last best friend. Likewise, within a family, it is the parents who must govern. For similar reasons, monarchs are called, in law, *parens patriae* or 'parent of their country'.[4] Just as the ancient Roman word for 'Emperor', that is, *Imperator*, means 'commander', the office of any leader must, like that of a responsible commander, be one of accepting responsibility, taking charge, and serving those one leads, sacrificing selfish desires for the greater common good. That is the ideal of Christian leadership and monarchy, the supreme example being that of Christ the King, the Servant-King who took the fullest responsibility for His people, even for their sins and even unto death upon the Cross. This, indeed, is the theological meaning of the Crown of Thorns (as royal crown), the Reed (as royal sceptre) and the seamless garment (as royal alb), symbols of service, sacrifice and redemptive suffering. In turn, they are consciously and symbolically reproduced in the ceremonial vesture and regalia of kings and emperors alike, such as the alb, stole, cincture, cope, sceptre, orb and crown. For the emperors, this latter was the crown of Charlemagne, worn by them for a thousand years from AD 800 until AD 1806, when Napoleon Bonaparte effectively dissolved the Holy Roman Empire.

In our time, these symbols are now only preserved live in the ceremonial vesture and regalia of the British monarch, last seen in full array at the coronation of Queen Elizabeth II in 1952. This, then, is a gift of which the Anglican cultural heritage can still give testimony to the rest of the Christian world. It preserves and exemplifies the kingly aspect of the Christian vocation, one of the three roles of the baptized, that is, prophet, priest and king.[5] The kingly role is a symbol for Christian leadership at all levels of society, paradigmatically that of a king but likewise any other leadership role. The monarchy, being an explicitly and expressly Christian institution, inevitably operates as a brake upon the increasing secularization of society.

Moreover, monarchy, particularly Christian monarchy, is a form of government that is centred upon a family at the apex of the social organism, not merely upon a group of individuals who have, by fair means or foul, managed to claw their way to the summit of political power. Monarchy has the added advantage that, unlike a republic, it is forever young since, being based upon a family, it will have new and younger members every time a royal princess gives birth to another child. This tends to give monarchy a more human quality than other forms of government. By contrast, a republic does not produce children in a line of succession but only a selection of often ageing and greying politicians, of no particular background beyond the world of narrow party politics, who have merely managed to attain high office by outwitting, outlasting or outmanoeuvring (sometimes corruptly) their opponents. Higher and nobler feelings of loyalty, self-sacrifice and duty fit naturally towards one's monarch and sovereign, as to a father or mother, but perhaps not quite so well towards a mere politician who has managed to climb the greasy pole of political ambition. Perhaps ironically, it was an early-twentieth-century Irish Catholic Archbishop, Dr John Healey of Tuam, who best described the nobility of spirit engendered by monarchy:

> The character of kings is sacred; their persons are inviolable; they are the anointed of the Lord, if not with sacred oil, at least by virtue of their office. Their power is broad – based upon the will of God, and not on the shifting sands of the people's will ... They will be spoken of with becoming reverence, instead of being in public estimation fitting butts for all foul tongues. It becomes a sacrilege to violate their persons, and every indignity offered to them in word or act, becomes an indignity offered to God Himself. It is this view of kingly rule that alone can keep alive, in a scoffing and licentious age, the spirit of ancient loyalty, that spirit begotten of faith, combining in itself obedience, reverence, and love for the majesty of kings which was at once a bond of social union, an incentive to noble daring, and a salt to purify the heart from its grosser tendencies, preserving it from all that is mean, selfish and contemptible.[6]

As a result of the once widespread geographical and global reach of the British Empire, the British monarch is a familiar figure in all but the most remote parts of the globe. This, in turn, has given the monarchy an influence and import that the institutions of very few other small countries, the size of Britain, have. There can be little doubt that this influence partly arises because of its origin in Christianity and the Gospel.

This influence, with obvious exceptions, has mostly been for good, in recent times due, not least, to the personal qualities of the current monarch, Queen Elizabeth II, a woman almost universally admired, even, it must be said, by the enemies of monarchy. That she is a devout member of the Church of which she is the Supreme Governor is a fact known by almost everyone, not least as a result of her annual broadcast at Christmas which invariably focuses first upon the Commonwealth, of which she is head, then on her family and the nation and last, but far from least, upon the Christian Gospel and the person of Jesus Christ, both of which have clearly shaped her own personal life.

As a result of careful and flexible constitutional development, the British monarchy has evolved in a surprisingly adaptable manner. This, in turn, has ensured its survival in an egalitarian age. Indeed, one of the chief roles, now, of the Monarch is to be the last resort of protection for democracy, not only in Britain but also in countries where others act in her name. In Australia, for instance, the Governor General still has powers, called prerogative or reserve powers and derived from the monarch but written into the Australian Constitution by the founding fathers (all themselves monarchists), to dismiss the prime minister and government and to dissolve the elected Parliament in order to protect Australian democracy from abuse of power by politicians.[7] That this is no mere empty symbol can be seen from the fact that this power was used in living memory, as recently as 1975, to dismiss the then Labour government of Prime Minister the Rt Hon. Edward Gough Whitlam AC QC who, despite not having a sufficient majority in the elected upper house to govern, had refused to submit to an election.[8] Although the Governor General's actions were regarded by many – particularly republicans – as highly controversial and considered by some as a remnant of times past, his intention was clearly to protect democracy and to restore democratic accountability to the people. The people responded by voting out the Whitlam government with one of the largest majorities in Australian electoral history.[9] A stronger endorsement by the people of the importance of these viceregal (and thus monarchical) powers could hardly be imagined.

It can reasonably be argued that the republican constitution of Germany, under the pre-Nazi Weimar Republic, enabled the Nazis to seize power in a way that would have been far more difficult under a monarchical constitution. As President von Hindenburg was ageing and dying, Hitler, as chancellor, grasped the opportunity to manufacture a crisis (not least by conniving at the *Reichstag* fire, probably started by his supporters), to rush through legislation, albeit illegally and unconstitutionally, hugely to magnify his own power, to abolish democracy and to merge the offices of president and chancellor into a new dictatorial office entitled 'leader' or, more familiarly, '*Fuehrer*'. The process was called *Gleichschaltung* ('synchronization'), begun before Hindenburg died and completed thereafter. It included, in 1933, the *Reichstagsbrandverordnung* (the *Reichstag* Fire Decree), the *Ermächtigungsgesetz* (the Enabling Act) and, in 1934, the *Gesetz über den Neuaufbau des Reiches* (the Law Concerning the Reconstruction of the *Reich*) and the *Gesetz über das Staatsoberhaupt des Deutschen Reiches* (the Law Concerning the Highest State Office of the German *Reich*) passed by the cabinet on 1 August 1934 immediately before Hindenburg died, among numerous other acts. They carefully ignored Hindenburg's last wish that the Hohenzollern monarchy be restored. For want of a sovereign to prevent it, Hitler illegally seized power and became dictator. He then held a referendum to endorse his seizure of power, but the voting was widely corrupted and manipulated by SA intimidation, vote-rigging and ballot-fixing.

If Germany had still been a monarchy, the king could have used his residual royal prerogative powers to veto any such attempted unconstitutional *coup*, dismiss the chancellor and government and compel them to submit to the people in an election. The lack of such an impartial royal guardian or 'umpire' of the Weimar Constitution opened a fracture which an evil and dictatorial genius was able to exploit with the most far-reaching, and ultimately devastating, consequences. Hitler cleverly exploited and perverted the word '*Reich*', meaning 'Empire', 'Realm' or 'Commonwealth', to give Germans the impression that he was returning Germany to its roots when, in fact, he was, as a republican, permanently cutting those roots.

Unlike a presidency which, when the occupant dies in office, necessitates an inevitable, and exploitable, time lag between death and a fresh election, a monarch is immediately succeeded by his or her heir, in accordance with the hereditary principle. This, a principle that many see as anachronistic and outdated, is, in fact, a powerful and important bulwark against tyranny and a potentially vital protection for democracy. Indeed, this combination of the two principles – hereditary and democratic – may be the best constitutional safeguard for any state.

On a broader historical canvas, the history of Christianity is intimately interlinked with monarchy. It is a matter of historical record that Christianity, beginning with the birth, ministry and death of Jesus Christ, commenced within the framework of the Roman Empire and owed its early rapid spread to the existence of that empire, into which Christ was born and through which Christianity grew and came to flourish (albeit enduring numerous strong persecutions at the outset). Ultimately, Christianity was victorious over the pagan Roman power that sought to persecute and eradicate it, so much so that even the Roman Emperor himself became Christian, beginning with Emperor Constantine I the Great. He, it is said, won a famous victory over his enemies after seeing an extraordinary vision of the *Chi-Rho* symbol – the first two letters in the Greek word for Christ, Χριστος or 'Christos', and later a potent Christian symbol.[10] It is said that he also saw the words (in

Greek) Εν Τούτῳ Νίκα ('en toutō níka'), rendered in Latin as *'in hoc signo vinces'* and in English as 'in this sign ye shall conquer', meaning that, under the sign of Christ he would gain the victory.[11] Constantine ordered that the letters of the *Chi-Rho* be painted on the shields of his troops and he then went on to win a resounding victory over his enemies at the Battle of the Milvian Bridge on 28 October AD 312. Thereafter he favoured Christianity, allowing it to spread all over the Roman Empire (including to Britain, the country of his acclamation as *Caesar* and Western Emperor, by the army, at *Eboracum*, now the city of York, in AD 306 after his father, also Western Emperor, died). He, himself, was later baptized a Christian.

His later successor, the Emperor Theodosius I the Great, made Christianity the official state religion of the Roman Empire replacing the old pagan Roman religion.[12] From that time, the laws of the Roman Empire were conformed to the teachings of Christ and of the Christian religion and, gradually, over time, the majority of the people of the Empire became Christian, including in Romanized Britain. This, then, was the beginning of that concept once familiar to all Christians, and still familiar to Anglicanism today, that the State is officially Christian, though recognizing the freedom of its members to follow other religious traditions. In the historical context this unique arrangement was called 'Christendom', or the temporal (i.e. social and political) kingdom of Christ upon the earth.

It is one of the remarkable facts of our time that, in many of the formerly Catholic countries, the idea of Christendom has gradually been eclipsed by the advent of an increasingly secularist state, however, in the historically Protestant countries, like Britain, the Netherlands and the Scandinavian countries, although secularism has advanced in many ways just as rapidly there, nevertheless the traditional idea of a Christian monarchical state has survived surprisingly well.

In Britain, Christianity first found fertile soil among the ancient *Prythani*, or 'Britons', who were soon persuaded to abandon their pagan beliefs as readily as the woad that their warriors had worn as war paint when the Romans first arrived under Julius Caesar in 55 BC. When a new wave of pagan barbarians, coming from the East, began to overrun the Roman Empire, by then still a fledgling Christian Commonwealth, the legions were compelled to withdraw from the furthest reaches of the Empire, leaving behind Romano-Christianized native populations to fend for themselves.

Britain was no exception and the Romanized-Celts (the ancestors of the *Cymri*, or Welsh people) who remained continued to build and defend their Christian civilization to such an extent that legends have famously survived, giving rise to later embellishments, for example the legendary tales of King Arthur and his Knights of the Round Table, all Christian Romanized-Britons.

Whilst these Romanized-Britons were eventually defeated militarily by invading pagan Germanic tribes, their Christian religion eventually won over the invading Anglo-Saxons and Jutes, for it is part of the genius of Christianity that it prefers to conquer its enemies by turning them into friends.

Queen St Bertha (or St Aldeberge, *c.*565–601) was the Queen of Kent whose influence led to the Christianization of Anglo-Saxon England. She was a Frankish princess and great-granddaughter of King Clovis I, the first Christian King of the Franks, and his Queen, St Clotilde, who, in turn, had converted him.[13]

In similar fashion, in AD 580, Queen St Bertha married, and eventually converted, King St Æthelberht of Kent who, thereafter, endorsed and supported the missionary Benedictine monks, led by St Augustine of Canterbury, sent, in AD 596, by Pope St Gregory I the Great to restore Christianity to Britain.[14]

Famously, Pope Gregory had seen blonde-haired and blue-eyed pagan Anglo-Saxon children being held as prisoners in the Roman captives forum and marvelled at their appearance, likening them to little angels.[15] On being informed that they were Angles, St Gregory remarked '*non Angli, sed angeli si forent Christiani*' – 'not Angles but angels, if they were Christian' – and vowed to send a mission to their country to evangelize them.[16] So began the genuinely Anglo-Saxon, later English, form of Christianity.

Because, after the later Norman Conquest, so much was lost of Anglo-Saxon culture, only remnants have been bequeathed to later generations but, from what has remained, we are able to catch a glimpse of a deeply Christian society founded upon a strong monarchy.

Anglo-Saxon monarchy is also famous for its remarkable number of royal saints such as St Edmund, king and martyr, the original Patron Saint of England before St George became more popular, introduced from the East by crusader knights. Others in that glorious array[17] include King St Alfred the Great (by popular acclaim, rather than canonical process), Kings St Athelstan I, St Edward the Martyr and St Edward the Confessor and Princesses

St Æthelburh of Wilton, St Frideswide of Oxford and St Edith of Wilton and Kemsing, to name but a few.[18]

In Scotland, Christianity was introduced to the Picts and Scots during the Roman occupation of Britain. After the Anglo-Saxon invasion, paganism returned to southern Scotland but, in the sixth century, missionaries like St Ninian (Finnian), St Kentigern (Mungo) and St Columba arrived, the latter founding the monastery at Iona from where he carried out missions to the Scots of *Dál Riata*. Early kings like Fergus the Great (*Fergus Mòr Mac Earca*), Constantine (*Causaintin*) and Angus (*Oengus*) were Christian, as was Kenneth I MacAlpin (*Cináed mac Ailpín*). Most of Ireland had remained Christian since after the time of St Patrick, himself a Romanized-Briton, its high kings emulating the other monarchs of Christendom.

By this time, the centre of Christendom had moved, after the barbarian invasions, to the East, at Constantinople, the city of Constantine the Great. The ancient, flourishing culture of Byzantium and Eastern Christianity stems from this transfer. The political structure was again monarchical with the Eastern Roman Emperor as the cynosure and central figure alongside the Pope. All of Christendom, including the kings of England and the high kings of Scotland and of Ireland, recognized Byzantium as the genuine Christian successor of the original Christian Roman Empire based on Rome.

However, with the decline of the Eastern Empire, partly due to Islamic invasion, and threatened by a new wave of barbarian invasions, the people of Rome and the West began to fear for their very survival. Since they were unable to rely any longer upon the Eastern Roman Emperor for aid, they turned to Charlemagne, the newly powerful Christian king of the evergrowing nation of the Franks.

Famously, on Christmas Day AD 800, with the sanction and blessing of Pope St Leo III, the nobility, clergy and freemen of the city of Rome gathered in St Peter's Basilica and elected, by acclamation, Charlemagne as the revived Roman Emperor in the West.[19] This development had a huge impact upon Western culture, not least in England, Scotland and Ireland. Thereafter Christian kings in the West began to model themselves upon the person, cult and court of Charlemagne. The English monarchy was no exception and it, and the high kings of Scotland and of Ireland, directly imitated the Frankish imperial court. The central position of the Christian Emperor was so clearly endorsed by the Church that, from time out of mind, until the Bugnini reforms of 1954–5, the universal Church prayed expressly for the Emperor, directly after the Pope and clergy, in the Great Intercessions on Good Friday and in the *Exultet* on Holy Saturday at the Solemn Easter Vigil.[20] These imperial prayers, in Latin, extolling the special position of the Holy Roman Emperor, included a Great Intercession on Good Friday which may be translated thus: 'Let us pray also for the most Christian Emperor ... that the Lord God may reduce to his obedience all barbarous nations for our perpetual peace', and a post-communion prayer beginning thus: 'O God, who prepared the Roman Empire for the preaching of the Gospel of the eternal King.'

Court ceremonial was developed, from ancient Roman rituals, under Charlemagne, partly influenced by his chief minister of education, the Anglo-Saxon Benedictine monk, Alcuin of York, venerated as a saint in the Anglican Communion. The imperial coronation ceremonial, once so prominent in Western Christendom, now only survives, in its full form, in the British coronation ceremonial and therefore remains part of the Anglican cultural heritage.

Although the imperial office, by reason of time-honoured Roman tradition, was an elective office, most other Christian monarchies (but not all) retained the hereditary principle as primary. Originally, both imperial and papal electors were the same, namely the nobility, clergy and freemen of the city of Rome but, as the civil disorders often engendered by such forms of election became evident, the electoral privilege was deputed to colleges of electors (a concept familiar to American presidential elections).

For a pope this became the College of Cardinal-Princes. For an emperor it became the College of Prince-Electors (originally numbering seven) each also holding ancient Roman imperial offices, reflecting their closeness to, and personal service upon, the Roman Emperor. The number seven is often held, in Christian tradition, to be the number of completion, hence seven Sacraments, seven deadly sins and contrary virtues, seven days of the week, seven orders of clergy, seven day hours of the Divine Office (Lauds, Prime, Terce, Sext, None, Vespers and Compline – Matins being a night office) and so on. The original seven Prince-Electors of the Holy Roman Empire were the three principal archbishops, namely of Cologne, Mainz and Trier (Arch-Chancellors of Italy, Germany and Gaul & Arles, i.e. Burgundy, respectively), the King of Bohemia (Imperial Arch-Cupbearer or Arch-Butler), the Duke of Saxony (Imperial

Arch-Marshal), the Margrave of Brandenburg (Imperial Arch-Chamberlain) and the Count-Palatine of the Rhine (the Imperial Arch-Steward or Arch-Seneschal). The Prince-Electors, being concerned with the government of their own states, delegated by 'commission' to other nobles, the performance of these imperial offices, later also in a hereditary succession. For example, the Imperial Hereditary Lord High Steward of the Holy Roman Empire, or *Reichserbtruchsess*, holding 'in commission' from the Count-Palatine of the Rhine, was the Count-Imperial of Waldburg zu Zeil und Trauchburg. Palatine and Imperial counts held their estates directly (or 'immediately') from the Emperor, Palatine nobles having, historically, the closest relationship to the Emperor, being successors of the Paladins of Charlemagne, his closest peers. The term derives from the fact that the Roman Emperor's closest peers dwelt with him on the Palatine hill in Rome (the Roman hill traditionally thought to be the location of the cave where the founders of Rome, Romulus and Remus are said to have been suckled as infants by a she-wolf). The word 'palace' likewise derives therefrom. The title exists in Britain, too. For example, the English counties of Durham, Cheshire and Lancashire are all counties palatine.

The same or similar titles were reproduced in the Great Officers of State of all the kingdoms and principalities of Christendom. England, Scotland and Ireland were no exception but the important difference, so far as the Anglican heritage is concerned, is that these Great Officers of State continue to exist (as also in Ireland until it became a republic in 1948) as part of the Christian Constitution of those kingdoms.

In England, these Great Officers of State were – and still are – the Lord High Steward (vacant now except for coronations and trials in the House of Lords), the Lord High Chancellor, the Lord High Treasurer (now usually held in commission by the Prime Minister of the day as First Lord of the Treasury), the Lord President of the Council, the Lord Privy Seal, the Lord Great Chamberlain (permanently held 'in gross'[21] by a number of ladies and gentlemen but exercised by the Marquess of Cholmondeley) and the Lord High Constable (whose function is now largely deputed to another Great Officer of State, the Earl Marshal, an ancient office not originally one of the seven Great Offices). The office of Earl Marshal is hereditarily held by the Roman Catholic dukes of Norfolk.

The office of Lord High Admiral, also not originally one of the seven Great Offices but which dates back to the fifteenth century, has been, since the eighteenth century, held in commission by the Commissioners for Exercising the Office of Lord High Admiral of Great Britain ('the Admiralty Board') headed by the First Lord of the Admiralty. When the Ministry of Defence was created in 1964, the office of Lord High Admiral was re-vested in the Monarch but her Majesty has since conferred it upon her husband, Admiral of the Fleet Prince Philip, the Duke of Edinburgh.

Scotland has similar Great Officers of State, although some were lost or forfeited after the unsuccessful Jacobite[22] uprisings of 1715 and 1745 against the new choice of dynasty, the German Hanoverians,[23] following the revolution of 1688.

There were originally seven Great Officers of State in England, Scotland and Ireland, just as there had originally been seven Prince-Electors of the Holy Roman Empire. The currency of these Great Offices is such that even until 1948, when the Attlee government abolished the process,[24] peers were still tried in the House of Lords with the Lord High Steward, the highest Great Officer of State after the monarch, presiding over the trial. In such cases, the Lord High Chancellor, the usual presiding officer in the House of Lords,[25] was appointed temporarily to be Lord High Steward.

The last such trial was that of Edward Russell, 26th Baron de Clifford, in 1935 for motor manslaughter.[26] The case so caught the public imagination that it provided the central theme for one of the novels of Dorothy Sayers (herself a devout Anglican), entitled *Clouds of Witness*, in which the fictional Duke of Denver, brother of the eponymous Lord Peter Wimsey, is tried for murder.

In Britain, as in the rest of Christendom, the monarchical principle remained, for most of Christian history, the central political reality of the Christian world. Even those Christian states that called themselves 'republics' were, in reality, variants of monarchy, for example, the Italian maritime republics of Florence, Genoa, Siena and Venice.

Indeed, so great has been the influence of Christian monarchy that even modern republics, like that of the United States of America, retain many hallmarks that derive from the monarchical past, for example, the classical architecture adorning many American state buildings or the US dollar which derived from the imperial *thaler*,[27] the wide powers of the US president (originally based upon those of King George III whom the presidency replaced) and various procedures in the Congress such as, for example, trial by impeachment.

Conversely, many so-called 'modernizers' today so often think that 'modernizing' must necessarily mean abolishing colour, pageantry and tradition, replacing it with the monochrome, the dull, the oppressive and even, occasionally, the outright tyrannical. They even pretend to call this 'progress' or 'progressive'. It is, in reality, neither.

The idea of Christendom – the social Kingdom of Christ upon the earth – once so hugely important to the temporal Constitution of Catholic Christendom, is now, as noted above, in some ways better preserved by the Anglican heritage than in many once Catholic countries.

Even when King Henry VIII broke with Rome, he was determined to retain all the customs and traditions of imperial Christendom and expressly regarded his own kingdom as an 'empire' of its own, with himself as the new emperor. As some modern historians are now arguing, the cause of the break was not just his matrimonial disputes, but also his anger at having lost the imperial election of 1519 to Emperor Charles V, his Spanish wife's Habsburg nephew. He later determined to start an empire of his own.

Thus, by a twist of fate, monarchy continued to be seen as an essential ingredient in English Christianity, even after the Protestant Reformation. It has since become a permanent and prominent feature of the Anglican cultural heritage.

Arguably, the preference for monarchy has preserved Britain, and parts of the Commonwealth, from tyranny, not least the tyrannies of Communism and Nazism. The Monarchy has, indeed, become so much a part of the warp and weft of British and Commonwealth society that ancient traditions associated with the Monarchy continue to this day, for example the so-called 'Maundy money' is still given out by the Monarch on Maundy Thursday,[28] in memory of the royal doles given out to the poor by the Christian monarchs of times past.

The chivalric orders bestowed by the Monarch remain deeply Christian in symbolism, for example the Order of the Garter is still given in the name of 'God, our Lady and St George'.

Monarchy in Britain is expressly and openly Christian and so remains an important part of the Anglican cultural heritage. As a consequence, reverence for our Christian monarchy and monarch continues to play a role in the lives of many members of the Ordinariate and other British Commonwealth Catholics today.

Notwithstanding contrary trends in British society, the Monarchy still provides a wholesome testimony to Christian governance, a form of government that has enjoyed the favour of the Church and the Christian people for most of Christian history, time out of mind.

Notes

1. James H. Huston, 'John Adams' Title Campaign', *New England Quarterly* 41, no. 1 (March 1968), pp. 30–9.
2. As of May 2017, thirty-one out of the fifty-three member states of the Commonwealth were republics.
3. Gilbert and Sullivan, *The Gondoliers* (1889), Act II.
4. The concept dates, in English law, from the beginning of Christian monarchy and, in 1608, was cited in Sir Edward Coke's report of *Calvin's Case* which stated 'that moral law, *honora patrem* ... doubtless doth extend to him that is *pater patriæ*'. *Calvin's Case* (1572) 77 ER 377; (1608) Co Rep 1a.
5. *Catechism of the Catholic Church*, Part 1, section 2, chapter 3, article 9, paragraph 2, pp. 783–6.
6. P. J. Joyce, *John Healy* (Dublin: M. H. Gill & Son, 1931), pp. 68–9.
7. *The Federal Constitution of the Commonwealth of Australia* (1901) (as amended), Sections 57 and 64.
8. Sir John Kerr, the Governor General, by letter dated 11 November 1975, and served in person upon the Prime Minister at Government House, Yarralumla, Canberra, on the same day, determined his commission of office under Section 64 of the Australian Constitution.
9. http://australianpolitics.com/elections/federal-1975.
10. L.C.F. Lactantius, 'Lucii Caecilii liber ad Donatum Confessorem from De Mortibus Persecutorum', in *The Works of Lactantius* II, Ante-Nicene Christian Library: translations of the Writings of the Fathers down to AD 325. XXII (Edinburgh: T & T Clark, 1867 to 1885), p. 203.
11. Eusebius of Caesaria, *Vita Constantini*, AD 339 (London: Samuel Bagster and sons, 1845), chapters 28–31, available at www.documentacatholicaomnia.eu, pp. 943–6.
12. *Edictum Gratiani, Valentiniani et Theodosii De Fide Catholica*, 27 February AD 380, in *Codex Theodosianus*, XVI, 1, 2 Magnou-Nortier, Paris, 2002.
13. She was the daughter of King Charibert I and Queen Ingoberga, and granddaughter of King Chlothar I.

14 St Bede, *Historia Ecclesiastica Gentis Anglorum* (Ecclesiastical History of the English People), trans. A. M Sellar (London: George Bell and Sons, 1907), Book I, chapter 25, Book II, chapter 5.

15 There being few prisons in those days, it was the ancient custom to reduce captive prisoners of war, and sometimes their families, to indentured servitude for a fixed term (release often taking place at the Biblical Jubilee). Christianity ensured that the captives were treated fairly and humanely. This was to be distinguished from true or 'chattel' slavery and it was Christianity that eventually caused chattel slavery to be abolished altogether.

16 St Bede, *Historia Ecclesiastica Gentis Anglorum* , Book II, chapter 1.

17 Susan J. Ridyard, *The Royal Saints of Anglo-Saxon England* (Cambridge: Cambridge University Press, 1989).

18 By contrast, the number of republican presidents canonized by the Church is non-existent although it is possible that Gabriel Garcia Moreno, nineteenth-century president of Ecuador, might one day be canonized (but then, it must be said, he was a lifelong monarchist). See Mary Monica Maxwell-Scott, *Gabriel Garcia Moreno, Regenerator of Ecuador* (London: R & T Washbourne, 1914).

19 Eginhard, *Vita Caroli Magni*, trans. A. J. Grant (Ontario: Medieval Latin Series, 1999), p. 28.

20 These prayers were later replaced, in the new liturgy after the Second Vatican Council (perhaps significantly by the same Archbishop Annibale Bugnini), with a prayer *pro omnibus res publicas moderantibus* ('for those in public office') and placed right at the end of the intercessions, behind the prayers for unbelievers and atheists.

21 Offices of State are held 'in gross' by the principal hereditary office holders and 'in commission' by delegates of the principal hereditary office holders, chosen by the monarch on the advice of the prime minister.

22 The Jacobites, so named after King James II of England and Ireland and VII of Scotland, were those who sought to restore the Catholic Stuarts who had been illegally and unconstitutionally ousted by the revolution of 1688 largely for being Roman Catholics and for tolerating Catholicism and other minority religions (including Jews and Muslims). The Jacobites also sought to restore the ancient constitution of the kingdoms of England, Scotland and Ireland, each as separate kingdoms, with their own parliaments, all under one Crown. The legitimist Jacobites were, however, eventually defeated by the religiously intolerant, and exclusively Protestant, Hanoverian government whom Jacobites rejected as illegitimate revolutionaries. Many under the Hanoverian regime seized the opportunity to enrich

themselves at the expense of the urban and rural poor, by the slave trade and by financial chicanery in the city of London. Furthermore, the post-1688 revolutionary government imposed a savage penal code against any who did not conform to the state religion, Anglicanism in England and Ireland and Presbyterianism in Scotland. Some commentators claim that the present Royal Family lack all legitimacy as a result of the 1688 revolution, but this extreme view is not only entirely impractical (since it would render all laws since 1688 null and void), but it is also deeply unfair to the present queen whose character and policy have been exemplary from any viewpoint. As a matter of historical fact, King George III, far more reasonable and tolerant than his grandfather and great-grandfather, was eventually recognized widely (including by the Pope) except, of course, by the rebellious American colonists. Nevertheless, even his government eventually recognized, by the formal Treaty of Paris of 3 September 1783, the existence of the new United States of America. Some have thus argued that true constitutionalists ought to celebrate that date as the beginning of the new American republic, rather than 4 July.

23 In an early ecumenical gesture, the Duke of Brunswick-Lüneburg (Hanover), despite being Protestant, was promoted to prince-electoral status within the Catholic Holy Roman Empire. This was acceptable to Catholic rulers because the Prince-Elector of Brandenburg had remained an imperial elector even after he had become a Protestant during the Reformation. The Hanoverians, even after being chosen by the anti-Catholic English government to be king of Great Britain and Ireland, remained Imperial Prince-Electors and are referred to as such, in documents and letters, by the rebellious American Colonists. It is a simple historical fact, however, that the anti-Catholic English Parliament, after the revolution of 1688, unconstitutionally excluded from the throne no less than fifty-five princes, forty-eight of whom were bypassed for the sole and only reason that they were Roman Catholics, choosing the Prince-Elector of Hanover, later King George I, solely because he was a Protestant. Upon arrival in England, the parliament-appointed King George I (with a mistress on each arm, his wife remaining locked in a castle back in Hanover) was jeered by the people. Of his two German mistresses (Frau Schulemberg, later Duchess of Kendal, and Countess von Platen, later Countess of Darlington) one put her head out of the window of the carriage and called out in poor English 'Good people, why you wrong us? We have come for all your goods!' (meaning 'good'), to which one wag in the crowd replied, 'And for all our chattels, too, I think!' (see the review of James Hogg's The 'Jacobite Relics of Scotland' in *The Scots Magazine – the Edinburgh Magazine and Literary Miscellany* VI (1820), p. 35). George I and his son, King George II, were unpopular with the majority of the British and Irish people; there was rioting at the coronation of George I on 20 October 1714 in over twenty

towns in England alone, and the Jacobite cause to restore the Royal Stuarts was at its height during their reigns. The following year, on 6 September 1715, the standard was raised at Braemar by the Earl of Mar, beginning the first of several attempted Stuart restorations.

24   By the *Criminal Justice Act* (1948), however, the House of Lords still has the power to try by impeachment or by attainder.

25   Now replaced, since the Constitutional Reform Act 2005, by the entirely confected office of 'Lord Speaker', a constitutionally illiterate title devised by the Blair government who clearly did not understand (or care about) the constitutional significance of the Great Officers of State. The Speaker is the presiding officer of the House of Commons, not the Lords, and represents the Commons to the monarch and the House of Lords. The obvious choice to be presiding officer of the Lords would have been the Lord High Steward as the most senior Great Officer of State.

26   *Hansard* HL Deb 4 December 1935, volume 99, cc48-9, cc145-50 *et seq*.

27   From New Netherland (New York) the *leeuwendaalder* or 'lion dollar', deriving from the imperial *thaler*, spread to all Thirteen Colonies.

28   At the Royal Maundy Service, annually.

11

A personal reflection on Our Lady of Eton and the place of Marian devotion in English culture

Rev. Alexander Sherbrooke

William Byrd's setting of *Cantiones Sacrae* (1573) – a work he developed with Thomas Tallis – indicates how the focus of minds might have changed from the zealous adoration of the Mother of God typical of late medievalism through the revolutions of the Reformation. The composers of the Chapel Royal dedicate the work to Queen Elizabeth who, in a strange, enforced and political way, replaces Mary in their devotional musical aesthetics. Our Lady of Eton survives maybe, in part, because of Elizabeth's personal domination of her realm: her shadow cast long after her death. The *Cantiones Sacrae* echo the supernatural devotion articulated by King Henry VI in his declaration of the foundation of Eton College:

> We ... have considered in zealous contemplation, in what manner, how, or by what kind of royal gift, according to our devotion and the custom of our elders, we can make suitable honour to the same lady and our most holy Mother, to the satisfaction of her spouse; and finally, having contemplated such things in intimate

meditation, it was settled in our heart that ... we will fund a college in the parish Church of Eton, upon Windsor, which is not far from our place of birth.[1]

It is, however, only an echo, King Henry VI, in his 'royal gift' – the charter dated 11 October 1440 – established Eton College and its title (Our Lady of Eton College), articulating both his inspiration and what he assumed would be an inextricable bond to the Church Universal, together with a specific association to his birthplace. He states clearly what a later observer might call a fruit of discernment, inspired by prayer. This royal articulation was deemed to draw protection, inspiration and a sense of sacred purpose from being under the mantle of Mary.[2] This act should also be seen as part of the living tradition of Henry's ancestors, the divine right[3] of the House of Lancaster and its particular 'munus'[4] to protect the Church from heresy whether it be the assaults of Lollardy or the assaults of John Wycliffe.

For the current purpose it is important to accept that Henry's intention subsumed an existing parish church – dedicated to the Assumption of the Blessed Virgin Mary – where devotion to Our Lady was of consequence, showing continuity with what already existed. It may be useful to suggest how well Henry's intention and the earlier dedication of the parish fit within the patterns of English Marian devotion, a considerable history of devotion through the centuries, expressed both in polity and culture, through literature, poetry and art and, of course, through the lives of ordinary people. Devotion to Mary was the social, cultural and, of course, religious air breathed: it can be drawn in from Chaucer, Bede and Anselm. It was articulated in song – both in popular and contemplative settings – and invoked regularly by Queens, Kings, their sustaining nobility and the ordinary subjects of that sustenance. From before the Anglo-Saxon settlement until the shattering of the bonds with Rome under Henry VIII, no monarch had failed to invoke Mary, or neglected to ask for the protection of her mantle. Most undertook the pilgrimage to Walsingham, even the shrine's desecrator, King Henry VIII. That devotion also spread to Europe, with many finding their way to what had become known as England's Nazareth in Norfolk. Mary, Walsingham and kingship combined as the air drawn in by English lungs. As Henry VI drew on an existing devotion of the Parish Church, more widely did the country and its people know that Mary was their intercessor and particular confidante. Marian devotion was interwoven with the complexities of English Catholic life from the mission of Augustine, through the writings of Bede until their apogee in the consecration of England to Mary by both Edward the Confessor and, later, King Richard II.[5]

Perhaps there is no better-preserved artefact or object of devotion expressing this rich vein of motherly supervision and trust as well as divine elements of intercession as the Wilton Diptych. Now displayed at the National Gallery,[6] the diptych was painted between 1395 and 1399 for the devotional practice of King Richard II himself and expresses a complex of signs and symbols.[7] This was epitomized by the title of Dowry of Mary proclaiming that England had been given to Mary as if one was to give a dower house to a widow. As Ronald Knox explained:

> It is to originate from the reign of St Edward the Confessor ... it had become widespread by the middle of the 14th Century and around the year 1350 a mendicant preacher stated ... it is commonly said that the land of England is the Virgin's dowry ... in 1399 Thomas Arundel Archbishop of Canterbury wrote to his suffragen bishops ... we English being the servants of her special inheritance and her own dowry ... ought to surpass others in the fervour and our praises and devotions.[8]

Perhaps primarily it symbolically speaks of the devotion to Mary of her dowry, England, as shown by the image of the island in the orb at the top of the standard which could refer both to England under the protection of St George and the Resurrection or to the Agnus Dei.[9] Mary seems almost to lose the child Jesus who stretches out to bless both the standard and Richard. She holds the child's foot ready for the devotion of the King. Saint Edmund King and Martyr, Saint Edward the Confessor and John the Baptist present Richard and his kingdom – represented in the St George's cross standard towards which Jesus reaches – to the mother so the Son may bless him and his realm. On the outside of the diptych are Richard's arms plus his special emblematic – ironically so – white hart. This was considered analogous to the Agnus Dei. Other artefacts that survived the dissolution that found safety in European seminaries set up for training of priests for the English Mission, such as Vallalodid, Seville and Rome, portray this extraordinary devotion to Mary in how she was seen as protectress and Queen of England. A contemporaneous altarpiece to the Wilton Diptych has Richard II handing the orb to

Mary with the inscription '*Dos tua Virgo pia haec est*' meaning 'this is thy dowry, O Holy Virgin'. Like the image of the Assumption at Eton on Lupton's Tower, the Wilton diptych has survived as one of the most remarkable works of medievalism, explaining in iconic form how political and devotional life were infused by devotion to Mary. Henry VI's foundation was part of a whole which made the 1530 and 1560 Reformist desecrations of Eton such a watershed in the construction of English identity. Reformist zeal as it scrabbled for legitimacy helped define an English identity as it materialized over the next century. Part of this scrabbling was to explain the inevitability of the dissolution of the monasteries as essential to a new golden age – that of the Virgin Queen rather that Blessed Virgin. The as yet unexplored parallel is interesting. Somehow that maternal intercession felt through Marian devotion and attendant feminine culture survive, resurfacing after the Protestant settlement lost its vigour. It would take four hundred years, but that spiritual vitality – an expression of the unique patterns of English Marian devotion – may have returned.

Conflicted innards

In institutions – made up of members, government and those charged with governance – there are always conflicting loyalties.[10] For those charged to rule, there must be an intention to preserve the institutional environment, even if this means lying as a modus operandi. Those who constitute a membership, fill the pews or belong to a body because they believe in it, can be less contrary and readier to compromise. The late Lancastrian then Tudor polity tries to align itself with the iconic structure of the Wilton Diptych but conversion was absent and replaced by absolute and increasingly terrifying royal power. Some one hundred years after its foundation, Eton was an established, noble and royal polity aware of its proximity to the centres of royal power at Windsor, Hampton Court and Whitehall. In order to survive political turbulence, Eton – like many organizations – trimmed to survive. Even so, the Blessed Edward Powell, for a short time Headmaster of Eton, called Henry VIII a 'common adulterer' to his face. He did not last long and was hung, drawn and quartered at Smithfield in 1540. The Act of Supremacy came just before Provost Roger Lupton resigned in 1536 having bequeathed his chapel, tower and most significantly the statue of Our Lady's Assumption completed around 1533. Such an act of devotion not only expresses piety but also suggests there was little fear or understanding that such piety would be outlawed by political developments. Later, Eton's ready desire to accommodate any new settlement, to trim it if need be, so business could carry on as normal – to trim with the wind – ironically threw a protective political mantle over the statue. Christopher Hill touches on such accommodating behaviour.[11] It is not unusual: the Vichy regime is a modern case in point.[12]

The year 1538 witnessed the first waves of serious, officially sanctioned iconoclasm; it was perhaps that moment when the governance of the school – namely the Provost, Fellows and chaplains – became aware that it could not resist Henry's overwhelmingly powerful and intrusive mandate. In the surrounding country, images in churches were still permitted but anything associated with pilgrimage and shrines was considered idolatrous.[13] The campaign against such expressions of faith went hand in hand with the destruction of places of pilgrimage and the foci of devotion. The dissolution of the friaries that supported such activity was more rapid than the dissolution of the monasteries: it was complete by the end of 1538.[14] Thomas Cromwell's main agent in dissolving the friaries and their shrines was Dr John London, a priest and Warden of New College. The fluidity of the times could not be better embodied. Although suspected of Roman, anti-reformist tendencies and eventually to die in prison, he dissolved friaries, monasteries and convents with vigour, destroying several shrines, notably Our Lady of Caversham near Reading.[15] The surviving correspondence is only London's to Cromwell but suggests that the defacing of churches attached to friaries went beyond what Cromwell wanted and London was instructed to stop. There is no evidence of London visiting Eton but an interesting gap exists in his correspondence between 18 September and 1 October 1538. On the 18 September he was at Reading; having destroyed Caversham, he planned to travel to Aylesbury, Bedford and possibly Northampton. He may have returned to Oxford though the possibility of hospitality as a royal commissioner and warden to the royal foundation of Eton may have been enough to bring him to Windsor. After all, it would fit well with London's successful destruction of the shrine of Our Lady of Eton as a place of pilgrimage. Eton's shrine may have been dismantled by late 1538. This could also have been the moment that popular devotion to Our Lady – see below – led in part by the scholars of Eton, came face to face with Protestant Erastianism. This ideology was a force that wanted to crush Catholic practices of filial devotion to Mary, and pitted Henry VIII's court – a heterogenous group[16] – against Eton's scholars and choristers, and the poor parishioners who depended on shrines such as Eton's. The scholars, choristers and poor had principles they were ready to stand by and this protected Eton's welcoming statue. The Reformation settlement was, however, soon to be applied with precision and ruthlessness at Eton.

Eton in the 1970s

For the majority of Etonians, school days were happy coloured by friendship, kindness and silver spoons jutting awkwardly from most mouths. This privilege meant, for most, few mundane cares. Typically, in English private educational establishments there was no theological clarity, only a vague liberal Protestantism.

In this context my experience of Catholic culture could only be limited, despite good and holy Catholic priests who somehow managed to tack through the shallow waterways patrolled by the rusty gunboats of the *Ecclesia Anglicana*. Any history of the period communicated a particular understanding of the break with Rome and the inevitability of a Protestant settlement lacking of and indeed rejecting Marian or Eucharistic devotion. It was some years before Eamon Duffy's groundbreaking work, *Stripping of the Altars: Traditional Religion in England 1400–1580*, was able to correct the imbalance.[17] History clearly is written and taught by the winners,[18] but I wonder now at what I once considered comfortable neutrality. Everything we were routinely taught about Henry's 1537 Act of Supremacy, the Edwardian and the definitive Elizabethan settlements – the latter in 1558 – of how these evolved until their collapse into civil war, about the struggle against the practices of the past, struggles that lasted until the death of the last Catholic Martyr, Saint Oliver Plunkett in 1679, and the accession of William and Mary in 1683 were part of the Enlightenment's unrelenting assault on Catholic devotional life. Comfortably neutral they certainly were not.

Seen as a cancer, Marian devotion needed precise, politically competent and determined agents such as London to root it out. Eamon Duffy shows persuasively how English Catholicism was never a corrupt and weak religious polity ready for the plucking, but had a depth, a vigour and perseverance. Plentiful rosaries among the remains of the Mary Rose which sank in 1545 is evidence of the slow death of Marian piety. Prayers for the dead, the Holy Week Liturgy, recusant life and hopes for a Catholic revival lived on despite everything. The clandestine Catholic language of Shakespeare as well as Thomas Tallis's Catholic compositions finding receptive ears at Elizabeth's supposedly Protestant court suggest the Old Faith lingered on, rumours of its death being greatly exaggerated. As late as 1679 Charles II converted, making a confession to Father Huddlestone on his death bed. This, then, was the background noise to my career as a student of history.

Monsignor Alfred Gilbey (1901–1998), for thirty years Catholic chaplain to Cambridge University, who perhaps more than any Catholic priest was able to glide easily between various ecclesiastical communities, said that if you scratch the surface of a civilized English personage you will find deep anti-Catholic prejudice or at least patterns of suspicion.[19] Fear of such prejudice was written into the codes of conversion and practice. In 1925, Alfred Lord Braye, an old Etonian convert, built a Catholic chapel dedicated to Our Lady of Sorrows in reparation for the wanton destruction of the Shrine of Our Lady of Eton. The conditions attached stipulated its location – at the south end of the High Street in Eton – without windows at street level, preventing worshippers looking out or – more importantly – Protestant passers-by looking in. There is a beautiful irony in that most polite but implacable opponent of Catholicism or certainly in mainland Europe Freemasonry legislated the same window regulations for its temples.

Perhaps the Protestant evangelical backstory meant there was something particularly masculine and untender in the Christianity we met at Eton – an element which ran contrary to the supportive and nurturing secular lives lived there. Our Lady was missing either by fault or design. Marian festivals or indeed the continuing dedication to Our Lady of Eton did not much impinge. Talk of the call to vulnerability, acknowledgement of need for healing or the tenderness of God's love was not on the curricula of establishment Divinity Schools. Any educational establishment deep in the Anglican tradition didn't genuflect often, unless to civic icons. Some might call it an effortless superiority which had been imparted with civility, kindness and – sometimes – humour.

My dear father saved me, as he thought, from what he considered the mysterious and suspicious ways of Ampleforth with its cowel clad monks, where my brothers were sent. I was to become sixth in a line of fathers to sons sent to Eton. But, somehow, a seed was sown and a vine grew, taking me to seminary and now over thirty years as a priest. Perhaps that most subtle and heavenly touch of 'Our Lady of Eton' had stilled a restless soul – who knows.

The founder's intention

Indulgences are easily dismissed by non-Catholic and even Catholics as an abusive practice, sold to build St Peters or support crusades. They are easy to dismiss for their rationality is not immediately apparent. The proper application springs from the teaching of God's infinite mercies which the Church is charged to transmit. As with all medieval shrines or places of pilgrimage, Our Lady of Eton had both partial and plenary (perpetual) indulgencies associated with it under the normal conditions especially granted by the Pope in 1441 and 1442.[20] In 1445 an extra thirty beds were hired for confessors at the time of the patronal Feast of Our Lady's Assumption on the 15 August.[21] This suggests a strong Marian devotional life which meant pilgrims, prayers, penances and graces received. Due to the vicissitudes of King Henry VI's reign, we cannot be confident that after the 1440s and 1450s the number of pilgrims increased. There were, however, the Provost (a priest), ten Fellows (also priests), ten chaplains, ten clerks, sixteen boy choristers aged under twelve, a schoolmaster, an usher, seventy poor scholars and thirteen weak almsmen provided for under Henry VI's statutes of 1453.[22] This suggests that Eton was a place of prayer and devotion where pilgrims and residents could pray, lead lives of devotion, aspire to holiness and be faithful to God's Word. All of which would bear fruit in the Treasury of Grace. There are no limits to the efficaciousness of God's grace across history. Prayers both for the Holy Souls as well as for our descendants cry out continually for God's mercy. How could those years of devotion to Our Lady fail to yield fruit?

A spiritual legacy and modern story

Etonian blood runs thick but towards neither Rome nor Mary. For non-believing ears it is not easy to explain the workings of God's grace, yet an insight may be gained from the *familia Etoniensis*, where the bonds of friendship and proximity to that remarkable institution instil a camaraderie and mutual familiarity which extend throughout life.

Some years after ordination, I heard of a beautiful story of an Etonian who had gone to work with the Missionaries of Charity. The Missionaries of Charity were founded in 1950 by Mother Teresa of Calcutta with the particular charism of meeting, serving and loving Jesus among the poorest of the poor wherever they should be found in the world. The account recalled how this man, while working with the sisters, was often to be found washing, caring for and giving dignity to those abandoned and brought in from the street. I never found out the identity of this man or where he operated but was profoundly touched by how – from a very particular Etonian culture – the strength of the tender love of Christ could shine out. That most vital part of a Marian dispensation instituted and engineered by the first one hundred years of Eton's life was a spiritual legacy of a political failure and can never be underestimated. The Reformation was not always kind to Marian devotion, deeming it misplaced, unscriptural and superstitious. Despite the intensity of such devotion and its zeal, the tender love of Christ, infused by Mary, withstands the vagaries of history.

We are what we will be and our formative experiences can be neither forgotten nor denied. Without in any way belittling the kindness of what this young man did amongst the poorest, the implicit strength and reality of tender and vulnerable love should not be something trumpeted. This would not be part of his narrative, but somehow that young Etonian had found a hidden strength and, in his way, was participating in the sanctification of the poorest of the poor.

Mary – the voice of the poor

Mary's great hymn of praise at the Visitation, the *Magnificat*, was sung by the assembled priests, choristers, chaplains, scholars and the poor at every Vespers in the Chapel of Our Lady of Eton. One of the finest extant examples of medieval polyphony that survived the English Reformation is the *Eton Choir Book* rich in chants and antiphons composed for Our Lady. In the *Magnificat* she reminds us how God humbles the rich, raises the poor and feeds the hungry.

In this journey to Grace there is a trace of the paradigm which King Henry VI intended and provided for in his foundation of Eton. It may have been obscured, forgotten or even ignored, but nothing is lost in God's providence. Catholics, among others, believe in the power and potency of Mary's prayers. That beautiful combination continues to look lovingly down on the college from the heights of Lupton's Tower. Roger Lupton, Provost from 1504 to 1535, constructed 'the new gateway ... [it] was decorated in its brickwork with Madonna lilies and the statue of the Assumption ... this building, together with the fine Chantry Chapel added to College Chapel at his own expense indicates that on the eve of the Reformation, there was no decline in religious devotion, or in veneration of Our Lady'.[23] Our Lady is physically close to heaven but interceding for her sons and showing them the way to heaven.

For five years I quizzically examined it and wondered how it had survived. The particular devotion of the founder was to the Assumption of Our Lady into Heaven. At the top of the tower is the Della Robbia-like ornament, portraying Mary being guided to heaven by angels. Catholic life was pulverized by Thomas Cromwell's men, who tore into vestments, altars and statutory. The shrine of Our Lady in College Chapel was demolished and the exquisite cycle of the life of Our Lady on both south and north walls of the chapel whitewashed and hidden behind timbers.[24] Why and particularly how did the statue on the Tower survive? My musings as a mischievous teenager were that the iconoclasts had been too idle to climb so far. In recent years I learnt that the cause was not idleness but white martyrs.[25]

An old Hindu Etonian recalled how edified he had been by the courage, faith and Marian devotion of the scholars who stared down King Henry VIII's troops. The story tells how Thomas Cromwell sent troops – in all likelihood under Dr John London – between September and October 1538 to demolish the shrine. They arrived in School Yard where the ordained beaks (masters) were hiding but the King's Scholars refused to let the soldiers pass.[26] King's Scholars against the king's soldiers in combat would not have been a pretty sight. These scholars were white martyrs refusing to let the axe be put to the sweet Mother of God who was their patron and teacher and exemplar of the educational and spiritual project on which they were engaged. It is for that reason of passive resistance that Our Lady of the Assumption continues to smile benignly on School Yard to this day, her survival nothing to do with idleness. Who knows how efficacious her glance is in the workings of God's grace? A question we can tentatively answer only in our contemplative prayer and which will be fully answered when we gaze upon eternal beatitude.

Our Lady Mediatrix of Grace

In the Anglican firmament it is challenging to move from seeing devotion to Our Lady as something purely symbolic and decorative (indeed an attitude held at times also in Catholic circles) to that which is about active engagement in world affairs; she is the promoter of peace and divine justice and the cause of the defeat of evil. With eyes of faith, Catholics have recognized, both in the private sphere and the public, the power and efficacy of Mary's prayers whether it be the healing of the sick at Lourdes or the defeat of the British by the Americans at the Battle of New Orleans in 1815, which seems to have been effected by the city's Ursuline nuns praying before a statue of Our Lady of Prompt Succour. The so-called 'miracle on the Wisła' is, perhaps, an even more poignant example of Marian intervention – the defeat of the Soviet Red Army in Warsaw on the Feast of the Assumption 1920. The Soviet Army reportedly fled from Warsaw when large numbers of its soldiers reported seeing a vision of the Virgin Mary over two of the battlefields.

Similarly, Our Lady appeared in Walsingham in 1061 at the start of a decade which saw invasions from Norway and Normandy, the near annihilation of the Anglo-Saxon ruling class and genocidal violence during William the Conqueror's harrying of the North in 1069–70. Our Lady's gift of letting England be called her dowry, from the late fourteenth century onwards, again came during a difficult period for the country and the Church. Heresy had emerged through John Wycliffe and the Hussites which was the first major challenge to the truth of Catholicism since the pagan Vikings invaded in the ninth century. Within living memory, a third of the population had died during the Black Death (1348–9). The Hundred Years' War with France (1337–1453) was well underway.

The terrified sailors who transported Columbus across the Atlantic in 1492 took comfort in their hope of the protection of Our Lady. Contemplating the end of wide-scale child sacrifice in Mexico and the conversion of the Aztecs after the appearance of Our Lady to the shepherd Juan Diego, just as Cromwell and his men were demolishing Marian shrines at Eton and beyond, any fearful Catholic would have given thanks for her intercession. The Spanish missionaries had been unsuccessful in calling the Aztecs to depart from their murder of children. No show of strength or considerate words had any effect. The miraculous intervention of Mary and the representation of her on Juan Diego's *tilma*, the traditional Aztec cloak, changed everything.[27] Sacrifices ceased and were replaced by baptism. The seeds of a Marian civilization had been sown, as had been intended by Henry VI at Eton.

Furthermore, at the Battle of Lepanto in 1571 Don Juan of Austria defeated the Turks against overwhelming odds, having diligently prayed the rosary with all his soldiers and sailors. She intervened and Pope Pius V instituted the Feast of Our Lady of Victories in recognition and thanksgiving. A decade later, the Old Etonian St Ralph Sherwin – the first of many martyrs trained at the English College in Rome – was hanged, drawn and quartered at Tyburn for daring to celebrate Mass and encouraging and proclaiming devotion to Our Lady. The protection of Our Lady of Eton – never absent, albeit physically destroyed – had shown her hand in this man's remarkable witness, courage and refusal of Queen Elizabeth's bribes of offering him a bishopric and all sorts of blandishments.

The narrative of Mary's prophecies and interventions lies in a continuum, from the Annunciation two thousand years ago to her presence in the twentieth century. Her prophecies in the Portuguese village of Fatima in 1917 encompassed the Russian Revolution and rise of Communism and Fascism, the horrors of the world wars and the attempted assassination of Pope John Paul II. Our Lady is no harbinger of violence but rather warns humanity to step away from disobedience and look towards the righteousness, justice and love of God. When His tender love – exemplified by that Old Etonian working and caring for the dispossessed of Calcutta– is rejected and stamped upon, the consequences are manifold and terrible. Those consequences are shown in the wide-scale destruction of the innocent unborn, euthanistic threats to the elderly, the complicity in poverty and many kinds of human degradation and the accelerated attack upon the Judaeo-Christian dispensation's teaching regarding marriage and the family.

Catholic filial devotion to Mary encourages the believer to hand him- or herself over to her 'who heard the Word of God and kept it' so that she can intercede for us to God. Her participation in our humanity means that all parts of our human experience, and in particular family, parenting and home, are graced by her presence. Why these locations in particular? Her presence works vitally in other, less domestic, settings. Do not those who cry to her from the all too human experiences of loss, bereavement, imprisonment, torture and exclusion have a more particular reason to be graced by her presence? She brings an assurance and a certainty to what our dispensation teaches and reminds us that we must be zealous in its preservation.

It may seem a long, unjustified and unnecessary journey from the cloisters and Gothic buttresses of College Chapel to the slums of Calcutta. It is nevertheless a necessary one if we are to read, mark and learn and internally digest the Founder's determination to assure that his charges should be formed under the mantle of Our Lady while remaining close to the poor and destitute, the better to build a Christian civilization. Inherent in this is the need to embrace and accept fully both historically and spiritually how deep, real and actual devotion to Mary was in Our Lady's Dowry – 'this sceptred isle'. For some years that devotion may have been outlawed or may have raised suspicion, but it never completely disappeared. The architecture of statues, music, churches and literature was taken away, but there was still a Marian architecture of the soul. Its contours are defined by a desire to reach out to the vulnerable; a readiness to search out the will of God and, therefore, a willing docility to become daughters and sons of Mary so as to be subsumed into Christ: 'It is not I who lives but Christ who lives in me' (Gal. 2.20).

Many speak today of a fractured environment and of how human selfishness is causing irreparable damage to our ecology; it is claimed that if action is not taken soon, widespread extinctions as well as the destruction of human prosperity will become inevitable. Such predictions of doom need to be analysed but ignore what has happened periodically to the human race since our ancestors stepped out of Africa. The history of poverty, hunger and genocide weighs heavily on the shoulders of political elites, crying out for God's justice and mercy:

> Go away from me with your curse upon you, to the eternal fire prepared for the devil and his angels. For I was hungry and you never gave me food; I was thirsty and you never gave me anything to drink. ... Insofar as you neglected to do this to one of the last, you neglected to do it to me. (Mt. 25.42-45)

The deliberate, determined murder of ethnic minorities from Armenia, the Caucasus, Siberia, Western China, Germany, Rwanda and the Middle East call to heaven for justice.[28] Manifestations of Our Lady have increased in recent centuries and perhaps because of the darkness of war, massacres of the vulnerable and genocides that have coloured the twentieth century so red. She has spoken and prophesized the destruction caused by Communism, the Balkan civil wars and Rwandan genocide. It might well be asked why have we become so deaf and stubborn to the pleas of God? Is it because we have forgotten how to be the children of a Mary so beautifully portrayed in the Wilton Diptych and Lupton's Tower statue?[29] The motherhood and queenship of Mary held by generations of kings, nobles and subjects were not empty mantras but expressions of how the world was seen, ordered and to be governed. The *Communist Manifesto* has the DNA of all that has followed in its name so with the diptych and Lupton's Tower they both expressed what had preceded and what would most certainly follow – or at least they believed.

I spent my first Christmas as a priest with Mother Teresa and her Sisters, working as a volunteer in Calcutta. During that unforgettable Calcutta Christmas she asked me to help her write to Saddam Hussain and President Bush, asking them to step back from war after the 1990 invasion of Kuwait. She did not engage in political argument but simply spoke about the threats to those poorest and most vulnerable, those to be killed or wounded, those orphaned, those to be rendered homeless. In other words, whatever the rights and wrongs of political and military argument, the poorest are easily forgotten at such moments. We must all answer before God for our actions and He must have had His fill of ogres. Catholic arguments for a just war seem spiritually tortuous for they are words which will have to be brought to the judgement seat of God.

Mother Teresa is one of the most recognized figures of our age, but recognition of her face does not acknowledge what drove her. The melody of her being was drawn from her direct, personal encounter with Christ and His Mother, which was only known and published posthumously. These writings speak simply and directly of how Christ and his Mother pleaded with her to go to the poor and communicate the gentle, sanctifying love of God. This was not an inspired reading of scripture, a learned act or a considered response to *kairos* but an obedient and humble response to a pleading from Calvary.[30] The agony of the Crucifixion continues across the twentieth and into the twenty-first century. Our Lady pleaded with Mother Teresa from the Cross, as she did with the three shepherding children – Jacinta, Francisco and Lucia – at Fatima, predicting the destruction occasioned by Fascism and Communism and the Second World War. She also appeared and warned at Kibeho and Medjugorje before the Rwandan genocide and Balkan wars.

I suspect it needs the heart of a believer to make the connections, but we still need to contemplate and explain the enormity of destruction and of humanity's ability and willingness to authorize murder, to allow poverty and cruelty. Devotion and belonging to Mary are both integral to a Catholic understanding of history and the Church's engagement with human affairs. So many have knowingly or unknowingly turned their backs on these foundations, with consequences. The destruction of the shrine of Our Lady of Eton and other similar sacrileges have been instrumental in this consequentialism. Mary's *Magnificat* and *Fiat* at the Annunciation teach us how to see both the particular and the universal. The particular is how she hears the cry of the poor and dispossessed and brings down the proud and powerful. One who lives under the mantle of Mary cannot fail to hear the cry of the poor. Henry VI's foundation of Eton embraced the poor and destitute for they, as children of Mary, help us to be true to the Gospel and obedience to God.

If we do not have, as Pope Benedict XVI has said, a 'true human ecology', material ecology will be a house without solid foundations. Marian devotion was, I would suggest, at the heart of the intentions of the founding fathers of the Council of Europe. This is evidenced by the twelve stars surrounding the Lady in the Apocalypse appearing on the Council's flag, later adopted by the European Union. The European Union's founding charter, the Treaty of Rome, was signed on Our Lady's feast of the Annunciation, which for centuries in this country not only signalled the beginning of the year but also signalled, for most of the founding fathers, the intention that the European Union should sit under Mary's protection.[31] As with the secularization of England so with the European Union: its Catholic and Marian roots continue to be undermined.

In Henry VI's profoundly Catholic paradigm, devotion to Mary was essential to building a Christian civilization of justice, *noblesse oblige* and care for the poor and abandoned. This in no way denies the wars, political manoeuvrings and dynastic unrest to which he was party – he was a prince of his age. There was, however, an inner light to his spiritual acts – such as his foundation of Eton – which have shone despite the failure, indecision and wretched end in the Tower.[32] He heard the call to listen to, learn from and ask Our Lady's intercession. Mary teaches us to listen to and obey God in a response to the consequences of original sin. She teaches, indeed pleads, that we be especially close to the poor and abandoned. Above all, through her glorious Assumption, she shows us a road to heaven.

The achievements of Eton are many. Ronald Knox and Harold Macmillan were almost contemporaries, in the years before the First World War, and Knox tutored Macmillan in classics. Knox was destined for Canterbury and Macmillan for Downing Street. Knox later crossed the Tiber and spoke of Westminster Abbey on the feast of St Edward the Confessor. He asked: who would one want to be on the day of Judgement? An explorer, general, inventor, acclaimed statesman? Or a political incompetent and failed politician like Edward, who was beloved by the poor, who nursed the sick and gave succour to the destitute under the mantle of Our Lady? Neither Edward the Confessor nor Henry VI was a skilled politician. Neither aspired to worldly or secular acclaim, to be masters of intrigue, or to any kind of advancement. They were seen as powerful intercessors for the sick, poor and beleaguered. Many miracles were attributed to them, witnessed by pilgrimages and precious objects given to the Confessor's tomb at Westminster Abbey (plundered by his successor Henry VIII) and Henry VI's at Chertsey and latterly Windsor.

Both men were determined, like Mother Teresa, to give glory to God in all things through Mary. Both recognized and believed that Christ deliberately aligns Himself most intimately and closely with the poor, broken, vulnerable and disadvantaged. St Lawrence, brought before the Roman Emperor Valerian, was instructed to bring his most precious vessels and material wealth. He brought instead his spiritual wealth – the poor, outcast and destitute. The same spirituality may be witnessed in these two saintly but, arguably, apolitical kings. A Catholic polity such as theirs, under Our Lady's mantle, must chart the turbulent waters of political affairs, but it cannot fail to be close to the poor as was evidenced by the poor and destitute who besieged Edward in his lifetime and came to his tomb after his death.

It might be argued that the belittling, then surgical amputation, of Marian devotion was brutal, unkind and against the mission of the Holy Spirit, of whom she is the spouse. Was the Reformation necessary, part of a kind of historical inevitability, and does it therefore represent the promised end of Marian life in England?[33] The answer should be in the negative; if Mary is forgotten the Gospel becomes incomplete: believers experience a ruptured hermeneutic. More important are the consequences for building a just and ordered society where God's love penetrates into all areas of public, civil and private life. Without the vessel of that love, Mary, there is injustice, the marginalization of the unwanted and masculine intolerance. We need to rediscover Mary and repair the damage caused by the destruction of so many shrines, not least that of Our Lady of Eton.

Conclusion

A week after the death of Princess Diana, Mother Teresa was called home to God. A cartoon of the pearly gates shows St Peter asking whether Diana should be allowed in. Mother Teresa holds Diana's hand and says 'she's with me'. Those days were heady but my privilege was that I had been with the two of them on various occasions: I could hear the deep pain and suffering of that most Marian of modern saints, Mother Teresa. She was deeply concerned for how marriage and family blessed by God in that most privileged position needed to be protected, exalted, even fought for. Diana was drawn to Mother Teresa without being able to articulate the spirituality but sensing it expressed – in this lover of the poor – someone profoundly consecrated to Mary.

Perhaps rooted in prayer there was some kind of anticipation of what would happen after their respective deaths. Thousands thronged the Loreto Convent in Calcutta as did those paying their respects outside Kensington Palace. All of us are flawed, but perhaps those strange days suggested an unarticulated English hunger for Our Lady's motherly and tender protection. Somehow Diana, despite all her very human failings, suggested that the English can sometimes, if not always, be a moderate, feminine and kind-hearted nation which does not baulk at Catholic and Marian sensitivities.

Ven. the Hon. Fr Ignatius Spencer, CP, is a servant of God, a great-great-great uncle of Princess Diana and, of course, an old Etonian. As an Anglican clergyman he was an evangelical missionary working towards the unity of Christians. As was the case with St John Henry Newman, this evangelizing zeal propelled him into the Catholic

Church. He travelled back to Eton, to the palaces of Windsor and London, to the slums of Manchester and Birmingham to call people back to Christ under the mantle of Mary. How from heaven would he have viewed his relation's death and weird political wake? We will have to wait to find out but can surmise he would have seen something of a search for Mary among those who came to mourn.

The emergence of Christendom in a savaged and morally confused post-Roman Europe brought much; not least the Judaeo-Christian dispensation concerning marriage, the right to property and its proper regulation, as well as the call to sanctity, to love the poor and the inherent and God given dignity to be given to every human being from the moment of conception to natural death. Devotion to Our Lady as exemplified by the founder of Eton placed marriage, the sanctity of life and the care for the poor as inherent and divinely blessed but never to be trifled with. Today liberal secularism and the gospel of atheistic humanism are like the king's soldiers confronting the King's Scholars in School Yard before Lupton's Tower and the crowned virgin, whom they still considered the Queen of England. Some years back a constituent of the penultimate old Etonian Prime Minister wrote to him saying, 'Many would congratulate you on changing the laws of marriage. I would however like to thank you for giving us a referendum on Europe.' The two for our story are connected. Many members of his party were so outraged at same-sex marriage that his hand may have been forced to give a vote on Europe to pacify them. Changing the laws on marriage cut to the heart of the Judaeo-Christian dispensation and was another blow to Mary's protection of this land. Perhaps the subsequent referendum was a stirring in the hearts of many – as evidenced by Diana's wake – that all was not well. When Mary is not proclaimed and sung of, fissures begin to appear, but all is not lost for us as G. K. Chesterton put it in *The Secret People*, published in 1907: 'Smile at us, pay us, pass us, but do not quite forget; for we are the people of England, that have never spoken yet.'

It is observable that since the 1980s Anglican cathedrals, along with parish churches, have seen an explosion of devotion to Mary in statues, icons, flowers, candles and beautification. Somehow Mary is knocking on the doors of the hearts of believers and non-believers alike. Eton may not see a revival of the shrine of Our Lady of Eton but the sad and painful history of Henry VIII's attacks is not lost. Such a history only needs to be cherished again so it can be understood and – I pray – learnt from.

The Chapel of Our Lady of Sorrows just off the High Street in Eton is dwarfed by the buildings, houses and corridors of excellence belonging to the College. Unsurprisingly in my five years as a school boy, I never knew of its existence, only later as a priest did I cross its threshold to celebrate the sacrifice of the Mass; that supreme prayer which Our Lady humbly adores and reverences. This small and discreet chapel was built in reparation for the destruction of the shrine of Our Lady of Eton. It is a reminder to us that she who the chapel exalts is always humble, quiet, tender and faithful. It is through this smallness that she becomes the most powerful intercessor of all. How much she pleaded at Fatima for reparation for sins against her Immaculate Heart so now from this little chapel pleads for our sorrow at what was done to her shrine only a few hundred yards away. The Catholic community of England on 29 March 2020 renewed the dedication of itself to Our Blessed Lady repeating that of Richard II who in his dedication promised this land and its people as the Dowry of Our Lady in 1381. Let this little chapel reminds us all of what it means to be children of Mary – lover of the poor and broken-hearted, small, tender-hearted and zealous for the truth always desirous of letting Mary show us the way to heaven and so build God's Kingdom upon earth. Only she can teach us how to receive and love God's will for us. Then let us be ready to return to Our Lady of Eton. In the words of Henry VI, otherwise known as the Founder's Prayer:

> *Domine, Jesu Christe, qui me creasti, redemisti, et preordinasti ad hoc quod sum; tu scis quæ de me facere vis; fac de me secundum voluntatem tuam cum misericordia. Amen.*
>
> *[O Lord Jesus Christ, who hast created and redeemed me and hast foreordained me unto that which now I am; thou knowest what thou wouldst do with me; do with me according to thy will, in thy mercy. Amen.]*

Notes

1. David Grummitt, *Henry VI* (London: Routledge, 2015), p. 110.
2. 'Mantle' derives from Middle English, meaning a sleeveless cloak. In medieval portrayals of Mary, she is often portrayed with a mantle spread around her, the faithful gathered into its protection.

See, for example, di Pietro's fifteenth-century *Virgin of Mercy* or Erhart's *Ravensburger Schutzmantelmadonna*, the Bode Museum, Berlin (in which sculpture Mary's mantel is evoked in the popular title).

3 The concept of 'divine right' was not articulated until much later, while the Crown was assailed by those secular forces that became the Whig political consensus after 1660. There was, however, a sense for Lancastrians of divine right even if not so articulated.

4 *Munus* translates as duty and is a curate's egg of a theological term to denote the responsibilities and rights – the munies – associated with teaching, holiness and power: it is frequently used to describe the relationship of bishops to their clergy.

5 See T. Jones, R. Yeager, T. Dolan and A. Fletcher, *Who Murdered Chaucer?: A Medieval Mystery* (London: Methuen, 2003).

6 John Armitage, 'A New Dedication for Today', *Oremus* (February 2020), p. 8.

7 National Gallery, NG4451. The diptych may well have been painted in France which matters slightly more now than it did in the late fourteenth century. It may be important to note that the diptych is as much about royal power as Marian theology. This may explain in part its miraculous survival.

8 Ronald Knox, 'Sermon delivered at the Catholic Parish of St. Edward the Confessor in Golders Green, London, for the Feast of St Edward', as found in the Breviary for the readings of October 13.

9 Looking at the diptych, one reads from left to right and clearly the dominant figures are those of kings (albeit two canonized). This shows how devotion and political power went hand in hand – albeit one hand uncomfortably stronger and clad in mail. John the Baptist is almost incidental in the iconography. Mary reflects from a pool of blue the blinding gold of the left-hand panel. Analysis of these layers of meaning can be found in D. Gordon, *Making and Meaning: The Wilton Diptych* (London, National Gallery, 1993). See M. A. Michael, 'Creating Cultural Identity: Opus Anglicanum and its Place in the History of English Medieval Art', *Journal of The British Archaeological Association* 170, no. 1 (2017), pp. 30–60.

10 Conflating institutions with organizations should be avoided. An institution is a legal construct, a pattern of rules and policies. An organization lives and contains people that pattern themselves into parties and governments and exhibit intersecting loyalties, some of which may not like sharing the space.

11 Christopher Hill, *The World Turned Upside Down: Radical Ideas During the English Revolution* (London: Penguin Books, 1991).

12 M. A. Baruch, *Le regime de Vichy: 1940–1944* (Paris: Texto, 2017).
13 M. Gaudio, 'The Space of Idolatry: Reformation, Incarnation, and the Ethnographic Image', *Anthropology and Aesthetics* 41, (2002), pp. 72–9.
14 Martin Heale, *Dissolution, Opposition, Accommodation: The Abbots and Priors of Late Medieval and Reformation England* (Oxford: Oxford University Press, 2016), see specifically chapter 8.
15 P. Preece and M. Kift, 'The Shrine of St Mary, Caversham', *Oxford Architectural and Historical Society* (1995), pp. 431–2.
16 A. Weir, *Henry VIII: King and Court* (London: Vintage, 2008).
17 Eamon Duffy, *Stripping of the Altars: Traditional Religion in England 1400–1580* (New York: Yale University Press, 1992).
18 George Orwell, 'History Is Written by the Winners'. *Tribune* 12, no. 11 (1944), p. 11.
19 A. N. Gilbey, *The Commonplace Book of Monsignor A. N. Gilbey* (London: Bellew, 1993).
20 T. Card, *Eton Established: A History from 1440 to 1860* (London: John Murray, 2001), p. 5.
21 Ibid., p. 7.
22 Ibid., p. 28.
23 Ibid., p. 39.
24 Roger Rosewell, *The Eton College Chapel Wall Paintings: England's Forgotten Medieval Masterpiece* (Woodbridge: Boydell & Brewer, 2009).
25 A white martyr is someone who does not shed blood for the faith but suffers extreme social isolation and opprobrium.
26 At Eton College, a King's Scholar (known as a 'Colleger' or colloquially as a 'tug') is one who has passed the college election examination and has been awarded a foundation scholarship and admitted into a house known as 'College', the premises of which are situated within the original ancient purpose-built college.
27 If God intends irony there may be a touch in the use of this Aztec word for cloak.
28 The Middle East in particular has left a dark stain on the consciences of those who might have intervened but didn't, or did intervene and shouldn't. Burke calls this, the aggregate activities of evil people, more succinctly, 'an unpitied sacrifice in a contemptible struggle'.
29 The statue is no great work of art but its position on the tower – able to be viewed from anywhere in School Yard – gives it a prominence and power for those with eyes to see and hearts to understand. The

Wilton Diptych also survived the iconoclasms of the sixteenth and seventeenth centuries: it is now a reminder of the previous, tender beauties of English Marian devotion.

30 καιρός, the perfect moment, the moment when God acts (Mk 1.15).
31 Robert Schumann, Alcide De Gasperi and Konrad Adenauer were all devout Catholics.
32 Henry was almost certainly murdered, having lost the throne for a second time. St Thomas More believed that Henry was killed by Richard, Duke of Gloucester (later the ill-fated Richard III).
33 In a riposte to Marx and determinism more generally, Isaiah Berlin writes eloquently against patterning history in such ways. See Isaiah Berlin, *Liberty* (Oxford: Oxford University Press, 2002).

Appendix: BENEDICT XVI – APOSTOLIC CONSTITUTION *ANGLICANORUM COETIBUS*

PROVIDING FOR PERSONAL ORDINARIATES FOR ANGLICANS
ENTERING INTO FULL COMMUNION WITH THE CATHOLIC CHURCH

In recent times the Holy Spirit has moved groups of Anglicans to petition repeatedly and insistently to be received into full Catholic communion individually as well as corporately. The Apostolic See has responded favourably to such petitions. Indeed, the successor of Peter, mandated by the Lord Jesus to guarantee the unity of the episcopate and to preside over and safeguard the universal communion of all the Churches,[1] could not fail to make available the means necessary to bring this holy desire to realization.

The Church, a people gathered into the unity of the Father, the Son and the Holy Spirit,[2] was instituted by our Lord Jesus Christ, as 'a sacrament – a sign and instrument, that is, of communion with God and of unity among all people'.[3] Every division among the baptized in Jesus Christ wounds that which the Church is and that for which the Church exists; in fact, 'such division openly contradicts the will of Christ, scandalizes the world, and damages that most holy cause, the preaching the Gospel to every creature'.[4] Precisely for this reason, before shedding his blood for the salvation of the world, the Lord Jesus prayed to the Father for the unity of his disciples.[5]

It is the Holy Spirit, the principle of unity, which establishes the Church as a communion.[6] He is the principle of the unity of the faithful in the teaching of the Apostles, in the breaking of the bread and in prayer.[7] The Church, however, analogous to the mystery of the Incarnate Word, is not only an invisible spiritual communion, but is also visible;[8] in fact, 'the society structured with hierarchical organs and the Mystical Body of Christ, the visible society and the spiritual community, the earthly Church and the Church endowed with heavenly riches, are not to be thought of as two realities. On the contrary, they form one complex reality formed from a two-fold element, human and divine.'[9] The communion of the baptized in the teaching of the Apostles and in the breaking of the eucharistic bread is visibly manifested in the bonds of the profession of the faith in its entirety, of the celebration of all of the sacraments instituted by Christ, and of the governance of the College of Bishops united with its head, the Roman Pontiff.[10]

This single Church of Christ, which we profess in the Creed as one, holy, catholic and apostolic 'subsists in the Catholic Church, which is governed by the successor of Peter and by the Bishops in communion with him. Nevertheless, many elements of sanctification and of truth are found outside her visible confines. Since these are gifts properly belonging to the Church of Christ, they are forces impelling towards Catholic unity.'[11]

In the light of these ecclesiological principles, this Apostolic Constitution provides the general normative structure for regulating the institution and life of Personal Ordinariates for those Anglican faithful who desire to enter into the full communion of the Catholic Church in a corporate manner. This Constitution is completed by Complementary Norms issued by the Apostolic See.

I. §1 Personal Ordinariates for Anglicans entering into full communion with the Catholic Church are erected by the Congregation for the Doctrine of the Faith within the confines of the territorial boundaries of a particular Conference of Bishops in consultation with that same Conference.

§2 Within the territory of a particular Conference of Bishops, one or more Ordinariates may be erected as needed.

§3 Each Ordinariate possesses public juridic personality by the law itself (ipso iure); it is juridically comparable to a diocese.[12]

§4 The Ordinariate is composed of lay faithful, clerics and members of Institutes of Consecrated Life and Societies of Apostolic Life, originally belonging to the Anglican Communion and now in full communion with the Catholic Church, or those who receive the Sacraments of Initiation within the jurisdiction of the Ordinariate.

§5 The *Catechism of the Catholic Church* is the authoritative expression of the Catholic faith professed by members of the Ordinariate.

II. The Personal Ordinariate is governed according to the norms of universal law and the present Apostolic Constitution and is subject to the Congregation for the Doctrine of the Faith, and the other Dicasteries of the Roman Curia in accordance with their competencies. It is also governed by the Complementary Norms as well as any other specific Norms given for each Ordinariate.

III. Without excluding liturgical celebrations according to the Roman Rite, the Ordinariate has the faculty to celebrate the Holy Eucharist and the other Sacraments, the Liturgy of the Hours and other liturgical celebrations according to the liturgical books proper to the Anglican tradition, which have been approved by the Holy See, so as to maintain the liturgical, spiritual and pastoral traditions of the Anglican Communion within the Catholic Church, as a precious gift nourishing the faith of the members of the Ordinariate and as a treasure to be shared.

IV. A Personal Ordinariate is entrusted to the pastoral care of an Ordinary appointed by the Roman Pontiff.

V. The power (*potestas*) of the Ordinary is:

a. *ordinary*: connected by the law itself to the office entrusted to him by the Roman Pontiff, for both the internal forum and external forum;

b. *vicarious*: exercised in the name of the Roman Pontiff;

c. *personal*: exercised over all who belong to the Ordinariate;

This power is *to be exercised jointly* with that of the local Diocesan Bishop, in those cases provided for in the Complementary Norms.

VI. § 1. Those who ministered as Anglican deacons, priests, or bishops, and who fulfil the requisites established by canon law[13] and are not impeded by irregularities or other impediments[14] may be accepted by the Ordinary as candidates for Holy Orders in the Catholic Church. In the case of married ministers, the norms established in the Encyclical Letter of Pope Paul VI *Sacerdotalis coelibatus*, n. 42[15] and in the Statement *In June*[16] are to be observed. Unmarried ministers must submit to the norm of clerical celibacy of CIC can. 277, §1.

§ 2. The Ordinary, in full observance of the discipline of celibate clergy in the Latin Church, as a rule (*pro regula*) will admit only celibate men to the order of presbyter. He may also petition the Roman Pontiff, as a derogation from can. 277, §1, for the admission of married men to the order of presbyter on a case by case basis, according to objective criteria approved by the Holy See.

§ 3. Incardination of clerics will be regulated according to the norms of canon law.

§ 4. Priests incardinated into an Ordinariate, who constitute the presbyterate of the Ordinariate, are also to cultivate bonds of unity with the presbyterate of the Diocese in which they exercise their ministry. They should promote common pastoral and charitable initiatives and activities, which can be the object of agreements between the Ordinary and the local Diocesan Bishop.

§ 5. Candidates for Holy Orders in an Ordinariate should be prepared alongside other seminarians, especially in the areas of doctrinal and pastoral formation. In order to address the particular needs of seminarians of the Ordinariate and formation in Anglican patrimony, the Ordinary may also establish seminary programs or houses of formation which would relate to existing Catholic faculties of theology.

VII. The Ordinary, with the approval of the Holy See, can erect new Institutes of Consecrated Life and Societies of Apostolic Life, with the right to call their members to Holy Orders, according to the norms of canon law. Institutes of Consecrated Life originating in the Anglican Communion and entering into full communion with the Catholic Church may also be placed under his jurisdiction by mutual consent.

VIII. § 1. The Ordinary, according to the norm of law, after having heard the opinion of the Diocesan Bishop of the place, may erect, with the consent of the Holy See, personal parishes for the faithful who belong to the Ordinariate.

§ 2. Pastors of the Ordinariate enjoy all the rights and are held to all the obligations established in the Code of Canon Law and, in cases established by the Complementary Norms, such rights and obligations are to be exercised in mutual pastoral assistance together with the pastors of the local Diocese where the personal parish of the Ordinariate has been established.

IX. Both the lay faithful as well as members of Institutes of Consecrated Life and Societies of Apostolic Life, originally part of the Anglican Communion, who wish to enter the Personal Ordinariate, must manifest this desire in writing.

X. § 1. The Ordinary is aided in his governance by a Governing Council with its own statutes approved by the Ordinary and confirmed by the Holy See.[17]

§ 2. The Governing Council, presided over by the Ordinary, is composed of at least six priests. It exercises the functions specified in the Code of Canon Law for the Presbyteral Council and the College of Consultors, as well as those areas specified in the Complementary Norms.

§ 3. The Ordinary is to establish a Finance Council according to the norms established by the Code of Canon Law which will exercise the duties specified therein.[18]

§ 4. In order to provide for the consultation of the faithful, a Pastoral Council is to be constituted in the Ordinariate.[19]

XI. Every five years the Ordinary is required to come to Rome for an *ad limina Apostolorum* visit and present to the Roman Pontiff, through the Congregation for the Doctrine of the Faith and in consultation with the Congregation for Bishops and the Congregation for the Evangelization of Peoples, a report on the status of the Ordinariate.

XII. For judicial cases, the competent tribunal is that of the Diocese in which one of the parties is domiciled, unless the Ordinariate has constituted its own tribunal, in which case the tribunal of second instance is the one designated by the Ordinariate and approved by the Holy See. In both cases, the different titles of competence established by the Code of Canon Law are to be taken into account.[20]

XIII. The Decree establishing an Ordinariate will determine the location of the See and, if appropriate, the principal church.

We desire that our dispositions and norms be valid and effective now and in the future, notwithstanding, should it be necessary, the Apostolic Constitutions and ordinances issued by our predecessors, or any other prescriptions, even those requiring special mention or derogation.

Given in Rome, at St. Peter's, on November 4, 2009, the Memorial of St. Charles Borromeo.

BENEDICTUS PP. XVI

© Copyright - Libreria Editrice Vaticana
Loading...

Notes

1. Cf. Second Vatican Council, Dogmatic Constitution *Lumen gentium*, 23; Congregation for the Doctrine of the Faith, Letter *Communionis notio*, 12; 13.
2. Cf. Dogmatic Constitution *Lumen gentium*, 4; Decree *Unitatis redintegratio*, 2.
3. Dogmatic Constitution *Lumen gentium*, 1.
4. Decree *Unitatis redintegratio*, 1.
5. Cf. Jn 17:20–21; Decree *Unitatis redintegratio*, 2.
6. Cf. Dogmatic Constitution *Lumen gentium*, 13.
7. Cf. *ibid*; Acts 2:42.
8. Cf. Dogmatic Constitution *Lumen gentium*, 8; Letter *Communionis notio*, 4.
9. Dogmatic Constitution *Lumen gentium*, 8.
10. Cf. CIC, can. 205; Dogmatic Constitution *Lumen gentium*, 13; 14; 21; 22; Decree *Unitatis redintegratio*, 2; 3; 4; 15; 20; Decree *Christus Dominus*, 4; Decree *Ad gentes*, 22.
11. Dogmatic Constitution *Lumen gentium*, 8.
12. Cf. John Paul II, Ap. Const. *Spirituali militium curae*, 21 April 1986, I § 1.
13. Cf. *CIC*, cann. 1026–1032.
14. Cf. *CIC*, cann. 1040–1049.
15. Cf. *AAS* 59 (1967) 674.
16. Cf. Congregation for the Doctrine of the Faith, *Statement of 1 April 1981*, in *Enchiridion Vaticanum* 7, 1213.
17. Cf. *CIC*, cann. 495–502.
18. Cf. *CIC*, cann. 492–494.
19. Cf. *CIC*, can. 511.
20. Cf. *CIC*, cann. 1410–1414 and 1673.

BIBLIOGRAPHY

Albertson, C. *Anglo-Saxon Saints and Heroes* (New York: Fordham University Press, 1967).

Alencherry, Joseph. 'Newman, the Liturgist: An Introduction to the Liturgical Theology of John Henry Newman', *Newman Studies Journal* 13 (2016): 6–21.

Anderson, Digby. 'English Gentlemen', *New Directions* (October, 2008): 29–30.

Andrewes, Lancelot. *Sermons by the Right Honorable and Reverend Father in God, Lancelot Andrevves, Late Lord Bishop of Winchester. Published by His Majesties Speciall Command* (London: George Miller, 1629).

Aquinas, Thomas. *Summa Theologiae*, Thomas Gilby and T. C. O'Brien (eds) (Oxford: Blackfriars, 1964).

Archbishops of Westminster and Canterbury. 'Joint Statement by the Archbishop of Westminster and the Archbishop of Canterbury', 20 October 2009, *Messenger of the Catholic League* 292, April–August (2010).

Arrieta, Juan Ignacio. *Governance Structures within the Catholic Church* (Montreal: Wilson and Lafleur, 2000).

Arrieta, Juan Ignacio. 'Gli ordinariati personali', *Ius ecclesiae* 22 (2010): 151–72.

Barlow, Bernard. *'A Brother Knocking at the Door': The Malines Conversations 1921–1925* (Norwich: Canterbury Press, 1996).

Baruch, M. A. *Le regime de Vichy: 1940–1944* (Paris: Texto, 2017).

Baura, Eduardo. 'Personal Ecclesiastical Circumscriptions', *Philippine Canonical Forum* 12 (2010): 103–30.

Barry, William. 'Oxford Movement', in *The Catholic Encyclopedia* vol. xi, Charles G. Herbermann et al. (eds), 370–7 (New York: The Universal Knowledge Foundation, 1911).

Bede the Venerable. *Ecclesiastical History of the English People*, trans. Leo Sherley-Price (London: Penguin Books, 1990).

Berlin, Isaiah. *Liberty* (Oxford University Press, 2002).

Best, Geoffrey. 'The Constitutional Revolution, 1828–1832 and Its Consequence for the Established Church', *Theology* 62 (468) (1959): 226–34.

Bliss, Frederick. *Anglicans in Rome: A History* (Norwich: Canterbury Press, 2006).
Bolton, W. F. 'How Boethian Is Alfred's *Boethius*?', in *Studies in Earlier Old English Prose*, P. E. Szarmach (ed.) (Albany: State University of New York Press, 1986).
Bourne, E. C. E. *The Anglicanism of William Laud* (London: SPCK, 1947).
Bouyer, Louis. *The Spirit and Forms of Protestantism*, trans. A. V. Littledale (Westminster, MD: Newman Press, 1961).
Brand, Clinton A. 'That Nothing Be Lost: America, Texas, and the Making of *Anglicanorum coetibus*', *Catholic Southwest: A Journal of History and Culture* 22 (2011): 48–67.
Brand, Clinton A. 'Restoring All Things in Christ: Some Reflections on the Pastoral Provision for the Anglican Use of the Roman Rite', in *Mapping the Catholic Cultural Landscape*, Paula Jean Miller, FSE, and Richard Fossey (eds), 259–74 (Lanham, MD: Rowman & Littlefield, 2004).
Brook, Stella. *The Language of the Book of Common Prayer* (London: Andre Deutsch, 1965).
Brown, M. *The Lindisfarne Gospels: Society, Spirituality and the Scribe* (London: British Library, 2003).
Bullough, D. A. *Alcuin: Achievement and Reputation: Being Part of the Ford Lectures Delivered in Oxford in Hilary Term 1980* (Leiden: Brill, 2004).
Burnham, Andrew, and Nichols, Aidan (eds). *Customary of Our Lady of Walsingham: Daily Prayer for the Ordinariate* (London: Canterbury Press, 2012).
Card, T. *Eton Established: A History from 1440 to 1860* (London: John Murray, 2001).
Carnicelli, T. A. (ed.). *King Alfred's Version of St Augustine's Soliloquies* (Cambridge, MA: Harvard University Press, 1969).
Chapman, Raymond. *Firmly I Believe: An Oxford Movement Reader* (Norwich: Canterbury Press, 2006).
Clark, J. C. D. *English Society 1660–1832*, 2nd edn (Cambridge: Cambridge University Press, 2000).
Chesterton, G. K. *Orthodoxy* (San Francisco: Ignatius Press, 1995).
Clark, Kenneth. *Civilisation* (London: BBC & John Murray, 1969).
Congar, Yves. *Dialogue between Christians: Catholic Contributions to Ecumenism* (London: Geoffrey Chapman, 1966).
Congar, Yves. *Diversités et communion* (Paris: Éditions du Cerf, 1982).
Congregation for the Oriental Churches. *Nobilis Galliæ natio*, 27 July 1954, *AAS* 47 (1955): 612–13.
Congregation for Oriental Churches. *Orientalium Ecclesiarum, Instruction for Applying the Liturgical Prescriptions of the Code of Canons of the Eastern Churches* (Città del Vaticano: Libreria Editrice Vaticana, 1996).
Congregation for the Doctrine of the Faith. *Complementary Norms for Anglicanorum coetibus* (Vatican City Portal, 2019).

Coulson, John. *Newman and the Common Tradition: A Study of the Language of Church and Society* (Oxford: Clarendon Press, 1970).
Coulson, John. *Religion and Imagination* (Oxford: Clarendon Press, 1981).
Coulson, John. 'Faith and Imagination', *The Furrow* 34 (9) (1983): 535–42.
Crawford, Samuel. *Anglo-Saxon Influence on Western Christendom, 600–800* (Oxford: Oxford University Press, 1933).
Crosby, John F. *The Personalism of John Henry Newman* (Washington, DC: Catholic University of America Press, 2014).
Cummings, Brian (ed.). *The Book of Common Prayer: The Texts of 1549, 1559, and 1662* (Oxford: Oxford World's Classics, 2011).
Dalgairns, J. B. *The Cistercian Saints of England: St Stephen, Abbot* (London: James Toovey, 1845).
Danby, John F. *Shakespeare's Doctrine of Nature: A Study of King Lear* (London: Faber & Faber, 1949).
Dawson, Christopher. *The Spirit of the Oxford Movement* (London: Sheed & Ward, 1945).
Dawson, Christopher. *Religion and the Rise of Western Culture* (New York: Sheed & Ward, 1950).
Dessain, C. S. *The Spirituality of John Henry Newman* (Minneapolis: Winston Press, 1977).
Di Noia, J. Augustine. '*Divine Worship* and the Liturgical Vitality of the Church', *Antiphon* 19 (2015): 109–15.
Donohoe, R. '*Continuity or Discontinuity? Apostolicae curae to Anglicanorum coetibus*', Doctoral thesis at the Pontifical Gregorian University: n. 416590, 269 (Rome, 2014).
Duckett, Eleanor. *Anglo-Saxon Saints and Scholars* (London: Macmillan, 1947).
Duffy, Eamon. *The Stripping of the Altars*, 2nd edn (New Haven, CT: Yale University Press, 2005).
Dulles, Avery. *Newman* (London: Continuum, 2002).
Dulles, Avery. 'Newman, Conversion, and Ecumenism', in *Church and Society: The Laurence J. McGinley Lectures, 1988–2007* (New York: Fordham University Press, 2008).
Dreher, Rod. *The Benedict Option: A Strategy for Christian in a Post-Christian Nation* (New York: Sentinel, 2017).
Pope Francis. *Evangelii Gaudium* (Rome: Editrice Vaticane, 2013).
Gaudio, M. 'The Space of Idolatry: Reformation, Incarnation, and the Ethnographic Image', *Anthropology and Aesthetics* 41 (2002): 72–9.
Gilbey, A. N. *The Commonplace Book of Monsignor A. N. Gilbey* (London: Bellew, 1993).
Gordon, Dillian. *Making and Meaning: The Wilton Diptych* (London: The National Gallery, 1994).
Gregory, Jeremy. 'Introduction', in *The Oxford History of Anglicanism Volume II: Establishment and Empire, 1662–1829*, Jeremy Gregory (ed.), 1–21 (Oxford: Oxford University Press, 2017).

Guyer, Benjamin. *The Beauty of Holiness: The Caroline Divines and their Writings* (London: Canterbury Press, 2012).
Hargrove, H. L. *King Alfred's Old English Version of Augustine's Soliloquies*, Yale Studies in English XXII (New York: Henry Holt, 1904).
Heale, Martin. *Dissolution, Opposition, Accommodation: The Abbots and Priors of Late Medieval and Reformation England* (Oxford: Oxford University Press, 2016).
Hempton, David. *Religion and Political Culture in Britain and Ireland: From the Glorious Revolution to the Decline of Empire* (Cambridge: Cambridge University Press, 1996).
Herbert, George. *The Works of George Herbert in Verse and Prose* (London: George Routledge, 1854).
Herbert, George. *The Poems of George Herbert* (Oxford: Oxford University Press, 1961).
Herbert, George, in R. Blythe (ed.). *A Priest to the Temple or the Country Parson* (Norwich: Canterbury Press, 2003).
Herring, George. *What Was the Oxford Movement?* (London: Continuum, 2002).
Hill, Christopher. *The World Turned Upside Down: Radical Ideas During the English Revolution* (London: Penguin, 1991).
Holmes, Peter. *Resistance and Compromise: The Political Thought of the Elizabethan Catholics* (Cambridge: Cambridge University Press, 1982).
Hutson, James H. 'John Adams' Title Campaign', *New England Quarterly* 41 (1) (March 1968): 30–9.
Jaki, Stanley. *Newman to Converts: An Existential Ecclesiology* (Pinckney, MI: True View Books, 2001).
John Paul II. *Spirituali militum curæ* (Vatican City Portal, 1986).
John Paul II. Apostolic Constitution *Fidei depositum* (Rome: Editrice Vaticane, 1992).
John Paul II. *Veritatis Splendor* (Rome: Editrice Vaticane, 1993).
Johnson, Paul. *A History of Christianity* (Harmondsworth: Penguin Books, 1976).
Jones, T., Yeager, R., Dolan, T., and Fletcher, A. *Who Murdered Chaucer?: A Medieval Mystery* (London: Methuen, 2003).
Keble, John. *The Christian Year* (Oxford: J. Parker, 1827).
Keble, John. *National Apostasy Considered in a Sermon Preached in St. Mary's, Oxford, before His Majesty's Judges of Assize, on Sunday, July 14, 1833* (Oxford: J. H. Parker, 1833).
Ker, Ian. *Healing the Wound of Humanity: The Spirituality of John Henry Newman* (London: Darton, Longman & Todd, 1993).
Ker, Ian. 'Newman on Imagination and Religious Belief', *Logos: A Journal of Catholic Thought and Culture* 1 (1) (1997): 96–110.
Ker, Ian. *Newman on Vatican II* (Oxford: Oxford University Press, 2014).
Jacob, W. M. *The Clerical Profession in the Long Eighteenth Century, 1680–1840* (Oxford: Oxford University Press, 2007).

Lambert, Malcolm. *Christians and Pagans: The Conversion of England from Alban to Bede* (New Haven, CT: Yale University Press, 2010).
Lang, Uwe Michael. 'Newman and the Fathers of the Church', *New Blackfriars* 92 (1038) (2011): 144–56.
Langham, Mark. *The Caroline Divines and the Church of Rome: A Contribution to Current Ecumenical Dialogue* (London: Routledge, 2018).
Langland, W. *The Vision of Piers Plowman*, XI, trans. H. W. Wells (New York: Sheed & Ward, 1935).
Leclercq, J. *The Love of Learning and the Desire for God: A Study of Monastic Culture*, 3rd edn (New York: Fordham University Press, 1982).
Levison, William. *England and the Continent in the Eighth Century* (Oxford: Clarendon Press, 1946).
Liddon, H. P. *The Life of Edward Bouverie Pusey* (London: Longmans, Green, 1893).
Lopes, Steven. '"Divine Worship: Occasional Services": A Presentation', *The Jurist* 74 (2014): 79–89.
Lopes, Steven. 'A Missal for the Ordinariates: The Work of the Anglicanae Traditiones Inter-dicasterial Commission', *Antiphon* 19 (2015): 116–31.
Lopes, Steven. 'Letter to the Priests and Deacons of the Ordinariate of the Chair of Saint Peter', 9 April 2019.
Magill, Gerard (ed.). *Personality and Belief: Interdisciplinary Essays on John Henry Newman* (Lanham, MD: University Press of America, 1994).
Magill, Gerard. *Religious Morality in John Henry Newman: Hermeneutics of the Imagination* (New York: Springer, 2015).
McAdoo, Henry Robert. 'Anglican/Roman Catholic Relations', in *Rome and the Anglicans: Historical and Doctrinal Aspects of Anglican – Roman Catholic Relations*, J. Averling et al. (eds) (Berlin: Walter De Gruyter, 1982).
MacCulloch, Diarmaid. *The Later Reformation in England: 1547–1603* (New York: St Martin's Press, 1990).
MacCulloch, Diarmaid. 'The Myth of the English Reformation', *History Today*, July (1991): 28–35.
McGrade, A. S. (ed.). *Richard Hooker: Of the Laws of Ecclesiastical Polity. A Critical Edition with Modern Spelling* (Oxford: Oxford University Press, 2013).
Merton, Thomas. 'Marxism and Monastic Perspectives', in *A New Charter for Monasticism*, J. Moffitt (ed.) (Notre Dame, IN: University of Notre Dame Press, 1970).
DeMille, George E. *The Catholic Movement in the American Episcopal Church* (Philadelphia: Church Historical Society, 1950).
Michael, M. A. 'Creating Cultural Identity: Opus Anglicanum and its Place in the History of English Medieval Art', *Journal of the British Archaeological Association* 170 (1) (2017): 30–60.

Morris, Jeremy. *The High Church Revival in the Church of England: Arguments and Identities* (Leiden: Brill, 2016).
Mumford, Lewis. *Condition of Man* (New York: Harcourt, Brace, 1944).
Neale, John Mason. *The Bible, and the Bible Only, The Religion of Protestants* (London: Joseph Masters, 1852).
Neill, Stephen. *Anglicanism* (London: Pelican, [1958] 1977).
Newman, John Henry. *St. Aelred: Abbot of Rievaulx* (London: James Toovey, 1845).
Newman, John Henry. *Grammar of Assent* (Notre Dame, IN: University of Notre Dame Press, 1979).
Newman, John Henry. *Autobiographical Writings*, Henry Tristram (ed.) (New York: Sheed & Ward, 1957).
Newman, John Henry. *Apologia Pro Vita Sua*, David J. DeLaura (ed.) (New York: W. W. Norton, 1968).
Newman, John Henry *The Letters and Diaries of John Henry Newman*, Charles Stephen Dessain et al. (eds) (31 vols): I–X (Oxford: Clarendon Press, 1973–84); XI–XXII (London: Thomas Nelson & Sons, 1961–72); XXIII–XXXI (Oxford: Clarendon Pres, 1973–7).
Newman, John Henry. *Loss and Gain: The Story of a Convert*, Alan G. Hill (ed.) (Oxford: Oxford University Press, 1989).
Newman, John Henry. *Plain and Parochial Sermons* (San Francisco: Ignatius Press, 1997).
Nichols, Aidan. *The Panther and the Hind: A Theological History of Anglicanism* (Edinburgh: T&T Clark, 1993).
Nichols, Aidan. *The Realm: An Unfashionable Essay on the Conversion of England* (Oxford: Family Publications, 2008).
Nichols, A. 'Anglican Unitism: A Personal View', *Messenger of the Catholic League* 292 (2010): 13–20.
Nichols, Aidan. *Catholics of the Anglican Patrimony: The Personal Ordinariate of Our Lady of Walsingham* (Leominster: Gracewing, 2013).
Norris, Thomas J. *Newman and His Theological Method* (Leiden: E. J. Brill, 1977).
Oddie, William. *The Roman Option: Crisis and Realignment of English-Speaking Christianity* (London: HarperCollins, 1997).
Orwell, George. *Inside the Whale and Other Essays* (London: Penguin, 1972).
Pickering, W. S. F. *Anglo-Catholicism: A Study in Religious Ambiguity*, revised edn (Cambridge: James Clark, 2008).
Pickstock, Catherine. *After Writing: On the Liturgical Consummation of Philosophy* (London: Routledge, 1999).
Pius X. *Officium supremi Apostolatus*, 15 July 1912, *AAS* 4.
Preece, P., and Kift, M. 'The Shrine of St Mary, Caversham', *Oxford Architectural and Historical Society* (1995): 431–2.

Pritchard, Arnold. *Catholic Loyalism in Elizabethan England* (London: Scholar Press, 1979).
Pugin, Augustus Welby. *Contrasts: Or, A Parallel between the Noble Edifices of the Middle Ages, and Corresponding Buildings of the Present Day; Shewing the Present Decay of Taste; Accompanied by Appropriate Text*, 2nd edn (London: Charles Dolman, 1841).
Ratzinger, Joseph. 'Theological Commentary on the Third Secret of Fatima', *L'Osservatore Romano* (English weekly edition), 8 June 2000, Special Insert.
Ratzinger, Joseph. *The Spirit of the Liturgy* (San Francisco: Ignatius Press, 2000).
Ratzinger, Joseph. 'The Feeling of Things, the Contemplation of Beauty', Message to the Communion and Liberation Meeting at Rimini, 24–30 August 2002, in *The Essential Pope Benedict XVI: His Central Writings & Speeches*, John F. Thornton and Susan B. Varenne (eds) (New York: HarperCollins, 2007).
Rankin, S. (ed.). *The Winchester Troper: Facsimile Edition and Introduction* (London: Stainer and Bell, 2007).
Renken, J. 'The Personal Ordinariate of the Chair of St Peter: Some Canonical Reflections', *Studia Canonica* 46 (2012): 5–50.
Reynolds, Anna Maria CP. '"Courtesy" and "Homeliness" in the *Revelations* of Julian of Norwich', *Fourteenth-Century English Mystics Newsletter* 2 (1979): 12–20.
Riché, Pierre. *Écoles et Enseignement dans le Haut Moyen Age*, 3rd edn (Paris: Picard, 1999).
Ridyard, Susan J. *The Royal Saints of Anglo-Saxon England* (Cambridge: Cambridge University Press, 1989).
Rosewell, Roger. *The Eton College Chapel Wall Paintings: England's Forgotten Medieval Masterpiece* (Woodbridge: Boydell & Brewer, 2009).
Rowell, Geoffrey. 'Newman, the Church of England and the Catholic Church', *New Blackfriars* 92 (1038) (2011): 130–43.
Rowland, Tracey. *Ratzinger's Faith: The Theology of Pope Benedict XVI* (Oxford: Oxford University Press, 2008).
Rutler, George W. 'Newman and the Power of Personality', in *Essays in Honor of the Centenary of John Henry Cardinal Newman (1801–1890)*, Christendom Educational Corporation (ed.), 111–31 (Front Royal, VA: Christendom Press, 1989).
Sacred Congregation of the Sacred Consistory (CSC). '*Circa la giurisdizione dell'ordinario militare in italia*', 13 April, *Acta Apostolica Sedes* 32 (1940): 280–1.
Sacred Congregation of the Sacred Consistory (CSC). '*Solemne semper*', 24 April, *Acta Apostolica Sedes* 45 (1951): 562–5.

Sarah, Robert. *The Power of Silence: Against the Dictatorship of Noise* (San Francisco: Ignatius, 2017).
Saward, John. *The Beauty of Holiness and the Holiness of Beauty. Art, Sanctity, and the Truth of Catholicism* (San Francisco: Ignatius Press, 1997).
Scruton, Roger. *Beauty: A Very Short Introduction* (Oxford: Oxford University Press, 2011).
Scruton, Roger. *Our Church: A Personal History of the Church of England* (London: Atlantic Books, 2012).
Selby, Robin C. *The Principle of Reserve in the Writings of John Henry Newman* (Oxford: Oxford University Press, 1975).
Smith, James K. A. *How (Not) to Be Secular: Reading Charles Taylor* (Grand Rapids, MI: Eerdmans, 2014).
Stanwood, P. G. 'Patristic and Contemporary Borrowing in the Caroline Divines', *Renaissance Quarterly* 23 (4) (Winter, 1970): 421–9.
Stevenson, K. W. 'Caroline Divines', in *The Oxford Companion to Christian Thought*, Adrian Hastings (ed.) (Oxford: Oxford University Press, 2000).
Sutherland, Stewart. *Atheism and the Rejection of God: Contemporary Philosophy and the Brothers Karamazov* (Oxford: Blackwell, 1977).
Taylor, Charles. *A Secular Age* (Cambridge, MA: Harvard University Press, 2007).
Thomas, C. *Christianity in Roman Britain to AD 500* (Berkeley: University of California Press, 1981).
Thorndike, Herbert. *The Theological Works of Herbert Thorndike Volume V* (Oxford: Parker, 1854).
Tyacke, Nicholas (ed.). *England's Long Reformation: 1500–1800* (London: UCL Press, 1998).
Second Vatican Council. *Sacrosanctum concilium* (Vatican City Portal, 1963).
Second Vatican Council. *Unitatis redintegratio* (Vatican City Portal, 1964).
Second Vatican Council. *Lumen gentium* (Vatican City Portal, 1964).
Waddell, Richard. 'Canonical and Theological Aspects of the Personal Ordinariates Established Pursuant to the Apostolic Constitution *Anglicanorum coetibus*' (JCL thesis, Rome: Pontifical Gregorian University, 2016).
Waite, Terry. 'A Very Present Help in Trouble', in *The Book of Common Prayer: Past Present & Future*, Prudence Dailey (ed.), 193–8 (London: Continuum, 2011).
Walsham, Alexandra. *Church Papists: Catholicism, Conformity and Confessional Polemic in Early Modern England* (Woodbridge: Boydell Press, 1999).
Ward, Robin. *On Christian Priesthood* (London: Continuum, 2011).

Waterhouse, R. 'Tone in Alfred's Version of Augustine's Soliloquies', in *Studies in Earlier Old English Prose*, P. E. Szarmach (ed.), 47–86 (Albany: State University of New York Press, 1986).
Weir, Alison. *Henry VIII: King and Court* (London: Vintage, 2008).
Wheeler, Gordon in J. Heenan (ed.). *Christian Unity: A Catholic View* (London: Sheed & Ward, 1962).
Williams, Bernard. *Morality: An Introduction to Ethics* (New York: Harper and Row, 1972).
Williams, Bernard. *Utilitarianism For and Against* (Cambridge: Cambridge University Press, 1973).
Williams, Hugh. *Christianity in Early Britain* (Oxford: Clarendon Press, 1912).
Willey, Petroc. 'Blessed Alcuin, Deacon', *New Diaconal Review* 1 (8) (2013).
Yelton, Michael. *Anglican Papalism: A History 1900–1960* (Norwich: Canterbury Press, 2005).

AUTHOR INDEX

Anderson, Digby 3
Andrews, Robert, M. 4
Anson, Peter Frederick 118, 124
Aquinas, Thomas, Saint 76
Augustine of Hippo, Saint 76

Bogle, James, Colonel 5
Brant, Clinton 4
Brook, Stella 114

Congar, Yves 2, 19

Dawson, Christopher 109, 110, 144
Dessain, Charles Stephen 96
Di Noia, Joseph Augustine 50, 63, 75, 102
Dostoevsky, Fyodor 138
Duffy, Eamon 112, 144, 190

Francis, Pope 46, 162

John Henry Newman, Saint 81, 82
John Paul II, Saint and Pope 162, 196
Julian of Norwich, Saint 100

Ker, Ian 97

Langland, William 144
Leclercq, Jean 143
Levada, Cardinal William 4, 5

Lopes, Steven, Bishop 4, 5, 66, 67, 69

MacIntyre, Alasdair 5
Mumford, Lewis 140

Nichols, Aidan 122, 123, 155

Orwell, George 110

Perkins, Timothy, P. 4
Pickering, W. S. F. 122

Ratzinger, Joseph Cardinal 14, 20, 123, 124
Rowland, Tracey 124

Sarah, Cardinal Robert 163
Scruton, Roger 110, 111
Sherbrooke, Alexander 6
Sutherland, Stuart 138

Taylor, Charles 100
Thorndike, Herbert 153, 160

Waddell, Richard 4
Ward, Robin 78
Warner, Gerald of Craigenmaddie 6
Wheeler, Gordon 80, 81
Willey, Petroc 5
Williams, Bernard 136, 137

SUBJECT INDEX

Adrian, Saint 136, 143
Aelred of Rievaulx, Saint 140
Alban, Saint 140
Alcuin of York 138, 175
Alfred the Great, Saint 5, 136, 144
Andrews, Lancelot 110, 152, 154. 155
Anglicanorum coetibus 1, 3, 4, 6, 10, 11, 14, 15, 18, 19, 23, 25, 28, 30–3, 45, 48, 50, 56, 58, 63, 65, 72, 79, 82, 85, 92, 93, 101, 111, 123–5, 152, 155, 161, 164
Anglican patrimony 2, 4–6, 28, 69, 75, 102, 111, 152
Apostolicae Curae 19, 118
ARCIC 10–15, 27, 28, 122
Aristotle 152
Arundel, Thomas 187
Augustine of Canterbury, Saint 62
Augustine of Hippo, Saint 124, 135

Battle of Lepanto 196
Benedict, Saint 139
Benedict XVI, Pope 1, 3, 6, 10, 14, 15, 19, 23, 37, 46, 58, 65, 69, 75, 83, 91, 94, 124, 199
Bernard, Saint 140
Black Death 195
Boethius 142
Book of Common Prayer 46, 50, 52, 55, 113, 158, 164
Braye, Alfred Lord 191
Byrd, William 152, 185

Calvin, Jean 151
Caroline Divines 5, 49, 55, 152–8, 161, 164
Carolingian Renaissance 139
Catechism of the Catholic Church 12, 14, 15
Charles I, King 152, 153, 159
Charles II, King 153, 191
Charles V, Holy Roman Emperor 179
Chesterton, Keith Gilbert 137, 202
Children of Fatima 199
Cicero, Marcus Tullius 152
Coggan, Frederick Donald 11
Columbus, Christopher 195
Comper, Ninian 120
Complementary Norms 23, 30, 32, 35, 66, 67, 101
Congregation of the Doctrine of the Faith 11, 25, 27, 37, 68
Constantine the Great, Roman Emperor 175
corporate reunion 1
Cosin, John 153
Cranmer, Thomas 53, 111, 112, 114, 115, 117, 124
Cromwell, Thomas 189

Diana, Princess of Wales 201
Don Juan of Austria, General 196
Donne, John 153
Dowland, John 152

Eastern Catholic Churches 17, 18
Edward the Confessor, Saint and King 187, 200

SUBJECT INDEX

Edward, King and Martyr 187
Edward Powell, Blessed 188
Edward VI, King 48
Elizabeth I, Queen 116, 156
Elizabeth II, Queen 5
Eton College 5, 186, 189–203
Eucharist 12, 20, 32, 36, 47,
   68–70, 160
European Union 199

Fergus the Great 5
Flying bishops 11
Forty English Martyrs 26, 48
Frank, Mark 153

George III, King 179
George, Saint 179, 187
Gibbons, Orlando 152
Gilbey, Monsignor Alfred 191
Great Officers of State 178
Gregory the Great, Saint 62,
   136, 142

Harold Macmillan 200
Henry II, King 141
Henry VI, King 6, 185, 186, 188,
   192, 194, 196, 199, 200, 203
Henry VIII, King 48, 111, 179,
   186, 188, 190, 194, 200, 202
Herbert, George 132–3, 153
hieratic language 3
Holy See 23, 24, 26–8, 49–51, 70
Hooker, Richard 80, 81, 110, 151,
   157, 160, 161
Huddlestone, Fr. John 191
Hunt, William Holman 124
Hussain, Saddam 198

Inter insigniores 11

James I, King 153
James II, King 153
Jerome, Saint 135, 136
John Fisher, Saint 9

John Henry Newman, Saint 3, 4,
   19, 49, 85, 87, 89, 90, 92–101,
   103, 110, 115, 116, 139, 201
John Paul II, Saint and Pope 12, 14,
   15, 26, 46, 88, 93, 94, 196

Kasper, Cardinal Walter 12,
   154, 155
Keble, John 95, 97
King's Scholars 194, 202
Knox, Ronald 200

Laud, William 110, 153–5,
   157, 164.
Lawrence, Saint 200
Leo XIII, Pope 19
Lisle, Ambrose Phillips de 91
London, John 189, 194
Lord High Admiral 177, 178
Lord High Chancellor 177
Lord High Constable 177
Lord High Steward 177, 178
Lord High Treasurer 177
Lumen gentium 16, 20, 27, 51, 123
Lupton, Roger 188, 194
Luther, Martin 151

MacAlpin, Kenneth 5, 175
Malines Conversations 26, 121
Manning, Henry Edward
   Cardinal 87, 97
Marlowe, Christopher 152
Mercier, Désiré-Joseph
   Cardinal 121
Miracle on the Wisłą 195
Mother Teresa of Calcutta 193,
   198, 199, 201

Nouvelle Théologie 154
Novus Ordo Missal 3

Oliver Plunkett, Saint 190
Ordinariate of Chair of St. Peter
   34, 66, 67

Ordinariate of Our Lady of
  Walsingham 67, 68
Ordinariate of the Southern
  Cross 67
ordination of women 11
Ordinatio sacerdotalis 12
Our Lady of Eton 6, 185, 189,
  192, 194, 196, 201–3
Oxford Movement 49, 55, 86, 88,
  90, 92, 98, 110, 117, 122

Parker, Matthew 156
Patrick, Saint 142, 175
Paul VI, Pope 3, 11, 26, 48
Paul of Tarsus, Saint 115
Petroc, Saint 141
Pius V, Pope 46, 113, 196
Pius XII, Pope 1
Pontifical Council for the
  Promotion of Christian Unity 12
Prince Electors of the Holy Roman
  Empire 176, 177
Pugin, Augustus Welby 116
Puritan protectorate 49, 55
Pusey, Edward Bouverie 92, 93,
  98

Ramsay, Michael 2
Ratzinger, Joseph Cardinal 156
receptive ecumenism 2, 4
Richard II, King 187, 203
Romano-British Christianity 131

Russell, Edward 26th Baron de
  Clifford 178

Sayers, Dorothy 178
Second Vatican Council 15–17, 26,
  49, 53, 56, 79, 88, 123
Shakespeare, William 114, 152,
  159, 191
Spencer, Fr. Ignatius 201
Stephen Harding, Saint 139

Tallis, Thomas 152, 185, 191
Taylor, Jeremy 153
Theodore of Canterbury, Saint
  136, 143
Thirty-Nine Articles 112
Thomas Becket, Saint 140
Tractarians 90, 91, 117
Traditional Anglican Communion
  (TAC) 25, 26
Treaty of Rome 199

Unitatis redintegratio 18, 79, 155

Valerian, Emperor 200
virtue of religion 4

William the Conqueror, King 195
Williams, Rowan 14, 154
Wilton Diptych 187, 188, 198
Winefride, Saint 141
Wycliffe, John 186, 195

www.ingramcontent.com/pod-product-compliance
Lightning Source LLC
Chambersburg PA
CBHW060950230426
43665CB00015B/2136